ZEW Economic Studies

Publication Series of the Centre for
European Economic Research (ZEW),
Mannheim, Germany

ZEW Economic Studies

Vol. 1: O. Hohmeyer, K. Rennings (Eds.)
Man-Made Climate Change
Economic Aspects and Policy Options
1999. VIII, 401 pp. ISBN 3-7908-1146-7

Vol. 2: Th. Büttner
Agglomeration, Growth, and Adjustment
A Theoretical and Empirical Study
of Regional Labor Markets in Germany
1999. XI, 206 pp. ISBN 3-7908-1160-2

Vol. 3: P. Capros et al.
Climate Technology Strategies 1
Controlling Greenhouse Gases.
Policy and Technology Options
1999. XVIII, 365 pp. ISBN 3-7908-1229-3

Vol. 4: P. Capros et al.
Climate Technology Strategies 2
The Macro-Economic Cost and Benefit
of Reducing Greenhouse Gas Emissions
in the European Union
1999. XIII, 224 pp. ISBN 3-7908-1230-7

Vol. 5: P.A. Puhani
Evaluating Active Labour Market Policies
Empirical Evidence for Poland During
Transition
1999. XVI, 239 pp. ISBN 3-7908-1234-X

Vol. 6: B. Fitzenberger
Wages and Employment Across Skill Groups
An Analysis for West Germany
1999. XII, 251 pp. ISBN 3-7908-1235-8

Vol. 7: K. Rennings et al. (Eds.)
Social Costs and Sustainable Mobility
Strategies and Experiences in Europe
and the United States
1999. VI, 212 pp. ISBN 3-7908-1260-9

Vol. 8: H. Legler et al.
Germany's Technological Performance
2000. X, 191 pp. ISBN 3-7908-1281-1

Vol. 9: O. Bürgel
The Internationalization of British Start-up Companies in High-Technology Industries
2000. XIV, 230 pp. ISBN 3-7908-1292-7

Vol. 10: J. Hemmelskamp et al. (Eds.)
Innovation-Oriented Environmental Regulation
Theoretical Approaches and Empirical
Analysis
2000. VI, 348 pp. ISBN 3-7908-1313-3

Vol. 11: K.L. Brockmann, M. Stronzik
(Eds.)
Flexible Mechanisms
for an Efficient Climate Policy
Cost Saving Policies and Business
Opportunities
2000. VIII, 130 pp. ISBN 3-7908-1314-1

Vol. 12: W. Smolny
Endogenous Innovations
and Knowledge Spillovers
A Theoretical and Empirical Analysis
2000. VIII, 277 pp. ISBN 3-7908-1320-6

Vol. 13: M. Lechner, F. Pfeiffer (Eds.)
Econometric Evaluation
of Labour Market Policies
2001. X, 242 pp. ISBN 3-7908-1372-9

Vol. 14: M. Beise
Lead Markets
Country-Specific Success Factors of the
Global Diffusion of Innovations
2001. XVI, 305 pp. ISBN 3-7908-1430-X

Vol. 15: O.H. Jacobs, C. Spengel
Effective Tax Burden in Europe
Current Situation, Past Developments and
Simulations of Reforms
2002. X, 131 pp. ISBN 3-7908-1470-9

Jens Köke

Corporate Governance in Germany

An Empirical Investigation

With 7 Figures
and 50 Tables

Physica-Verlag
A Springer-Verlag Company

ZEW
Zentrum für Europäische
Wirtschaftsforschung GmbH
Centre for European
Economic Research

Series Editor
Prof. Dr. Wolfgang Franz

Author

Dr. Jens Köke
University of Mannheim
Mannheim Research Institute
for the Economics of Aging (MEA)
L 13,17
68131 Mannheim
Germany

ISBN 3-7908-1511-X Physica-Verlag Heidelberg New York

Cataloging-in-Publication Data applied for
Die Deutsche Bibliothek – CIP-Einheitsaufnahme
Köke, Jens: Corporate Governance in Europe / Jens Köke. – Heidelberg; New York: Physica-Verl., 2002
(ZEW economic studies; Vol. 16)
ISBN 3-7908-1511-X

Physica-Verlag Heidelberg New York
a member of BertelsmannSpringer Science+Business Media GmbH

Cover design: Erich Dichiser, ZEW, Mannheim

SPIN 10883329 88/2202-5 4 3 2 1 0 – Printed on acid-free paper

Preface

This study was written while I was a doctoral student at the University of Mannheim and a research fellow at the *Zentrum für Europäische Wirtschaftsforschung* (ZEW) in Mannheim; it has been accepted as a doctoral dissertation in December 2001. I am indebted to my advisor, Professor Axel Börsch-Supan at University of Mannheim, for his steady support and for many helpful discussions and comments. I also feel indebted to my second advisor, Professor Ulrich Schlieper at University of Mannheim, for his feedback and valuable suggestions.

During the process of writing various parts of this manuscript, I also benefitted from helpful comments, and fruitful discussions with Marco Becht, Eckehart Böhmer, Herbert Buscher, Rainer Feuerstack, Klaus Gugler, Friedrich Heinemann, Florian Heiss, Felix Hüfner, Silke Januszewski, Jens Kammerath, Mathias Nilsson, Luc Renneboog, Tanja Salem, Richard Stehle, Max Steiger, Tereza Tykvová, Peter Westerheide, and Bircin Yurtoglu. Especially I would like to thank Joachim Winter for his instantaneous help and invaluable feedback on any problem encountered during preparation of this study. I also appreciate the comments I received from seminar participants at the University of Mannheim and the ZEW. Similarly, I profited from comments that I received at the annual meetings of the *Verein für Socialpolitik* in Berlin, 2000, the European Economic Association in Bozen, 2000, the Financial Management Association in Paris, 2001, the European Finance Association in Barcelona, 2001, and the German Finance Association in Vienna, 2001. During preparation of the final manuscript and during construction of the database used for this study, excellent research assistance was provided by Matthias Braun, Gregor Führich, Timo Gieb, Dirk Günnemann, Monika Nilles, Elena Todorova, Heiko Truppel, and Dilek Turan. Financial support from *Deutsche Forschungsgemeinschaft* (research grant no. BO 934/7-2) and the ZEW is gratefully acknowledged.

Finally, I would like to thank my parents and my wife Justyna for their ongoing encouragement and moral support during this project. My beloved wife and our son Frederik, who had to get along without their husband and father for quite some nights and weekends, helped me to put the whole project into perspective.

Mannheim, December 2001 *Jens Köke*

Table of Contents

1 Introduction 1

2 Literature Review and Methodological Concerns 11
2.1 Reverse Causality 12
2.1.1 Tests 15
2.1.2 Lessons 16
2.2 Sample Selectivity 19
2.2.1 Tests 24
2.2.2 Lessons 24
2.3 Missing Variables 26
2.3.1 Lessons 30
2.4 Measurement Error in Variables 31
2.4.1 Tests 33
2.4.2 Lessons 33
2.5 Summary and Lessons 35

3 The German Corporations Database (GCD) 37
3.1 Data Sources 38
3.2 Sample Selection and Structure of GCD 42
3.3 Sample Representativeness 43

4 Frequency, Causes, and Consequences of Control Transfers 47
4.1 Hypotheses 48
4.2 Data 51
4.2.1 Characteristics of Entering and Exiting Firms 52
4.2.2 Concept of Control 53
4.3 Frequency of Control Transfers 58
4.3.1 Evidence Based on Aggregate Measures 58
4.3.2 Evidence Based on Changes in Individual Shareholders 60
4.4 Causes and Consequences of Control Transfers 64
4.4.1 Causes of Control Transfers 65
4.4.2 Consequences of Control Transfers 68
4.5 Summary and Lessons 73

5 Determinants of Acquisition and Failure 75
5.1 Hypotheses 77
5.2 Data and Frequency of Exit 79
5.3 Preliminary Evidence 82
5.3.1 Industry Distribution 82
5.3.2 Performance 83
5.3.3 Capital Structure 86
5.3.4 Ownership Structure 87
5.3.5 Restructuring and Firm Size 90
5.3.6 Summary 91
5.4 Estimation Results 92
5.4.1 Performance, Capital Structure, Ownership Concentration 93
5.4.2 Shareholder Types 94
5.4.3 Sensitivity of Results 98
5.5 Summary and Lessons 106

6 Corporate Governance, Market Discipline, and Productivity Growth 109
6.1 Hypotheses 111
6.2 Data and Measurement Issues 113
6.2.1 Measuring Corporate Governance 114
6.2.2 Measuring Market Discipline 115
6.3 Preliminary Evidence 116
6.4 Empirical Model of Productivity Growth 120
6.5 Estimation Results 122
6.5.1 Effects of Corporate Governance and Market Discipline 122
6.5.2 Sensitivity of Results 124
6.6 Summary and Lessons 128

7 Concluding Remarks 135

Appendix 141

Bibliography 155

List of Data Sources 167

List of Figures 169

List of Tables 171

1 Introduction

Corporate governance is the complex system of control mechanisms by which "the suppliers of finance to corporations assure themselves of getting a return on their investment" (Shleifer and Vishny, 1997: 737). The classical problem of corporate governance is the separation of ownership and control, or more exactly, the agency costs which result from a divergence of interest between the owners and the managers of the firm (Berle and Means, 1932; Jensen and Meckling, 1976).

Understanding corporate governance is important. The political changes in Eastern Europe after 1989 made it necessary to design efficient corporate governance systems virtually from scratch. In Russia, the weakness of corporate governance still leads to substantial diversion of assets by managers of many privatized firms (Boycko, Shleifer, and Vishny, 1995). Compared with the governance systems in transition and developing economies, the systems of Germany and the US are probably well developed. However, there is considerable disagreement on the merits and deficiencies of those developed systems. For example, Jensen (1993) argues that the US system, which is often labeled as 'market-based', is severely constrained by oversized boards, lack of independence of the chairman of the board, and too small equity holdings of managers. Roe (1993) suggests to replace the Anglo-Saxon system with those patterned in Germany or Japan, which are often labeled as 'bank-based'.[1] Vice versa, Börsch-Supan (1999) and Allen and Gale (2000) argue that weaker governance structures and less intense competition in product markets contribute to significantly lower productivity in continental Europe. According to Börsch-Supan (1999), Germany and France have lagged the US in terms of productivity growth by around 20% throughout the entire period of 1970–1995.

[1] For international comparisons of corporate governance systems, see Franks and Mayer (1990), Prowse (1994), Kaplan (1997), Mayer (1998), and Becht and Röell (1999). For descriptive evidence on European corporate governance systems, see Gugler et al. (2001) for Austria, Becht et al. (2001) for Belgium, Bloch and Kremp (2001) for France, Becht and Böhmer (2001) and Köke (2001c) for Germany, Bianchi et al. (2001) for Italy, De Jong et al. (2001) for the Netherlands, Crespi-Cladera and Garcia-Cestona (2001) for Spain, Agnblad et al. (2001) for Sweden, and Goergen and Renneboog (2001) for the UK.

In recent years, corporate governance has also attracted increasing attention from policy makers and practitioners. For example, in May 1999 the OECD approved Principles of Corporate Governance, which include recommendations regarding shareholder rights, disclosure, and transparency. In Germany, the Law on Control and Transparency in Corporations of May 1998 aims to improve the monitoring function of the general shareholders' meeting and to limit the use of voting caps. A Code of Best Practice, developed by practitioners, intends to make the German system of corporate governance more transparent for international investors. Recent developments in financial markets are likely to stimulate the interest in corporate governance further. For example, worldwide the assets under management of institutional investors (such as investment funds and pension funds) have grown substantially over the past two decades (Blommestein, 1998). This gives institutional investors a potentially more active role in corporate governance, as it is currently observed for the US (e.g., Smith, 1996; Carleton et al., 1998; OECD, 1998; Gerke and Steiger, 2001). In Germany, the transition from pay-as-you-go financing to a partially funded pension system is expected to channel a larger fraction of savings into the capital markets, further fostering institutional investment. If this new class of financial investors contributes to improving corporate governance, and if this, in turn, propels productivity growth, the result could be a reduced cost associated with the transition in the pension scheme (Börsch-Supan and Winter, 1999).

A very recent example demonstrating the relevance of corporate governance is the takeover of Mannesmann by Vodafone and the subsequent preparation of a mandatory takeover code for Germany. Leaving aside the benefits and shortcomings of the current proposal for this code, the case exemplifies that (hostile) changes in ownership are a new phenomenon for Germany, and our knowledge on the causes and consequences of control changes is very limited. This points to a need for scientific policy advice, particularly because the rate of acquisitions and divestitures is expected to increase substantially from 2002 on when sales of corporate assets essentially become tax-free.

Research on Corporate Governance

The theoretical literature on corporate governance enumerates six main different mechanisms that are supposed to limit agency costs. These are: ownership structure (Jensen and Meckling, 1976; Shleifer and Vishny, 1986), capital structure (Jensen, 1986; Zwiebel, 1996), board structure (Jensen, 1993; Maug, 1997; Warther, 1998), managerial remuneration (Jensen and Murphy, 1990), product market competition (Hart, 1983; Baily and Gersbach, 1995), and the takeover market (Jensen and Ruback, 1983; Jensen, 1988; Shleifer and Vishny, 1988). For a detailed survey of these and other studies, see Shleifer and Vishny (1997).

Unfortunately, theoretical analyses of corporate governance tend to deliver ambiguous answers because there are too many counteracting mechanisms which mask any clear picture (Hellwig, 1997). Empirical research intends to shed light on the relative weight of these counteracting mechanisms. In the following we briefly summarize important findings, with particular respect to Germany.

In contrast to the US and the UK, large shareholdings are common in the rest of the world (La Porta et al., 1999). In Germany ownership is also highly concentrated (Köke, 2001c; Becht and Böhmer, 2002). According to Shleifer and Vishny (1986), this should give large shareholders the incentive to collect information and to monitor management, ultimately reducing agency costs. The evidence suggests that large shareholders indeed play an active role in corporate governance.[2] For Japan, Kaplan and Minton (1994) find that poorly performing management is more likely to be replaced by a large blockholder. For Germany, Franks and Mayer (2001) find little association of ownership concentration with managerial disciplining. In contrast, Januszewski et al. (2002) show that ownership concentration is positively related to productivity growth. Regarding other characteristics of the ownership structure, such as ownership complexity or the type of owners, the evidence is similarly ambiguous. For Germany, Gorton and Schmid (2000) find a positive impact of bank ownership on accounting performance; in contrast, Edwards and Nibler (2000) cannot find evidence that the role of banks is different from that of other large corporate shareholders. Focusing on productivity growth, Januszewski et al. (2002) find that financial institutions as blockholders are harmful for productivity growth. The evidence on cross ownership and pyramids, which are of particular relevance for Germany, is weak (Franks and Mayer, 2001).

Similar to large shareholders, also creditors can play an important monitoring role. According to Jensen (1986), a large burden of debt can force management to make efficient use of resources, in particular to reduce free cash flow. Recent evidence from the UK (Nickell and Nicolitsas, 1999) and Belgium (Renneboog, 2000) indicates that high gearing has a positive impact on performance. For Germany the available evidence is similar, but it dates back to the early 1970s (Cable, 1985).

Regarding the mechanisms of board structure and managerial remuneration, the evidence is comparatively sparse. For recent surveys of the literature, which mainly focuses on the US, see Murphy (1998) on executive compensation and Hermalin and Weisbach (2002) on the board of directors. For Germany, there is hardly any evidence on both governance devices. Partly this is due to the fact that, in case of compensation, payment schemes such as stock options are relatively new, and appropriate data have been difficult to obtain until recently. Some evidence on pay-for-performance sensitivities in Germany is provided by Conyon and Schwalbach (1997a/1997b).

---

[2] For a survey of early empirical studies on the impact of ownership structure on corporate performance, see Short (1994). For a recent survey, see Holderness (2002).

In contrast to the sometimes sparse evidence on the mechanisms of internal control, there is a lot of evidence on the disciplinary role of intense product market competition; Allen and Gale (2000) provide a review. Studies examining the role of competition include Green and Mayes (1991) and Nickell (1996) for the UK, Klette (1999) for Norway, Bottasso and Sembenelli (2001) for Italy, and Caves (1992) and Porter (1992) for a range of industrialized countries. The evidence is relatively clear: Increased competition helps discipline management and often contributes to the long-term success of corporations. The available evidence for Germany is similar (Januszewski et al., 2002), but the interaction of competition with some important other corporate governance devices remains an open question.

Finally, the market for corporate control can exert considerable pressure on management. Jensen and Ruback (1983) argue that takeovers address governance problems. The intuition is that takeovers can serve to replace poorly performing management by a more able management team. Particularly active markets for corporate control have been described for the US (Jensen, 1988) and the UK (Franks and Mayer, 1990). To a large extent these markets are based on hostile takeovers.[3] Focusing solely on hostile takeovers, there is no market for corporate control in the bank-based economies of continental Europe (OECD, 1998), in particular not in Germany (Franks and Mayer, 1998). For Germany, this lack is typically attributed to bank voting power, complex ownership structures, and political resistance. However, recent case-study evidence suggests that in Germany changes in corporate ownership occur more frequently than often assumed (Jenkinson and Ljungqvist, 2001). What is lacking, so far, is a systematic analysis of the frequency, causes, and consequences of those changes.

Purpose of This Study

The above discussion shows that corporate governance is relevant but that the available evidence particularly for Germany is often scarce. Partially, previous empirical studies were limited through data availability. This has changed. Therefore, one contribution this study makes is to assemble a unique database – the German Corporations Database (GCD) – which provides a solid basis for corporate governance analysis (Chapter 3). The construction of GCD is guided by theoretical considerations as well as shortcomings of the samples used for previous empirical studies. These issues are discussed in a critical literature review (Chapter 2).

The second contribution is to examine three specific topics in corporate governance that have not been covered sufficiently before and are crucial to our understanding of corporate governance: the frequency, causes, and consequences of control transfers (Chapter 4), the determinants of acquisition and

[3] For a survey of the evidence from the 1980s, see Jarrell et al. (1988). For more recent evidence and perspectives on mergers, see Andrade et al. (2001).

failure (Chapter 5), and the role of corporate governance and market discipline for productivity growth (Chapter 6). Essentially, these three analyses are a direct application of GCD. Key questions they try to give an answer to are: Are German corporate governance structures as stable as often assumed? Does a change in corporate ownership act as a disciplining device, in particular, are changes in control related to poor performance? How does ownership affect the probability of acquisition or failure, or more specifically, are acquisitions hindered by complex ownership structures? How does corporate governance affect productivity growth, or more exactly, what is the role of shareholders, creditors, and the supervisory board? Does intense competition in product markets has a separate effect, or do these disciplinary devices reinforce each other?

Although these questions might appear to be quite diverse, they are closely related. In Chapter 2 we argue that all main governance mechanisms should be examined in combination because there might be important interactions. We also argue that understanding corporate governance requires to analyze dynamics in governance structures (such as ownership). In the remainder of this chapter we summarize the main lessons from previous empirical work on corporate governance, describe the main features of the German Corporations Database, and briefly discuss the approach and the main results of the three empirical analyses contained in this study. Figure 1.1 shows how the different parts of this study are related to each other.

Lessons From Previous Empirical Studies

Chapter 2 critically surveys previous empirical work on corporate governance. The intention is to derive data requirements for the construction of the German Corporations Database (GCD) in Chapter 3 as well as methodological lessons for the empirical analyses in Chapters 4–6. Of course, the lessons regarding data requirements and methodology apply to any other analysis of corporate governance as well.

We identify *endogeneity* of the right-hand side variables as the probably most common methodological problem of previous empirical studies. It generally occurs in two forms: structural reverse causality and unobserved firm heterogeneity. In both cases, panel data are a necessary condition to solve the endogeneity problem. With panel data on hand, fixed-effects models or models in first differences can be estimated to take into account the unobserved part of firm heterogeneity. But this approach fails if unobserved heterogeneity (e.g. ownership structure) is not constant over time. We conclude that GCD must be a panel of firms.

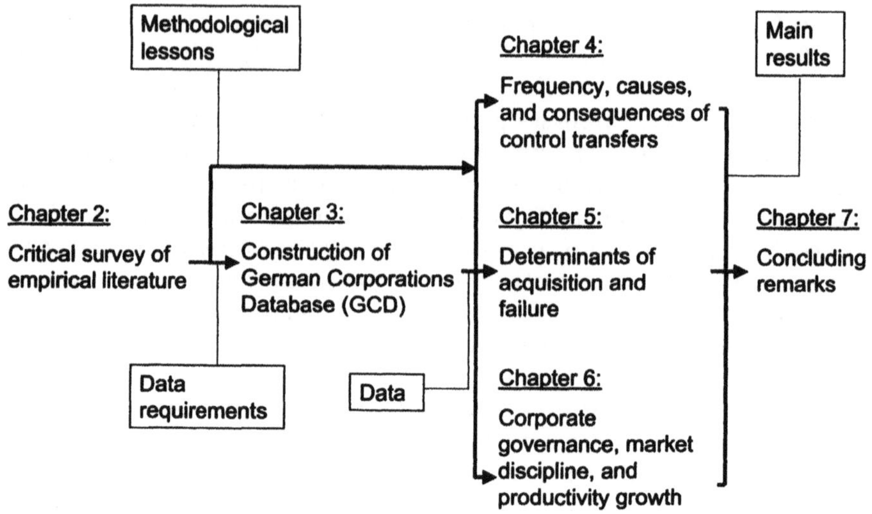

Figure 1.1. Structure of this study

A second common source of potential estimation bias is *sample selectivity.* There are two kinds of selection bias: First, the sample does not contain any information on some type of firm (e.g. non-listed corporations or private corporations); second, the sample contains all relevant firms but suffers from sample attrition. The first source of bias is best addressed by collecting data on all types of firms potentially suffering from a separation of ownership and control. Thus, GCD should contain listed and non-listed corporations, private as well as public. The second source of bias can be addressed by using econometric methods, e.g. by explicitly modeling sample attrition. This implies that GCD should contain information on the firms' survival status (i.e. information on acquisition or failure).

As a third problem the literature review identifies *missing variables.* It can only be avoided by including all theoretically relevant governance mechanisms in the empirical model. Thus, we need data on ownership structure, capital structure, board structure, product market competition, and possibly past takeover activity.

Finally, *measurement error in variables* can weaken, or in case of error in exogenous variables, bias estimation results. The direct approach to reduce measurement error is to improve the data on hand. This includes checks on data consistency (by making use of alternative sources of data) as well as choosing the correct measure for analysis. For example, German corporations typically show complex ownership structures. This implies that ownership must be measured at the *ultimate* level, not at the *direct* level. Another approach to address measurement error is to conduct sensitivity analyses or to instrument the mismeasured variable; both methods demand that alternative measures for the variable measured with error are available.

A Unique Database for Germany

The German Corporations Database (GCD) explicitly takes into account the data requirements identified in Chapter 2. Therefore, GCD allows to avoid serious methodological drawbacks constraining previous empirical studies. Chapter 3 provides information on the original data sources, the sample selection procedure, as well as sample representativeness.

This database is an unbalanced panel of medium-sized and large German corporations. With about 500 listed firms and about 2,500 non-listed firms observed through the years 1986–1997, GCD is significantly larger than any other database previously used for corporate governance analysis in Germany. Its panel structure allows to address problems of endogeneity.

GCD is highly representative for listed firms operating in non-financial industries such as manufacturing, construction, or trade. Since it also contains a significant number of private (*GmbH*) as well as public (*AG*) non-listed corporations, sample selection bias is much less likely compared with previously available data sets (e.g. *Deutsche Finanzdatenbank* at the University of Aachen). GCD does not include partnerships because in these firms there is typically no separation of ownership and control.

Furthermore, GCD contains information on all relevant governance mechanisms. This is important because problems resulting from missing variables can therefore be avoided in empirical analyses. In addition, GCD includes information on the intensity of product market competition. This allows to examine market discipline and its impact on firm performance as well as its interaction with corporate governance.

Finally, GCD offers information on a range of different measures for performance. This is important because it is not always clear how performance ought to be measured, making robustness checks in empirical analyses necessary. Likewise, GCD offers information on a range of alternative measures of product market competition and capital structure. This allows to reduce potential measurement error in these exogenous variables.

Three Empirical Analyses of Selected Topics in Corporate Governance

Chapter 4 examines the market for large share blocks in Germany, which is a potentially important governance device besides the internal governance mechanisms of ownership structure, capital structure, and board structure. The intention is to provide evidence on the frequency of changes in ownership as well as evidence on their causes and consequences. This analysis contributes to the literature in several ways: First, we provide evidence on the causes and consequences of changes in ownership, and hence complement the work of Denis and Sarin (1999) and Denis and Kruse (2000) who focus on the consequences. Second, previous studies focus on the market-based economy of the US, while this study examines a bank-based economy. Third, we develop a concept of control that takes into account the complex ownership structures often encountered in large German corporations and that clearly identifies one ultimate owner for each sample firm.

We find that – in contrast to the common perception – ownership structures in Germany exhibit significant variation over time; this confirms that panel data (on ownership) are essential for corporate governance analysis. Furthermore, there are some indications characterizing those changes in ownership as disciplinary; for example, poorly performing firms are more likely to experience a change in ownership. However, we also find that important aspects of the control transfer process work differently in listed and non-listed firms. This strongly suggests that corporate governance analyses should consider both types of firms.

Chapter 5 investigates the determinants of acquisition and failure of German corporations. It extends the analysis of Chapter 4 by explaining survival, acquisition, and failure simultaneously and by analyzing these issues within a multivariate framework. Therefore, it explicitly models sample selectivity. There are a number of novel elements contributing to the literature: First, the simultaneous analysis of acquisition and failure is new for Germany – the only exception being Heiss and Köke (2001) who examine these issues with a technically more refined econometric method. Second, we investigate the impact of different types of shareholders on the likelihood of acquisition and failure. Third, in contrast to standard bankruptcy and merger models we do not only focus on the year prior to exit because this would introduce a selection bias (Shumway, 2001). Rather, we consider different forward-looking time horizons from one year to four or more years.

Similar to Chapter 4 we find that acquisitions tend to occur in poorly performing firms, and that firm size as well as cross ownership act as a kind of takeover deterrent. These results give us some confidence in the methodology applied in Chapter 4, which essentially is a bivariate analysis only. Another important finding is that the determinants of acquisition and failure differ across shareholder types. This stresses the need for detailed data on all relevant governance mechanisms, in particular for data on different types of owners. Overall, we find that acquisition and failure tend to be influenced by common factors. This implies that they should be examined in combination, and models explaining one form of exit but disregarding the other are likely to suffer from sample selection bias.

Chapter 6 examines the role of corporate governance and market discipline for productivity growth. The focus is on productivity growth because, at the aggregate level, productivity plays a key role in determining future generations' welfare. This analysis contributes to the literature in several respects: First, we consider a larger range of governance mechanisms and their relation to productivity growth than previous studies. Second, this is the first study to examine the impact of financial pressure (from creditors) on productivity growth for a continental European country. Third, we explicitly address potential endogeneity of our explanatory variables using the generalized method of moments (GMM) estimator developed by Arellano and Bond (1991). This method is now standard in panel econometrics. However, it is not yet widely applied in studies on corporate governance with the exceptions of Nickell et al. (1997) and Januszewski et al. (2002).

One important finding is that firms under concentrated ownership tend to show higher productivity growth, and this effect is larger for firms operating in more competitive markets. Intense competition alone does not affect productivity growth. Hence, competition and owner control appear to be complements. Another key finding is that financial pressure from creditors also has a positive impact on productivity growth, particularly for firms in financial distress. Overall, the results show that corporate governance and product market competition should be examined simultaneously. Studies investigating only one or a few of all mechanisms, which potentially affect productivity growth, might come to misleading results.

2 Literature Review and Methodological Concerns

This chapter is a revised and adapted version of Börsch-Supan and Köke (2002). It critically reviews previous empirical work on corporate governance to point out important methodological problems constraining these studies. It also suggests solutions to these problems, paying particular attention to the institutional setting in Germany. The ultimate aim is to indicate which data should be collected for corporate governance analyses and which methodological drawbacks can be avoided when using those data. The construction of the German Corporations Database discussed in Chapter 3 as well as the empirical analyses presented in Chapters 4–6 are direct applications of the lessons suggested in this chapter.

As noted in Chapter 1, understanding corporate governance is important because agency costs are potentially large, reducing firm productivity and, if widespread, the productivity of an entire country (Börsch-Supan, 1999). Unfortunately, theoretical analyses of corporate governance tend to deliver ambiguous answers because there are too many counteracting mechanisms which mask any clear picture (Hellwig, 1997).

Empirical studies of corporate governance are supposed to shed light on the relative weight of these counteracting mechanisms. They usually regress some measure of performance, ideally the firm's equity value or total factor productivity, on measures of the stringency of corporate governance, such as ownership structure, capital structure, board structure, or the market for corporate control. Unfortunately, this is not an easy task. For reasons explained in this survey, empirical studies on corporate governance have more than the usual share of econometric problems. Quite frequently, firm variables are assumed to be exogenous but are actually endogenous; the sample is not selected randomly; relevant variables are left out; and variables are measured with large errors. In all of these cases it will be difficult to isolate the influence of corporate governance factors on firm performance.

This chapter is structured according to four categories of econometric problems that have to be solved to infer causal effects of corporate governance: reverse causality (Chapter 2.1), sample selectivity (Chapter 2.2), missing variables (Chapter 2.3), and measurement error in variables (Chapter 2.4). In each chapter, we briefly describe the econometric problem in a textbook fashion, give examples drawing on the recent empirical literature, provide some basic tests, and suggest practical solutions. The discussed solutions relate to the econometric methods applied and to the data collected for corporate governance analysis. Chapter 2.5 summarizes the main results of this survey by providing recommendations how to avoid the discussed methodological drawbacks.

2.1 Reverse Causality

The core task of empirical studies on corporate governance is to explain firm performance by firm-specific variables that describe owner control. High monitoring costs between shareholders and managers can make owner control ineffective when the shares are dispersed (Grossman and Hart, 1980), compared to a situation in which the shares are owned by only a few large shareholders (Shleifer and Vishny, 1986). However, the direction of causality between ownership structure and performance is not clear: Concentrated ownership can improve firm performance via better monitoring, but well-performing firms could also attract investors. This is an example of *structural reverse causality.*

Jensen and Meckling (1976) argue that the lower the participation of management in the firm's equity, the higher the agency costs. High managerial ownership aligns the managers' incentives with the incentives of other shareholders (Convergence-of-Interest Hypothesis). Vice versa, managers could hold equity especially in highly profitable firms because this increases their wealth (Leland and Pyle, 1977). Causality of ownership and performance is therefore not clear ex ante.

Similar problems arise when an unobserved variable simultaneously determines ownership and performance. This case of reverse causality is known as *spurious correlation.* To illustrate this, we borrow an example from Himmelberg et al. (1999). Assume that there are two types of firms: Firm A has a higher degree of market power than firm B. If competition has a disciplining effect on managerial decisions, closer monitoring is required for firm A. In consequence, managers of firm A might receive a relatively large fraction of equity to align their interests with those of the other shareholders. However, due to market power firm A shows higher profit rates than firm B. Empirically, we would measure a positive correlation between managerial ownership and profitability.[1] But the estimated coefficient of managerial ownership will reflect only spurious correlation, not a causal relationship.

In these examples, the explanatory variable (ownership structure) is codetermined with the variable to be explained (performance). In econometrics

[1] Note that this effect depends on the measure of performance applied: c.p., profitability is likely to be higher in firms with market power but not necessarily productivity or productivity growth. For example, Januszewski et al. (2002) find a negative impact of market power on the growth of total factor productivity.

speak, the explanatory variable is endogenous. Without structural assumptions, the impact of this corporate governance mechanism on performance cannot be identified.

More formally, assume that the true model can be written as

$$z = \beta x + \epsilon \quad \text{and} \tag{2.1}$$

$$x = \gamma z + \eta\,, \tag{2.2}$$

where $E(\epsilon) = E(\eta) = 0$ and $cov(\epsilon, \eta) = \sigma_{\epsilon\eta}$, z denotes firm performance and x ownership concentration. If only the first equation is estimated by OLS, we obtain

$$\hat{\beta} = \frac{cov(x,z)}{var(x)} = \frac{cov(x, \beta x + \epsilon)}{var(x)} = \beta + \frac{cov(x,\epsilon)}{var(x)}\,. \tag{2.3}$$

The second term can be evaluated by replacing x with the right-hand side of equation (2.2). We obtain

$$\begin{aligned} cov(x,\epsilon) &= cov(\gamma z + \eta, \epsilon) \\ &= cov[\gamma(\beta x + \epsilon) + \eta, \epsilon] \\ &= \gamma\sigma_\epsilon^2 + \beta\gamma\, cov(x,\epsilon) + \sigma_{\epsilon\eta}\,. \end{aligned} \tag{2.4}$$

It follows that $cov(x,\epsilon) = \frac{\gamma\sigma_\epsilon^2 + \sigma_{\epsilon\eta}}{1-\beta\gamma}$. If $\gamma \neq 0$ or $\sigma_{\epsilon\eta} \neq 0$, the estimated coefficient $\hat{\beta}$ will be biased and inconsistent. The first is true in our first example of structural reverse causality, the second if common unobserved factors are present. In the latter case, the empirically measured correlation between x and z is only spurious. Since both cases are very likely, endogeneity is, in our view, the most serious problem in studies on corporate governance.

The formal description in equations (2.1)–(2.4) is helpful in analyzing the problem. Suppose that poor performance leads to a takeover which results in higher ownership concentration. Assume further that the new owners replace management what in turn leads to improved performance. In terms of equations (2.1) and (2.2), β is the impact of ownership concentration on performance and γ the impact of performance on ownership concentration. According to our assumptions, β is positive and γ negative. If $\sigma_{\epsilon\eta} = 0$, we know that the covariance of x and ϵ is negative. This implies that the impact of ownership concentration on performance is underestimated because we neglected the endogeneity of concentration.

Another good example for the endogeneity problem is the widely cited study of Demsetz and Lehn (1985). They examine the effect of ownership concentration on a firm's average profit rate during the years 1976–1980. Using cross-section data for 511 US firms, they investigate

$$return_i = \alpha + \beta_1 log(A5)_i + \sum_{j=2}^{J} \beta_j x_{ij} + \epsilon_i \,. \tag{2.5}$$

Their central explanatory variable is $A5$, which denotes the equity share of the five largest shareholders.[2] As control variables x they use expenditures for advertising and R&D, firm size, the standard deviation of accounting rates of return, and the standard deviation of market rates of return to proxy for the instability of a firm's environment as well as industry dummies. Their main result is that ownership concentration has a negative, although insignificant impact on the firm's average profit rate. Demsetz and Lehn attribute this result to the endogeneity of ownership: Shareholders deciding to alter the ownership structure from concentration to dispersion of shares should do so in awareness of its consequences for loosening control over professional management (Demsetz and Lehn, 1985). Therefore, in their view, no relationship between ownership concentration and performance exists.

The study of Demsetz and Lehn (1985) exemplifies the approach of a host of other empirical studies examining the influence of ownership on performance. Morck et al. (1988) regress firm value measured by Tobin's q on the fraction of shares owned by management using a cross-section of 371 US firms. The main problem with their approach is that their cross-sectional data cannot provide for instruments which are necessary to control for potential endogeneity of ownership. In the same manner, McConnell and Servaes (1990) use a sample of 1,173 US firms. In contrast to Morck et al. (1988) they have intertemporal variation in their data because they use two sets of cross-sectional data. Being aware of the problem of potential spurious correlation, they determine the robustness of results by adjusting all variables for their industry mean. But McConnell and Servaes do not investigate the problem of structural reverse causality – probably due to the lack of valid instruments. Leech and Leahy (1991) use a sample of 470 listed UK firms. They directly address the problem of endogeneity by regressing ownership structure on firm age, firm size, and a measure of firm-specific risk. But there remain two problems with their approach. First, they do not explain performance and ownership structure simultaneously. Second, their explanatory variables are also likely to be endogenous. Thus they cannot avoid reverse causality.

Compelling evidence for an endogeneity problem created by unobserved common factors to both right-hand side and left-hand side variables is presented by Himmelberg et al. (1999). This example is particularly helpful because it shows that panel data are extremely important in getting rid of this second cause of endogeneity. To solve the endogeneity problem Himmelberg et al. use data from 1982–1992 to assemble an unbalanced panel with about 600 US firms. They explain the level of managerial ownership m_{it} with

[2] Demsetz and Lehn (1985) also use alternative measures of management ownership such as the share owned by the top 20 shareholders or a Herfindahl index which measures ownership concentration.

$$m_{it} = \beta_1 x_{it} + \gamma_1 u_{it} + \epsilon_{it}\,, \tag{2.6}$$

where x_{it} are observable and u_{it} unobservable firm characteristics. Assuming that the unobservable firm characteristics $u_{it} = u_i$ are constant over time, they calculate pooled and fixed-effect estimators. In the pooled regression, managerial ownership is explained by expenditures for R&D and advertisement, firm size, and firm's idiosyncratic risk. Then they calculate several variants of fixed-effect estimators, and most coefficients change sign or become insignificant while the adjusted R^2 rises significantly. This suggests that in the pooled OLS regression the error term is correlated with explanatory variables leading to biased coefficients.

Short (1994) provides an excellent survey of earlier empirical studies. She concludes that most studies are limited by the use of cross-sectional data because only panel data allow to fully capture the dynamic interactions of firm-specific variables.

2.1.1 Tests

The classical test for causality in panel data models goes back to Granger (1969).[3] The idea is simple: In terms of equation (2.1), if x causes z, then changes in x should precede changes in z. To say that, two conditions must hold. First, in a regression of z on past values of z, the addition of past values of x should contribute significantly to the explanatory power of the regression. Second, z should not help to predict x, otherwise it is likely that other factors are causing x and z. More formally, to test for causality we run an unrestricted regression

$$z_{it} = \sum_{j=1}^{J} \alpha_j z_{it-j} + \sum_{j=1}^{J} \beta_j x_{it-j} + \epsilon_{it} \tag{2.7}$$

and a restricted regression

$$z_{it} = \sum_{j=1}^{J} \alpha_j z_{it-j} + \epsilon_{it}\,, \tag{2.8}$$

and use the residuals from both equations to perform an F-test. The test should reject that the β-coefficients are jointly zero; and in a second step where we regress z on x, the respective coefficients should jointly be zero. To take into account that another factor y might be causing z, and y might be contemporaneously correlated with x, lagged values of y are included.

---

[3] For earlier tests, see Anderson and Rubin (1949) and Koopmans and Hood (1953).

2.1.2 Lessons

Theoretical considerations and empirical evidence show that no conclusions about the impact of any corporate governance mechanism on firm performance can be made without considering the problem of reverse causality. Two things can be learned for future empirical research:

- Use panel data: Cross-sectional data do not allow to correct for unobserved firm heterogeneity. Panel data are a necessary condition for the identification of any singular corporate governance mechanism because panel data can provide for instruments that are not available in cross-sectional data.
- Take the unobserved into account: When unobserved firm characteristics are correlated with the exogenous variables, estimated coefficients will be biased. Estimating fixed-effect models or models in first differences can help to solve this problem. However, when the unobserved firm characteristics are not constant over time, this econometric trick does not work because firm effects cannot be subtracted out of the specification (e.g. by calculating first differences). The only way out is to reduce the unobserved part of the model and to collect time-series information on all relevant firm-specific variables.

More formally, consider the following data generating process:

$$y_{it} = \beta x_{it} + \epsilon^*_{it}\,, \tag{2.9}$$

where ϵ^*_{it} is independently and identically distributed with mean zero and variance σ^2_ϵ. Furthermore, we suspect that x_{it} is endogenous with respect to y_{it}. In order to consistently estimate model (2.9), we need instrumental variables that are correlated with x_{it} but are uncorrelated with y_{it}. For panel data, values of x_{it} lagged j periods are such instruments, provided the following conditions hold:

$$cov(\epsilon^*_{it}, x_{it-j}) = 0 \quad \text{for} \quad j \geq 1 \quad \text{and} \tag{2.10}$$

$$cov(x_{it}, x_{it-j}) \neq 0 \quad \text{for} \quad j \geq 1\,. \tag{2.11}$$

While the second condition is likely to hold, for example because economic variables typically show some degree of persistence, the first condition is more problematic. In particular, when the true error structure is given by $\epsilon^*_{it} = \alpha_i + \epsilon_{it}$, i.e. when the error term contains a firm-specific effect α_i, which is constant for all t, and α_i is correlated with x_{it}, this condition does not hold. One solution to this problem of unobserved heterogeneity is to eliminate the individual effects by transforming the data to deviations from individual means, which is possible with panel data. We obtain

$$y_{it} - \bar{y_i} = \beta(x_{it} - \bar{x_i}) + (\epsilon_{it} - \bar{\epsilon_i})\,, \tag{2.12}$$

where the bars indicate means. The estimator β obtained from this transformation is often called the within estimator or fixed-effects estimator. It can be shown that this estimator has the interpretation of an instrumental variables estimator where each explanatory variable is instrumented by its value in deviation from the individual-specific mean (e.g., Verbeek, 2000). However, if the explanatory variable x_{it} is not strictly exogenous, for example because it represents a lagged endogenous variable y_{it-1}, the within estimator will also be biased.[4]

An alternative method to eliminate the firm-specific effect is to take first differences in panel data:

$$\Delta y_{it} = \beta \Delta x_{it} + \Delta \epsilon_{it} . \tag{2.13}$$

If ϵ_{it} is serially uncorrelated, $E(x_{it-j}, \Delta\epsilon_{it}) = 0$ holds for $j \geq 2$. Hence, explanatory variables lagged two or more periods (or their first differences) are valid instruments for Δx_{it} (Anderson and Hsiao, 1981). This instrumental variables estimator is consistent for $N \to \infty$ and/or $T \to \infty$.

In summary, the case for panel data is strong. Data sources suitable for analysis of corporate governance in German corporations are discussed in Chapter 3. Unfortunately, even with panel data two problems remain. First, estimating fixed effects does not explain why there is variation between firms. For corporate governance this could be of particular interest because we want to know which firm-specific arrangements improve performance. The true source of performance improvement can only partly be determined by interpreting within estimators. Second, as argued by Himmelberg et al. (1999), eliminating firm-specific effects by taking first differences is only appropriate as long as the α_i are indeed fixed. If the α_i are not constant over time, this is a problem of missing variables and estimated coefficients will be biased and inconsistent (Chapter 2.3). Therefore, more model structure is required to better understand how corporate governance influences performance. Denis and Sarin (1999) go a first step in this direction by challenging the commonly assumed persistence of ownership structure, showing for the US that firm ownership and the composition of the board of directors exhibit significant intertemporal variance. Changes in ownership are related to management turnover, stock performance, and the threat of takeover. Similarly, Köke (2000) shows that ownership structures in large German corporations vary significantly over time, and that major changes in ownership are preceded by poor performance and are followed by board turnover and corporate restructuring (see Chapter 4). Hence, studies examining the relation of ownership

---

[4] An alternative estimator is the between estimator or random-effects estimator. This estimator exploits the between dimension of the data (differences between individuals). However, this estimator also requires that the explanatory variables are strictly exogenous.

and performance should use panel data, both for financial and ownership variables.

But even including all firm-specific variables in panel format does not solve the problem that potentially all firm-specific variables are endogenous. Non-controversial instruments, crucial for identification, are those that are determined outside the firm and affect the firm. Prime candidates are macroeconomic variables (Nickell and Nicolitsas, 1999) or government regulation (Zingales, 1998; Garvey and Hanka, 1999).

Nickell and Nicolitsas (1999) investigate the impact of increases in financial pressure – the ratio of interest payments to cash flow – on company behavior. They find that an increase in financial pressure has a large negative impact on employment, a small negative impact on pay rises, and a minute positive impact on productivity. To cope with potential endogeneity of firm-specific financial pressure, Nickell and Nicolitsas apply a set of instruments: long lags on employment, output, wages, and capital stock. For their key financial variable, financial pressure, they make use of substantial exogenous shifts in interest rates, which have been instituted by government policy over the sample period.

Zingales (1998) shows how a change in the regulatory environment can help reveal information about firm processes. Zingales examines the market exit behavior in the US trucking industry following major industry deregulation in 1979 initiated by the Carter administration. Deregulation significantly lowered barriers to entry and allowed for increasing competition that was largely unexpected. Thus capital structure is not likely to have been chosen optimally beforehand. Zingales uses the change in competitive pressure to determine the role of capital structure for the firms' exit behavior. On a set of 889 trucking firms he examines the survival until 1985 with the following probit model:

$$Prob(survival_i^{1985}) = f(X_i^{1977}, leverage_i^{1977}) + \epsilon_i \,. \tag{2.14}$$

The variable of interest is the firms' leverage in 1977, i.e. before deregulation. Other factors potentially influencing the firms' survival are various measures of efficiency (X_i^{1977}). Among these are the level of intangibles (as a fraction of total assets), firm size, and return on sales. Leverage thus should catch any additional effect on survival other than efficiency. Zingales' results indicate that highly leveraged firms had a reduced chance of survival after deregulation. A reason for this may be that they had to curtail good investments.

Other good examples for the use of changes in regulation are the studies of Garvey and Hanka (1999) who study the impact of US anti-takeover laws on firm leverage, Kang (1998) who studies deregulation in the US textile industry, and Kole and Lehn (1997) who investigate deregulation in the US telecommunication and electric utilities industries. For Germany, the history of deregulation is still short. Only recently the markets for telecommunication and energy were opened to competition. The enactment of the Single European Market in 1992 might represent a useful instrument in panel studies, but only when it occurred as an exogenous shock. Allen et al. (1998) find that its enactment had a major impact on tariffs which in turn drove competition within the European Union.

In the context of dynamic panel data models, an alternative is to use lagged endogenous variables as instruments, provided they meet the conditions for valid instruments (see above). The standard instrumental variables (IV) estimator goes back to Anderson and Hsiao (1981) who use a version of a first-differenced two-stage least squares estimator to estimate a panel data model with a lagged dependent variable. Arellano and Bond (1991) propose a generalized method of moments (GMM) estimator that allows to exploit lags of the dependent variable as well as lags of the explanatory variables as instruments. Moreover, GMM estimators allow to use lagged values of the endogenous variable as instruments also in non-linear specifications such as the one used by Zingales (1998). Examples for the use of the GMM technique are the studies of Nickell et al. (1997) and Januszewski et al. (2002) both of which examine the effects of product market competition and corporate governance on productivity growth. Using an unbalanced panel of listed and non-listed German manufacturing firms, Januszewski et al. find that productivity growth tends to be higher in more competitive industries, but only for firms with concentrated ownership. Their results concerning the disciplining role of competition is consistent with the findings of Nickell et al. for the United Kingdom. Both studies are good examples how the endogeneity problem can be addressed using econometric methods without identifying exogenous events.

2.2 Sample Selectivity

An econometric issue that empirical researchers might be less familiar with is sample selectivity. To illustrate why this is an important issue consider recent empirical studies on corporate governance. Most of them focus on the largest and, among them, the listed companies. These companies are also likely to be the most profitable firms in the market. For example, Morck et al. (1988), Agrawal and Knoeber (1996), and Cho (1998) consider firms from the Fortune 500 in the US. Most studies on Germany also examine the top-performing firms (e.g., Cable, 1985; Seger, 1997; Edwards and Nibler, 2000; Gorton and Schmid, 2000). But performance is typically the variable that corporate governance is supposed to influence. Hence, these samples are obviously selected by the endogenous variable. This implies that most studies of corporate governance are likely to have a sample selection bias.

Take the example of management compensation, a governance mechanism which recently attracted increasing attention (Jensen and Murphy, 1990;

Murphy, 1998). If compensation is tied to performance, managers should become more focused on the respective performance measure. Empirical studies face the problem that data on management compensation are available only for those firms that enacted compensation programs. But these enterprises tend to be well-performing firms, often listed on the stock exchange. Hence, a selection bias is likely here.

More formally, estimated coefficients are unbiased only if the expectation of the error term given the exogenous variables is zero. In the model

$$y = \beta x + \epsilon , \tag{2.15}$$

the condition $E(\epsilon|x) = 0$ must be satisfied for $\hat{\beta}$ to be unbiased. If the sample is not randomly selected, i.e. if the probability for firms being in the sample is correlated with the endogenous variable, this condition does not hold.

To illustrate this, suppose that we have data for y only above a certain threshold y^*. Here y might represent firm performance and x the concentration of share ownership (Figure 2.1).

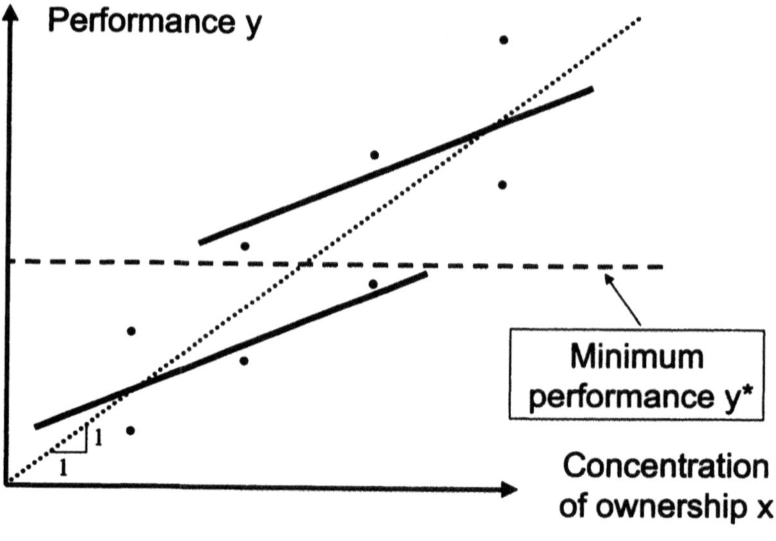

Figure 2.1. Estimation bias due to sample selection

The true slope coefficient is $\beta = 1$ and is depicted by the dotted line. We see that by excluding lower values of y from the regression – e.g. below a minimum performance of y^* – we systematically exclude residuals that are negative *at low values of* x. Thus, on average the error term will be positive given low values of x. But this implies a downward bias of $\hat{\beta}$ for performance values above y^* (bold lines). More generally, the direction of bias depends on the covariance of x and ϵ. If we knew $E(\epsilon|x)$, we could include it in the regression, resulting in unbiased estimates. Hence, sample selectivity is a special case of omitted variables.[5]

In particular, if we explain performance by the concentration of ownership, the impact will be underestimated when we use only firms with 'high' performance. 'Low' performers might not be in the sample because they were too small in size and hence were not required to report financial data. Our estimate with the 'high' performers would be misleading because not ownership structure forced the coefficient to be smaller than one but firm size. The true source of influence on performance would remain unclear.

To our knowledge, all empirical studies on corporate governance in Germany suffer from the econometric problem of selection bias. Table 2.1 lists the most recent of them and compares the selection criteria applied for sample construction.

Table 2.1. Comparison of criteria for sample selection

Study	Criteria
Cable (1985)	48 out of the 100 largest companies in 1970
Chirinko and Elston (1996)	270 companies that were continuously traded on a stock exchange during 1965–1990
Seger (1997)	144 companies that were continuously traded on a stock exchange during 1990–1992
Wenger and Kaserer (1998)	48 companies that were continuously traded on a stock exchange during 1973–1993
Edwards and Nibler (2000)	158 out of the 200 largest companies in 1992
Gorton and Schmid (2000)	Two cross-sections: 1. 88 out of the 100 largest companies in 1974 2. 57 out of the largest companies in 1985

Notes: All studies examine only public corporations (*AG*). Only the data set used by Edwards and Nibler (2000) includes a few private corporations (*GmbH*).

As can be seen from Table 2.1, in almost all cases only public corporations (*Aktiengesellschaft*) are selected for analysis. In addition, often a size criterion is applied since only the largest stock companies are used (Cable, 1985; Edwards and Nibler, 2000; Gorton and Schmid, 2000). The studies of Chirinko and Elston (1996), Seger (1997), and Wenger and Kaserer (1998) demand yet another criterion: The companies selected must have been continuously

[5] See Maddala (1983) on the econometrics of limited dependent variables.

traded on the stock exchange, in the case of Chirinko and Elston for 25 years in total. As understandable the selection of large companies might be – for example in the light of publication requirements (and hence availability of sufficient information), which are the strictest for the largest companies – in general these selection criteria potentially bias estimation results. We try to show this with some intuitive illustrations.

Firm behavior influences the probability that a particular firm will be in a sample for corporate governance analysis. If a firm exits its product market, for example due to bankruptcy or a takeover, it will drop out of our sample. If a firm goes public, it will be more likely to be in the data set because we often focus on firms listed on the stock exchange. Hence, both decisions – market exit and listing – influence the probability to be in the sample.

The firm's market value is often used as endogenous variable (e.g., Morck et al., 1988; McConnell and Servaes, 1990). But a precondition for this is that a market value for each firm is available. This is fulfilled only for listed firms, non-listed firms must be neglected. If the decision to go public depends on performance, the probability for a firm to be in the sample will be influenced by the endogenous variable. In this case parameters will be biased and inconsistent. Assuming that performance is irrelevant for the listing decision certainly is a strong assumption.

In Germany market capitalization was about 28% of GDP in 1996, while it was 114% in the US (OECD, 1998). This simple comparison shows that incentives to go public might be significantly different between countries. Even within Germany only a comparatively small number of corporations decided to have their shares traded. Out of 2,300 public corporations (*AG*) only about 500 were publicly traded. About 400,000 private corporations (*GmbH*) make the majority of all German corporations (Köke, 2001c). Hence, it is likely that the decision to go public is affected by possibly not observable firm-specific characteristics or institutional arrangements such as the strictness of disclosure rules. In turn, the decision on the legal form is likely to be influenced by regulations concerning codetermination (Hopt, 1997) or regulations concerning corporate institutions such as the board of directors (*Aufsichtsrat*) (Steiner, 1998). This is a problem if the same variables simultaneously influence performance.

Pagano and Röell (1996) suggest that an incentive for listing is a strong need of external funding, for example resulting from good investment opportunities. The probability of being in the sample could be determined as depicted in Figure 2.2. Similarly, if investment opportunities of listed firms improve, their market value will rise. In both cases the probability of being in the sample will be higher, when our sampling criterion is top-performing listed firms. Formally, the average correlation between the error term and the exogenous variable is positive. Hence, the impact of ownership concentration will be mismeasured, and probably all the studies shown in Table 2.1 suffer from this problem.

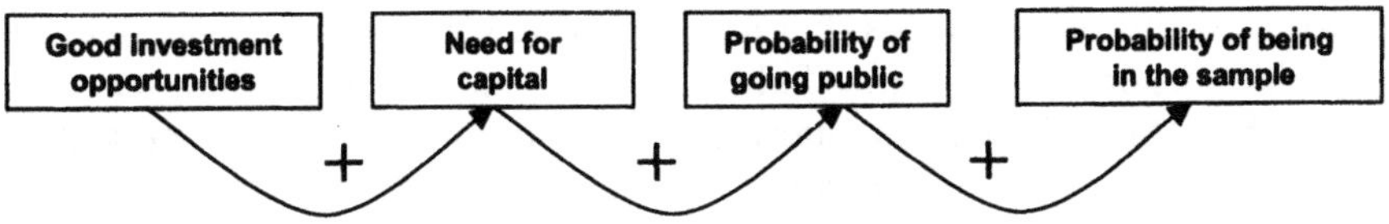

Figure 2.2. Causes for selection bias

The study of Holderness and Sheehan (1988) is an example how to appropriately address sample selectivity. For their analysis they use only firms listed either on the NYSE or on AMEX. To check whether there is a selection bias they replicate all estimations on a random sample from all firms in the 1980 Spectrum.[6] Showing that estimation results from both samples are generally the same they conclude that the original sample is not biased.

The firm's decision to exit a market can also bias a sample. Often researchers eliminate firms from their data set for which they do not have a performance history over the whole sample period – e.g. due to bankruptcy, takeover, or reporting failure – in order to obtain a balanced panel. However, sampling data only for surviving firms leaves them with the top- or well-performing firms; losers are eliminated. Thus, balanced panels are probably biased. In light of this, the studies of Chirinko and Elston (1996), Seger (1997), and Wenger and Kaserer (1998) are likely to suffer from this kind of selection bias.[7] Further selection criteria that might bias a sample are the firm's decision to diversify (Campa and Kedia, 2000) and the decision to announce corporate events such as debt or equity issues (Eckbo et al., 1990; Prabhala, 1997).

A good example that uses an unbalanced panel is the study of Himmelberg et al. (1999). They collect data for 600 firms from 1982 through 1992. When a firm drops out in a particular year, they keep the performance history of the firm. Nevertheless, sample bias also occurs when the exit decision is determined by the endogenous variable which in their case is firm performance measured by Tobin's q. Himmelberg et al. report that a simple probit model for exit refers to size as the main explanatory variable for exit, not firm failure. They conclude that selection bias is unlikely in their sample.

---

[6] The only additional criterion they use is that these firms must be in one of the manuals of Moody's.

[7] For an empirical study on the US, see for example Murali and Welch (1989). They require that the firms in their sample existed continuously during the years 1977–1981.

Economic intuition tells us that exit decisions are probably strongly correlated with corporate governance failure. If a firm exited the market, we would assume that this is important information about the firm. Not using this information means to include it in the error term. Therefore, firm decisions on market exit or listing are important vehicles for identification.

2.2.1 Tests

The above discussion shows that there are two types of selection bias: (1) The sample does not contain a particular type of firm at all (e.g., non-listed corporations or private corporations); (2) the sample contains all relevant firms but suffers from sample attrition (e.g. due to bankruptcy or takeover). The first type of bias is typically not testable because the sample does not contain any information on the missing firms. We need to rely on economic theory to detect which firms ought to be included in our analysis.

For the second type of bias, Verbeek and Nijman (1992) suggest a number of simple tests. One approach is based on the idea that the error terms should not depend on the selection indicators. Define the indicator variable r_{it} as $r_{it} = 1$ if (x_{it}, y_{it}) is observed and zero otherwise. To test that, one includes some function of $r_{i1}, ..., r_{iT}$ in the model and checks its significance. Verbeek and Nijman recommend to include $c_i = \prod_{t=1}^{T} r_{it}$, indicating whether unit i is observed over all periods, or $T_i = \sum_{t=1}^{T} r_{it}$, indicating the total number of periods i is observed. Another group of tests is based upon the idea that fixed- or random-effects estimators should suffer differently from selection bias, using either a balanced sub-panel or an unbalanced panel. Verbeek (2000: 346) argues that if different samples, selected on the basis of $r_{i1}, ..., r_{iT}$, lead to significantly different estimators, it is very likely that the selection process contains information about the unobservables in the model.

2.2.2 Lessons

Analogously to the discussion of tests, we now discuss solutions to selection bias, separately for both types of bias. The first source of bias is best be addressed by collecting data on the missing firms. What sounds simple, can in practice be a Herculean task. Whereas a number of databases contains information on large and listed German corporations, there is only a few that include balance sheet data on non-listed corporations. Among them are Balance Sheet Database from Hoppenstedt and Worldscope Global Researcher from Primark. Although disclosure requirements in essence are the same for listed and non-listed corporations (§266 ff. HGB), they are less strongly enforced for non-listed corporations. Even more difficult to obtain are data on ownership for non-listed corporations, preferably in panel format. Suitable data sources that contain information on private (GmbH) as well as public (AG) non-listed corporations are discussed in Chapter 3.1. A major obstacle is, however, that non-listed firms frequently change their name what makes it hard to track them through the full sample period.

The second source of bias can be addressed using econometric methods. This approach also requires some additional information. To appropriately correct for sample attrition due to bankruptcy or takeover, one needs information on these events. This implies that the researcher must verify why a particular firm stopped reporting in a particular year. Information about the status of a company (bankruptcy, voluntary liquidation, change in the legal form or the name etc.) are officially available only from courts (*Handelsregister*), which are accessible only locally at the place of registration of a particular firm. A more cost-efficient way to obtain this information is to conduct a survey among sampled firms, most simply by telephone. Of course, in case of liquidation without succession this strategy is not going to work.

The classical econometric approach to correct selection bias goes back to Heckman (1976). Essentially, we run an expanded regression to model $E(\epsilon|x)$. Assume that firm performance has a truncated distribution, as depicted in Figure 2.3.

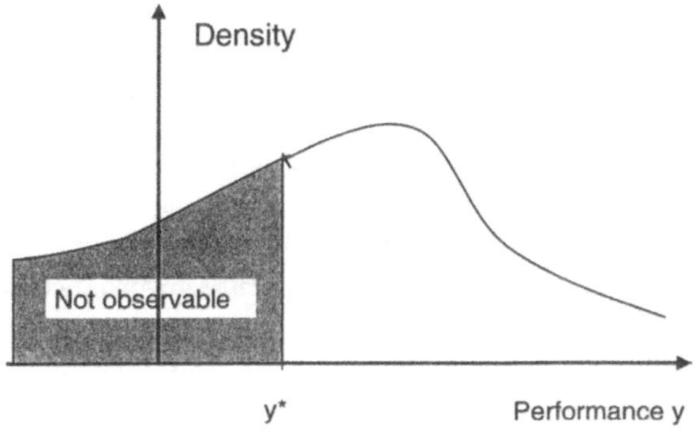

Figure 2.3. Truncation of the endogenous variable

The distribution is truncated at $y = y^*$. No information is available for firms below minimum performance y^*. Performance is observed conditional on the probability that the particular firm belongs to the sample. If we do not use this information, estimated coefficients will be biased and inconsistent.

More formally, the sample selection model consists of two parts, a linear performance equation and a binary choice type equation explaining exit:

$$y^*_{it} = \beta x_{it} + \epsilon_{it}\,, \tag{2.16}$$

where x_{it} is an exogenous characteristic and y^*_{it} is the firm's i performance, which is only observable for firms in the sample. Firm exit is described by

$$r^*_{it} = \gamma z_{it} + \eta_{it} \tag{2.17}$$

with the following observation rule:

$$y_{it} = y^*_{it},\ r_{it} = 1 \quad \text{if} \quad r^*_{it} > 0 \quad \text{and} \tag{2.18}$$

$$y_{it} \quad \text{not observed,} \quad r_{it} = 0 \quad \text{if} \quad r^*_{it} \leq 0, \tag{2.19}$$

where y_{it} is the firm's actual performance. The binary variable r_{it} indicates firm's survival or takeover. Alternatively, r_{it} could indicate firm's survival or bankruptcy.

The correction is done by adding a term $\sigma_{\epsilon\eta}\frac{\phi(\gamma z_{it})}{\Phi(\gamma z_{it})}$ to equation (2.16) as regressor. This term, also called Heckman's lambda, describes the probability that a particular performance value y_{it} is observed, given performance is above the minimum performance level. Since this ratio is probably endogenous we must explain it using information about firm exit as instrumental variables. Note that a naive application of the Heckman procedure generates problems of its own. Problems may arise because the functional form is wrongly specified, the assumption of a normal distribution does not hold, or some parameters are not identified. Other more recent techniques to deal with selection bias can be found in Verbeek and Nijman (1996) and Vella (1998).

The main lesson for empirical studies on corporate governance is that we need more firm-specific data that shed light on the sampling process. This is not an easy task since we usually use data that were collected for other purposes and hence are incomplete for our means.

2.3 Missing Variables

A third and probably well-known econometric problem plaguing empirical studies on corporate governance occurs when explanatory variables are missing in the estimated model. This occurs in two forms. First, for reasons of data availability typical in the entire industrial organization research, this literature features a more than normal number of estimated equations in which key explanatory variables are not available for inclusion. Second, knowing little about functional forms, the commonly employed linear specifications imply, if counterfactual, missing higher order terms in the equation that has been estimated.

An interesting example of a frequently missing variable is the intensity of product market competition (Baily and Gersbach, 1995). For example, more intense competition should increase pressure on management because profits shrink and, in consequence, non-performing managers might get fired (Hart, 1983).[8] Pressure resulting from high leverage could substitute for pressure from competition (Nickell et al., 1997). Hence, the interaction between competition and corporate governance mechanisms becomes important.

A prominent example for the second case is again the study of Demsetz and Lehn (1985). In their model, ownership concentration is supposed to influence the average profit rate. Their specification imposes the restriction that this influence is linear in nature. But this is not consistent with theory. Jensen and Meckling (1976) argue that managerial ownership should have a positive impact on performance. Fama and Jensen (1983) show that high managerial ownership could make managers too risk-averse. Hence, performance should be lower for high managerial ownership (Managerial-Entrenchment Hypothesis). Demsetz and Lehn's model does not allow for a non-linear influence of ownership. As we know, this could be corrected by using a polynomial, e.g. managerial ownership could enter the regression model in a linear and a quadratic term. In most studies the quadratic and higher order terms are left out, generating a left-out variable bias.

More generally, if the true structure of the model is

$$y = \alpha + \beta x + \gamma z + \epsilon\,, \tag{2.20}$$

but the regression leaves out the variable z, the OLS estimate of β is

$$\hat{\beta} = \beta + \gamma \frac{cov(x,z)}{var(x)}\,, \tag{2.21}$$

which is unbiased only if (1) $\gamma = 0$ or (2) the covariance of x and z is zero.

This textbook analysis generalizes to the multivariate case and may be used to sign the bias and to assess its relevance. Assume that y is the firm's profit, x is managerial ownership, and z measures the intensity of competition. Assume further that higher competition leads to lower profits, i.e. γ is negative, and that competition reduces agency costs. Then managers can be offered a lower equity share in the firm to align their incentives compared with a situation in which the firm has substantial market power. This means

[8] This result is not uncontroversial in the theoretical literature. Scharfstein (1988) shows that Hart's results depend on the extent of managers' assumed risk aversion. In a similar model but with a different utility function Scharfstein obtains the opposite result: more competition increases managerial slack. Hermalin (1992) shows that if agency goods are normal goods competition decreases agency costs.

that $cov(x, z) < 0$. If no measure of competition is included in the regression, the impact β of manager's equity on performance will be overestimated.

Taking the Demsetz and Lehn (1985) example, we also know the sign of the bias from a priori information. Jensen and Meckling (1976) predict a positive impact of managerial ownership, Fama and Jensen (1983) a negative impact at least for very large managerial stakes. Hence, we can expect an inversely U-shaped relationship. Leaving out the quadratic term will therefore cause the coefficient of the linear ownership variable to be underestimated.

Morck et al. (1988) provide evidence for this hypothesis. They regress Tobin's q on managerial ownership using a piecewise linear regression. They find that the relationship is non-linear with turning points at 5% and 25%. Below 5% the slope coefficient is positive, between 5% and 25% negative, and over 25% again positive. McConnell and Servaes (1990) confirm this result using a polynomial specification for managerial ownership. Hence, the result of Demsetz and Lehn (1985) who show that managerial ownership has no significant impact on performance might be due to an incomplete model.

Another difficulty is how a non-linear influence of right-hand side variables is detected. The way chosen by Morck et al. (1988) is to assume a priori that 5% and 25% represent the break-off points for the piecewise regression model. Since theory does not provide us with this specific kind of information, an econometrically better approach would be to estimate the break-off points themselves.

The general problem is that we do not know which variables are left out. If only one variable is missing in the model – for example because we do not have sufficient data on it – we can predict the direction of bias by using additional assumptions which themselves might not be testable. If more than one variable is omitted, it becomes more difficult to predict the direction of bias (Greene, 1997: 402). For example, if also the firm's leverage has a disciplining effect and is omitted from the model, the covariance of competition and ownership must be predicted, but net of the effect of leverage. Here economic intuition soon becomes unreliable.

This problem is particularly salient because the data requirements for empirical corporate governance analysis are high. As discussed in Chapter 1, the corporate governance literature enumerates six main different channels how managers can be disciplined: ownership structure, capital structure, board structure, management compensation, product market competition, and the takeover market. Let us further exemplify the missing variables problem by discussing specific studies dealing with the influence of ownership on performance.

Pound (1988) argues that the quality of monitoring depends on the type of owner. Institutional investors such as banks or insurers might have business relations with the firm they are supposed to monitor, and they do not want to endanger those relations by too harsh monitoring. Hence, private investors might be better monitors. Also institutional investors such as pension funds, which have no business relations with the firm, could be good monitors (Pound, 1988). Early studies indicate that pension funds have a significant influence on changes of the corporate charter (Gordon and Pound, 1993; Smith, 1996).[9]

A good example on the interaction of different governance mechanisms is the study of McWilliams and Sen (1997). They investigate whether managerial ownership has a negative effect on the market valuation of anti-takeover amendments of the corporate charter, or whether managerial board membership has a separate effect. In a first step, McWilliams and Sen show that higher managerial ownership is associated with a more negative stock market reaction. But they argue that managers' board membership should have a separate effect on the reaction of the market. In particular, if a manager holds equity and in addition sits on the board, the stock price should fall even more because managers would have much more power in the corporation. Just managerial stock ownership should not matter. Formally, if the probability for board membership is correlated negatively with the market reaction and if this probability is positively correlated with managerial equity, the impact of managerial equity on the market reaction will be underestimated. In other words, if the true impact of managerial ownership on the stock price reaction is zero but a mixed impact of board membership and equity ownership is measured by only using managerial ownership in the model, the true influence of equity ownership cannot be determined. For 265 US firms from 1980 to 1990 they run the following second regression:

$$p_{it} = \alpha + \beta_1 b_{it} + \beta_2 n_{it} + \epsilon_{it} , \tag{2.22}$$

where p_{it} is the price of stock i in year t, b_{it} is the fraction of shares owned managers sitting on the board, and n_{it} is the fraction of shares owned managers not sitting on the board. While the coefficient β_1 remains significantly negative, the coefficient β_2 is close to zero. Thus the results from the first regression were misleading: It is not managerial ownership that causes the negative stock market reaction to charter amendments but managers' board membership.

Nickell et al. (1997) examine the simultaneous impact of product market competition, capital structure, and ownership structure on productivity growth. Using data on 580 UK manufacturing firms from 1982 to 1994, they run the following model:

$$\Delta(y_{it} - k_{it}) = f(k_{it}, n_{it}, s_{it}, c_{it}, p_{it}) + \epsilon_{it} , \tag{2.23}$$

where y_{it} is real value added for firm i in year t, k_{it} is real capital stock, n_{it} is total employment, and s_{it} is shareholder control defined as the probability that the largest shareholder will win a vote under the assumption that all

[9] See Black (1998), Karpoff (1998), and del Guercio and Hawkins (1999) for critical surveys.

the other shareholders vote independently (Cubbin and Leech, 1983). Their measure of competition, c_{it}, is the inverse of ex post rents (profits less capital costs) normalized on value added. Financial pressure, p_{it}, is measured by interest payments normalized on cash flow. They find that all three factors improve productivity growth but that shareholder control and financial pressure can substitute for competition. Formally, if competition had been neglected in the model, the impact of shareholder control would have been underestimated because the covariance of shareholder control and competition is negative, and competition itself has a positive influence on productivity growth.

Typically, it is not possible to test for missing variables. As for the case of missing data for a particular type of firm (see Chapter 2.2), we must rely on economic theory to detect which variables are missing in a given empirical model.

2.3.1 Lessons

There are several lessons from these empirical studies. First, if theory suggests that particular variables have a non-linear influence on firm performance, the model must include polynomial terms of the relevant variables. Alternatively, piecewise regressions can be run. Forcing variables to have a linear impact can bias the estimated coefficients. Second, the influence of a particular corporate governance mechanism generally will not be measured correctly if other relevant mechanisms are omitted from the model. Coefficients will be biased and inconsistent if governance mechanisms can substitute or complement each other. This is, however, very likely for any firm-specific variable.

We have some clear requirements for data on hand. Earlier studies were limited through data availability. This has changed. The following specific data are required:

- Ownership data: shareholder type (e.g. managers, non-managing individuals, institutional shareholders, government), size of share blocks
- Financial data: debt structure (e.g. long-term versus short-term, bank versus industry credit, outside versus inside financing)
- Board structure: composition of the board (e.g. size, fraction of insiders or bankers, equity positions of board members, union representation)
- Competition measures: market power (e.g. number of competitors, industry-specific concentration indices, import penetration)
- Takeover activity: number of successful and unsuccessful takeover attempts.

If any of these variables are not used in estimation, a bias in coefficients will be likely. The problem with these requirements is that usually our data had been collected for other means. Therefore they are often incomplete over time and also do not contain the required details. This can significantly reduce panel size. Nevertheless, with currently available data sources it is possible to construct a full-fledged panel of significant size (Chapter 3).

2.4 Measurement Error in Variables

Measurement error is the fourth in our list of plagues to empirical corporate governance studies. This includes mismeasurement of the endogenous as well as the exogenous variables.

Corporate governance has the purpose to improve firm performance. However, it is not entirely clear how performance ought to be measured. Take the example of takeover studies. Economic theory suggests that the market for corporate control can serve as a governance device (Jensen and Ruback, 1983; Franks and Mayer, 1995). If firm value is lower than the expected value that can be achieved under a different management team, this signals that a corporate takeover followed by an exchange of management could improve firm value (Jensen, 1988).[10] The first empirical problem here is that in practice the true market value is particularly hard to measure in times of a takeover due to often erratic variation, and other corporate performance measures are not highly correlated.

Measurement error in the endogenous variable does not cause estimated coefficients to be biased because the error term catches this additional variation, but estimation results are likely to be weakened due to a low ratio of signal-to-noise. The additional variation may lead to insignificant and unusable estimation results. Estimated effects of corporate governance have a larger range of uncertainty than they have in reality.

As opposed to measurement of the endogenous variable, measurement error in exogenous variables causes coefficient estimates to be biased and inconsistent. This is most likely for variables that firms are not required to submit to the public. Competition measures are a good example. In the industrial organization literature, competition is typically measured using individual market shares, rents[11], price markups, or the elasticity of market demand. But since we cannot observe marginal costs, and prices are only reported jointly with the amount of goods sold (i.e. as sales), we have only vague information on price markups.

More formally, take the simple case with one regressor. Assume that the true regression model is $y = \beta x^* + \epsilon$ and the true x^* is measured with error ν. We observe $x = x^* + \nu$ and measure β with

---

[10] A problem with this argument is that the old management teams could enact the changes themselves. In addition, old management should generally have much better information about the company.

[11] Januszewski et al. (2002) define rents as operating surplus less costs of capital, normalized by total sales.

$$\hat{\beta} = \frac{cov(x,y)}{var(x)} = \frac{cov(x^* + \nu, \beta x^* + \epsilon)}{var(x)} . \tag{2.24}$$

Expanding the covariance by adding and subtracting $\beta\nu$ we obtain

$$\hat{\beta} = \frac{cov[x^* + \nu, \beta(x^* + \nu) - \beta\nu + \epsilon]}{var(x)} = \beta(1 - \frac{\sigma_\nu^2}{\sigma_x^2}) , \tag{2.25}$$

if $cov(\epsilon, \nu) = cov(x^*, \epsilon) = cov(x^*, \nu) = 0$. If $\sigma_\nu^2 > 0$, i.e. if there is noise in the measurement of the exogenous variable x, it follows that

$$|\beta| > [|\beta|(1 - \frac{\sigma_\nu^2}{\sigma_x^2})] > 0 , \tag{2.26}$$

because $\sigma_x^2 > \sigma_\nu^2$. Hence, β will be biased towards zero. Estimated effects of mismeasured variables are always smaller in absolute value than they are in reality.

Note that there are also theoretical problems concerning the above mentioned measures of market power. Even if we knew all participants in a market and their relative market shares, we would neglect the fact that most goods have more or less close substitutes. Moreover, even if we knew all market participants including those of substitutes, we would disregard competitive pressure resulting from the threat of market entry by new suppliers. In this case, public statistics report a too low size of an individual market and hence a too small degree of competition. Corts (1998) argues that a price markup measure is only appropriate if an industry is characterized by a conjectural variations game. This cannot be assumed for all industries. If an industry is characterized by efficient supergame collusion, the conduct parameter method will yield severely downward-biased estimates of market power in that industry. Since this downward bias will not be equal for all industries, measurement error will be even higher. Formally, if competition has a positive influence on firm performance and if competition is measured with some error, the estimated coefficient will be biased towards zero.

Many studies on corporate governance use Tobin's q as the key performance measure (e.g., Morck et al., 1988; Cho, 1998). Implicitly these studies assume that capital markets know the correct firm value and that it is reflected by current market value of shares. Although it is sometimes doubted that this assumption is correct, it might be the best measure available. Empirical studies on Germany usually use other measures (Table 2.2). The main reason lies in German accounting rules: In annual accounts, assets are not reported at their market value but at historical costs, i.e. at the value they had at the time of purchase.

If these different performance measures indeed proxied for the same (not directly observable) firm performance, they would be highly correlated. Unfortunately they are not. Geroski (1998) shows for British firms that the correlation between different performance measures and some preconditions for

Table 2.2. Comparison of performance measures

Study	Performance measure
Germany:	
Cable (1985)	Return on assets (ROA)
Chirinko and Elston (1996)	ROA
Edwards and Nibler (2000)	Market-to-book ratio
Gorton and Schmid (2000)	ROA, return on equity
US and UK:	
Demsetz and Lehn (1985), Holderness and Sheehan (1988)	Return on equity
Morck et al. (1988), McConnell and Servaes (1990), Cho (1998)	Tobin's q
Nickell et al. (1997), Nickell and Nicolitsas (1999)	Productivity growth

profitability, such as the number of major innovations or patents produced, is weak. In addition, even the correlation between performance measures such as accounting profits, market value, or the growth rate of market value is low. This is mainly due to differences in distributions of variables. Geroski shows that accounting profits normalized by total sales are almost normally distributed. In contrast, the number of patents produced, a precondition for profitability, is highly skewed. Hence, different measures of performance might be correlated only in a highly non-linear way.

2.4.1 Tests

Hausman (1978) proposes a simple test for measurement error in exogenous variables. This test is based on the idea that instrumental variables can help reduce measurement error. In the above notation, we need to specify one or more instrumental variables that are correlated with the exogenous variable x^*, which is measured with some error, but are uncorrelated with the error ν. Then we estimate the model $y = \beta x^* + \epsilon$ twice, once with and once without instrumental variables, to obtain estimates for β_{IV} and β, respectively. Under the null hypothesis of no measurement error, the difference of $\beta - \beta_{IV}$ is zero. As Hausman shows, this test statistic is asymptotically χ^2-distributed.

2.4.2 Lessons

There are several lessons for future research. First, selection of the endogenous variable can strongly influence estimation results. If different performance measures come from different distributions, estimated coefficients will depend on the model we have chosen. Only if our estimates for corporate governance variables are robust against using alternative performance measures, we can be more confident in our results. Robustness checks reduce the dependence on particular assumptions.

Second, if exogenous variables are measured with error, the problem is more serious. The direct approach to reduce measurement error is to improve the data on hand. Take the case of ownership data for large German corporations. Since there are several sources for ownership information, the researcher can use them to cross-check the relevant data to detect irregularities. But as discussed above, not only typos introduce measurement error. Also a theoretically wrong measure that is correlated with the correct measure is a mismeasured variable. In case of ownership concentration, due to complex ownership structures in large German corporations concentration should not be measured at the direct level but at the ultimate level of ownership (Köke, 2000; Becht and Böhmer, 2002).

Third, for some types of data there is only one source, hence cross checks are not possible. In case of industry-level competition, this data source is the Federal Anti-Trust Commission (*Monopolkommission*), which obtains the raw data from the Federal Statistical Office (*Statistisches Bundesamt*). These statistics report the number of suppliers and other measures of concentration for four-digit industries.[12] Even if these data are free from error, the researcher faces the problem to assign these industry-level data to firms, for which he typically has information on total sales only, not on sales for all the firm's market segments. The merge of both sources of data unavoidably introduces some error, particularly for the largest firms. To test whether this measurement error influences the estimated impact of competition on performance, the researcher might think of re-estimating the model without the largest firms. But this approach would create a serious selection problem.

Preferably, we consider additional measures of competition. For product market competition, this can be other industry-level measures such as import penetration, which need to be constructed from the foreign trade statistics (*Außenhandelsstatistik*) and the census of production (*Produktionsstatistik*) provided by the Federal Statistical Office, or firm-level measures such as ex post rents, which need to be constructed from balance sheet data. In absence of clear theoretical predictions how these different measures of competition interact, the researcher should experiment using several measures simultaneously in the empirical model and report adequate sensitivity analyses. Alternatively, the researcher chooses one measure and uses alternative measures as instruments to reduce the error in the prime measure.

A different but closely related method to deal with measurement error is the structural factor analysis. This approach explicitly specifies the relation between the unobservable attributes, which are supposed to influence the en-

---

[12] Note that these statistics include foreign competitors only then when they are registered at a German court. Therefore these competition data are likely to be measured with a bias depending on the industry.

dogenous variable, and the observable variables. Essentially, these observable variables are used to estimate (unobservable) latent variables, which in turn are applied to explain the endogenous variable of interest. In an analysis on firm's capital structure choice, Titman and Wessels (1988) estimate eight latent variables (such as growth opportunities, firm size, and profitability) using 15 observable firm characteristics. In a second step, these latent variables are applied to explain firm's capital structure. This approach is advantageous to simply using several proxy variables simultaneously when an observable firm characteristic influences several of the latent variables. However, for empirical corporate governance studies, which use measures of shareholder influence, creditor influence, or supervisory board influence, this overlap is typically not existent. This might change when further theoretical work offers more precise hypotheses on the interactions of different governance mechanisms.

2.5 Summary and Lessons

This chapter serves as a framework or checklist for future empirical corporate governance studies. It fulfills two purposes. First, going through this checklist should clarify where unavoidable problems are and how they can affect estimation and interpretation. Even better, it can prevent biases in the first place. Second, it should raise the awareness for careful data collection, in particular the need for panel data.

Endogeneity of the right-hand side variables is likely to be the most common problem. It generally occurs in two forms: structural reverse causality and unobserved firm heterogeneity. In both cases, panel data are a necessary condition to solve the endogeneity problem. With panel data on hand, fixed-effect models or models in first differences can be estimated to take into account the unobserved part of firm heterogeneity. But this approach fails if unobserved heterogeneity is not constant over time. What must be done is to reduce the unobserved part of the model by including other firm-specific variables. One econometric trick is to use long lags of right-hand side firm-specific variables. But these might be weak instruments; thus the crucial task to resolve structural reverse causality is the search for uncontroversial instruments.

Sample selectivity is the second source of potential estimation bias. To avoid sampling bias the researcher must take into account major firm decisions such as the decision to go public or to exit a product market. This is accomplished by extending the samples to non-listed firms, potentially of various sizes, and by not dropping observations of firms that exited the market. In a second step, information about market exit must enter the regression model.

The problem of missing variables must be avoided by including all theoretically relevant governance mechanisms in the empirical model. Hence, specific data are required on ownership structure, capital structure, board structure, the intensity of product market competition, and possibly past takeover activity. Since economic theory suggests that some of these variables might have a non-linear influence on performance, higher order polynomial terms are required.

Last but not least, measurement error in variables can bias estimation results. Measurement error in exogenous variables clearly biases estimated coefficients. Unfortunately this is likely to be the case for particular variables often used in corporate governance analysis, e.g. measures of competition or ownership. There is no simple solution to this problem. One way to reduce measurement error is to instrument the variables measured with error appropriately; however, such instruments are difficult to find. Another is to check the robustness of estimation results using alternative measures of the relevant firm characteristic. This also applies to the endogenous variable, although measurement error in this variable does not bias estimated coefficients. Previous empirical studies appear to follow this route because many different measures of performance are used. What they often fail to do, however, is to state clearly the assumptions on which their measures were selected. This is not a formalism: Many empirical contradictions could be dissolved if models were compared on an equal basis.

A final remark: What appears to be technical problems of econometric analyses, are in fact deep problems of any empirical analysis, independent of the technical tool. The discussed problems do not only occur in regression analyses. The same care should be taken in the interpretation of simple correlations and cross tables of variables whenever causal interpretations are attempted.

3 The German Corporations Database (GCD)

The key lesson from the literature review in Chapter 2 is that a solid database is essential. Only with data on hand that fulfill specific requirements, most methodological drawbacks plaguing previous empirical studies on corporate governance can be addressed.

The German Corporations Database (henceforth, GCD) to be described in the following has been constructed with these requirements in mind. Specifically, GCD is a panel of large and medium-sized German corporations, covering the years 1986–1997. It contains panel data on firms' capital structure and performance as well as panel data on firms' ownership and board structure. For Germany, this panel structure for a range of governance variables is new. It allows to address the endogeneity problems discussed in Chapter 2.1, for example by using instrumental variables in regression analyses. It also allows to model unobserved heterogeneity in specific variables, for example by providing information on changes in ownership or board structure.

GCD contains balance sheet information on 464 listed firms and 2,495 non-listed firms. For Germany, this significant coverage of non-listed firms is new. It allows to address a major sample selectivity problem that constrains previous studies which tend to focus on listed firms (Chapter 2.2). Similarly, it contains information on the reason for non-reporting. Therefore, sample attrition can be modeled explicitly.

Furthermore, GCD contains information on all relevant governance mechanisms. This is important because common problems resulting from missing variables, as described in Chapter 2.3, can be avoided. In addition, GCD includes information on the intensity of product market competition. This allows to examine market discipline and its impact on firm performance as well as its interaction with corporate governance.

Finally, GCD offers information on a range of different measures for performance. This is important because it is not always clear how performance ought to be measured (Chapter 2.4), making robustness checks in empirical analyses necessary. Likewise, GCD contains information on a range of alternative measures of product market competition and capital structure. This allows to address problems stemming from measurement error in exogenous variables, for example by using alternative measures as instruments.

In the following we describe the data sources used to construct GCD (Chapter 3.1), explain the selection procedure applied to assemble GCD and the resulting structure of GCD (Chapter 3.2), and examine to what extent GCD is representative for the population of large German corporations (Chapter 3.3). A detailed definition of all variables contained in GCD and used in the empirical analyses of Chapters 4, 5, and 6 is provided in the Appendix. For further information on data sources and data availability, see Köke (2001d).

3.1 Data Sources

GCD contains balance sheet data, stock price data, data on firms' ownership structure, data on firms' board structure, data on the intensity of product market competition, data on the reason for non-reporting, as well as some key macroeconomic and industry-specific data. Subsequently, we describe the sources of these types of data.

Balance sheet data The primary source of balance sheet data is Hoppenstedt's Balance Sheet Database (BSD), which is commercially available in electronic format.[1]

BSD contains the full annual accounts from all large listed German corporations (*Kapitalgesellschaften*), which are subject to compulsory disclosure according to §289 HGB and which do not operate primarily in the financial industry. Hence, banks, insurance companies, and other providers of financial services are not included. Additionally, BSD contains a range of large and medium-sized non-listed corporations, part of which are subsidiaries of conglomerate firms. BSD covers the years 1980–1997. For inclusion into GCD, only data from 1986–1997 are used (see Chapter 3.2).

The main advantage of BSD against alternative sources of balance sheet data (e.g. the part of German Finance Database (*Deutsche Finanzdatenbank*, DFDB) that is maintained at the University of Aachen) is the large number of non-listed corporations. In light of the issues raised in Chapter 2.2, this data source is particularly suitable for corporate governance analyses because it avoids some common sample selectivity problems.

A second source of balance sheet data is the annual Guide Through German Corporations (*Wegweiser durch deutsche Unternehmen*) from former Bayerische Hypotheken- and Wechselbank (henceforth, Hypobank).[2] This data source is mainly used to check for data consistency.

---

[1] For further information on this data source, see `http://www.hoppenstedt.de`.

[2] After the merge with Bayerische Vereinsbank in 1997, today this institution is Bayerische Hypotheken- und Vereinsbank.

Stock price data The primary source of stock price data is the part of German Finance Database (*Deutsche Finanzdatenbank*, DFDB) that is maintained at the University of Karlsruhe. DFDB contains stock price information on all stocks traded at the Frankfurt Stock exchange since the year 1960. From the year 1974 onwards it includes all stocks traded in any of the three segments of the Frankfurt Stock Exchange, and it contains the prices of stocks traded at other German stock exchanges as well.[3] For inclusion into GCD, data from 1986–1997 are used (see Chapter 3.2).

Stock prices as well as a market index (`dafox`) are observed one time per week (Wednesday). An essential characteristic of these data is that they are corrected for dividend payments, stock splits, equity issues, and other factors that induce stock price changes unrelated to changes in the underlying fundamental (Göppl, 1996). For example, the index is continuously corrected for listings and delistings, and thus does not suffer from a survivorship bias.

A second source of data is Hoppenstedt's Stock Guide (*Aktienführer*), which is mainly used to determine the total market value of the firms' shares.

Ownership data Data on the firms' ownership structure are obtained from two sources:

- 1986–1993: Guide Through German Corporations from Hypobank, printed format.
- 1994–1997: Group Structure Database (*Konzernstrukturdatenbank*, GSD) from Hoppenstedt, electronic format.[4]

Hypobank obtained its raw data from Hoppenstedt until the year 1993 when this series was discontinued. Therefore, in spite of apparently two different data sources, Hoppenstedt is actually the only ultimate source of data. This ensures consistency in data preparation.[5]

Both sources contain information on direct ownership of common stock (*Stammaktien*) for all listed German corporations. In addition, Hypobank provides information on direct ownership of common stock for large non-listed corporations (*Stammaktien* for the non-listed AG and *Gesellschafteranteile* for the GmbH, which cannot be listed). GSD differs from Hypobank in three important respects: First, ownership information is available electronically. Second, ownership structures can be traced back up to the 20th level. Third, GSD covers a much larger number of non-listed corporations. Both sources

---

[3] For further information on this data source, see `http://finance.wiwi.uni-karlsruhe.de/Forschung/Kkmdb/anfragen.html`.

[4] GSD is released four times per year. Since Hoppenstedt typically deletes data from previous years, only the following updates are available: 3-1994, 2-1995, 2-1996, and 1-1997.

[5] For further information on GSD, see `http://www.hoppenstedt.de`.

of data report the size and the name of a direct owner when the size of the ownership block exceeds five percent.

Note that ownership information from Hypobank cannot readily be used in our analysis for three reasons. First, in contrast to information from GSD, ownership information from Hypobank only refers to the *direct* level of owners. But due to the complexity of ownership of large German firms, empirical analyses should consider the *ultimate* level of owners. The concept of control, which is outlined in Chapter 4.2.2, describes how information on direct ownership rights is used to construct ownership pyramids in a bottom-up approach. A second drawback is that Hypobank does not directly reveal ownership information on medium-sized non-listed firms as does GSD. Other commercial data sources are also of little help because for the years 1986–1993 non-listed firms have not been subject to strictly enforced disclosure requirements. Therefore, we construct the relevant ownership structures by searching the information on investments in subsidiaries and affiliated companies, which is given in the appendix to each company in Hypobank. To further enlarge our sample, we search the Mannheim Company Database (*Mannheimer Unternehmenspanel*, MUP) located at the ZEW in Mannheim. We thereby obtain ownership information on many medium-sized non-listed firms, both for private and public corporations. Third, some firms change their name during the period of observation, for example following takeovers or restructuring of conglomerates. Since changes in ownership are crucial to the data collection procedure, we adjust for name changes.

Board data Analogously to data on firms' ownership structure, data on firms' board structure are obtained from two sources:

- 1986–1993: Guide Through German Corporations from Hypobank, printed format.
- 1994–1997: Group Structure Database (*Konzernstrukturdatenbank*, GSD) from Hoppenstedt, electronic format.

Both sources of data contain information on the management board (*Vorstand*) and the supervisory board (*Aufsichtsrat*). In contrast to information on ownership structure, there is no information on the board structure for non-listed firms before 1994. Similarly, for the years of 1994–1997 this information is often not available.

A major advantage of these data sources is that data on the supervisory board are available. Other data sources such as the Mannheim Company Database (MUP) do not contain this information.

Product market competition data Data on the intensity of product market competition are obtained from several sources:

- Industry-level data on domestic competition: measures of producer concentration, constructed from biannual reports of German Anti-Trust Commission (*Monopolkommission*).[6]
- Industry-level data on competition from abroad: measure of import penetration, constructed from Foreign Trade Statistics (*Außenhandelsstatistik*) and Census of Production (*Produktionsstatistik*, Fachserie 4, Reihe 3.1) of the Federal Statistical Office (*Statistisches Bundesamt*)
- Firm-level data on domestic competition: measure of ex post rents from production, constructed from balance sheet data of Hoppenstedt's BSD.

Firm-level measures of competition, which are based on balance sheet data, essentially are available for all observations with balance sheet data. Obtaining data on industry-level competition is a more difficult task. Data on import penetration are calculated at the two-digit industry level (on the basis of raw data obtained from the Federal Statistical Office) because data on imports are available only at this aggregate level. Data on (domestic) producer concentration are readily available at the four-digit industry-level from the German Anti-Trust Commission (henceforth, GATC). However, the major difficulty with both types of industry-level competition data is to assign the respective industry codes from the Federal Statistical Office and GATC to those of Hoppenstedt (for details, see Köke, 2001d).

Note that GCD contains industry-level data on producer concentration only for the manufacturing sector. GATC does not offer similarly detailed concentration data for other industries. Note also that our measures of competition are not perfect for theoretical as well as empirical reasons. From the theoretical point of view, both firm-level and industry-level measures are imperfect because neither do they take into account competitive pressure from substitutes nor do they consider the threat of market entry (see also Chapter 2.4). From the empirical point of view, at least the industry-level measures are imperfect because we cannot assign the GATC concentration measures to firms perfectly, i.e. separately to all their individual market segments but only to their primary product. Hence, some classification error is likely for conglomerate firms.

Reasons for non-reporting For some firms contained in GCD, time series of balance sheet data end before the final year of the sample. For these cases, information is collected on the firms' survival status for the years following the last year for which balance sheet data are reported. This is essential because modeling the firms' exit behavior (from the sample) requires information on the reason for why no balance sheet data have been submitted to Hoppenstedt any longer. In principle, firms can stop reporting for three reasons: (1) bankruptcy, (2) takeover, or (3) other reasons not related to bankruptcy or takeover (e.g. name change).

---

[6] See, e.g., Monopolkommission (1996).

Exit status is verified by examining text information contained in the Mannheim Company Database (MUP) and by conducting telephone interviews with the respective company or with its last owner.

Macroeconomic and industry-specific data To supplement firm-specific information contained in GCD, we add some key macroeconomic and industry-specific indicators. Data on prices are obtained from the Federal Statistical Office, data on interest rates from the Institute for the German Economy (*Institut der deutschen Wirtschaft*) in Cologne, and industry-specific data on business cycles from the ifo Institute in Munich.

3.2 Sample Selection and Structure of GCD

Balance Sheet Database (BSD) from Hoppenstedt contains a total of 6,302 firms (54,856 firm years). Since balance sheet data are a precondition for any empirical corporate governance analysis, we depart from BSD to construct the German Corporations Database. The selection procedure is summarized in Table 3.1.

Table 3.1. Sample selection for balance sheet data

Selection criterion	Firms	Firm years
Original sample	6,302	54,856
New disclosure rules	6,157	43,378
Full business years	6,157	43,136
Highest level of consolidation	6,157	35,338
Corporations (AG, KGaA, GmbH)	6,046	34,814
Years 1986–1997	6,046	34,759
Mining, manufacturing, construction, trade, hotels, and diversified holding companies	2,959	20,018

In 1985 several changes were introduced in German corporate law (§289 HGB), most of them triggered by the European Community's Fourth Company Law Directive on the harmonization of national requirements pertaining to financial statements. These changes hinder comparability of annual reports before and after 1986. Therefore, we exclude 145 firms that report under old disclosure rules only. Due to this change in disclosure rules, some firms report incomplete business years. These observations are also eliminated (242 firm years).

BSD contains annual reports for different levels of consolidation. We choose the highest level available for each firm to ensure that the data are not contaminated by accounting management within the firm. Essentially, this means that we use annual reports consolidated at the world level for conglomerate firms and annual reports consolidated at the firm level for all other firms, which have no subsidiaries. This selection causes 7,798 firm year deletions.

Further, we eliminate all observations on partnerships because GCD focuses on incorporated firms (111 firms, 524 firm years). The reason is that the separation of ownership and control is likely to occur in corporations, but not in partnerships because management typically owns one hundred percent of the shares in partnership firms. Furthermore, some firms had implemented the new disclosure rules as early as 1984. To ensure that all sample firms were subject to the new disclosure regulation, we exclude 55 firm years for the years 1984 and 1985.

Finally, we select by industry in three steps. First, we eliminate 3,087 firms from the utility, traffic, and telecommunications industries because they were still predominantly government-owned during the period of observation. Second, as a matter of better comparability we also eliminate firms that primarily operate in the banking and insurance business, while operating little in non-financial activities. Finally, we reclassify conglomerate firms according to their primary industry to ensure that the sample only includes firms operating predominantly in non-financial industries. This reclassification involves checking the individual firms' industry classifications and sorting them into appropriate categories. For 279 firms, this reclassification is not possible as no primary industry code can be identified; these diversified holding companies are not eliminated. In summary, this selection procedure leaves a sample of 2,959 firms (20,018 firm years).

This full sample is used when industry-adjusted measures of performance are calculated (see Appendix). Note that severe limitations in accessing appropriate data made it impossible to gather full information on every single observation contained in GCD. For example, data on ownership are available only for 1,759 firms. But compared with previous databases these numbers are still substantial. The structure of GCD can be described as depicted in Figure 3.1.

3.3 Sample Representativeness

The German Corporations Database (GCD) comprises large listed firms as well as large and medium-sized non-listed firms. All of these firms are incorporated firms (*Kapitalgesellschaften*). In total, GCD contains data on 464 listed firms and 2,495 non-listed firms. To put these figures into perspective, Table 3.2 shows the number of all German corporations and the number of sample firms, taking the year 1992 as reference. Table 3.2 distinguishes between listed and non-listed firms as well as public (AG, KGaA) and private firms (GmbH).

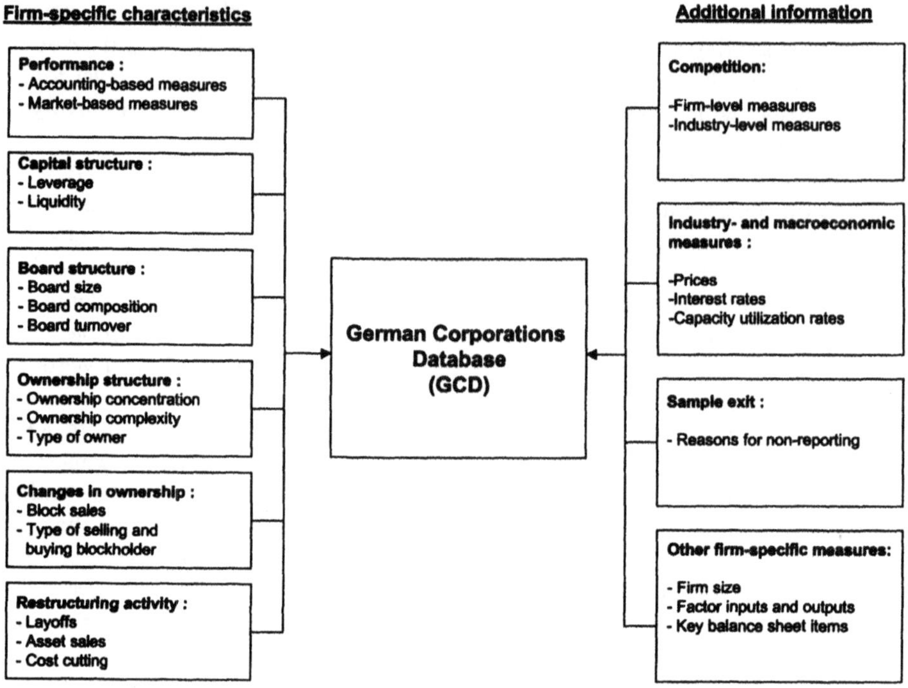

Figure 3.1. Structure of German Corporations Database

Table 3.2 shows that 26.2% of sample firms in 1992 are publicly traded. A significantly larger fraction of sample firms is not publicly traded, with 48.4% being non-listed public corporations (AG, KGaA) and 25.4% being non-listed private corporations (GmbH). Compared with the total number of German incorporated firms in 1992, coverage of listed firms is very high (82.3%). For non-listed firms, coverage is sufficiently high for public corporations (48.3%), but weak for private corporations (0.1%). However, choosing manufacturing corporations with total sales exceeding 10 million DM as the benchmark, the sample includes 86.8% of all large public corporations, and 2.5% percent of all large private corporations (not tabled). Hence, GCD achieves significant coverage of large incorporated firms, whether listed or not.

The sample comprises 2,680 firms from 32 industries (two-digit European NACE code) and 279 firms which cannot be classified into one primary industry. Most firms operate in manufacturing industries. Table 3.3 shows that the largest number of sample firms belong to the machinery, wholesale trade,

Table 3.2. Sample representativeness in 1992: listed and non-listed firms

Listing	Legal form	All German firms	Sample firms		
			total	in percent of total	in percent of all German firms
Yes	AG, KGaA	521	429	26.2%	82.3%
No	AG, KGaA	1,643	793	48.4%	48.3%
No	GmbH	359,358	415	25.4%	0.1%
Total		361,522	1,637	100.0%	0.5%

Notes: Column (1) shows the number of all German corporations in the year 1992, and column (2) the total number of sample firms (all incorporated) in 1992, separately for listed/non-listed public (AG, KGaA) and non-listed private firms (GmbH). Column (3) provides the fraction of sample firms that are listed or non-listed, separately by legal form. And column (4) relates the number of sample firms to the number of all German corporations, separately by type of firm. Data on the number of all German corporations are obtained from Statistisches Bundesamt, Umsatzsteuerstatistik, Fachserie 14, Reihe 8.

and food industries. Again taking the year 1992 as the reference, we find that the chemicals, food, machinery, synthetics, as well as rock, stone, and glass industries are well represented in GCD. Overall, manufacturing industries are well covered. Coverage of trade and construction industries is smaller but still significant.

Table 3.3. Sample representativeness in 1992: industry coverage

Industry	All large German firms	Sample firms total	Sample firms in percent of total	Sample firms in percent of all large German firms
Mining, energy	n.a.	44	2.7%	n.a.
Chemicals	103	101	6.2%	98.1%
Synthetics	107	52	3.2%	48.6%
Rock, stone, glass	117	74	4.5%	63.2%
Metals	216	111	6.8%	51.4%
Machinery	577	289	17.7%	50.1%
Electronics	377	79	4.8%	21.0%
Wood, paper, printing	366	73	4.5%	19.9%
Leather textiles	185	72	4.4%	38.9%
Food	237	170	10.4%	71.7%
Construction	693	74	4.5%	10.7%
Wholesales trade	785	208	12.7%	26.5%
Retail trade	610	65	4.0%	10.7%
Hotels and restaurants	96	19	1.2%	19.8%
Holding companies	n.a.	206	12.6%	n.a.
Total	n.a.	1,637	100.0%	n.a.

Notes: All statistics are calculated for the year 1992. The analysis can be conducted only for large firms because data obtained from Statistisches Bundesamt, Umsatzsteuerstatistik, Fachserie 14, Reihe 8, cover only large German firms. Firms producing in non-manufacturing industries are not contained in the sample. Most of the industries listed here are aggregates, i.e. contain several two-digit industries (European NACE code).

4 Frequency, Causes, and Consequences of Control Transfers

This chapter is a revised and adapted version of Köke (2000). It examines the market for large share blocks in Germany. Shleifer and Vishny (1997) argue that such a market for corporate control is an important element of corporate governance. Particularly active markets have been described for the US (e.g., Jensen and Ruback, 1983; Jarrell et al., 1988) and the UK (Franks and Mayer, 1990). To a large extent these markets are based on hostile takeovers. Focusing solely on hostile takeovers, there is no market for corporate control in the bank-based economies of continental Europe (OECD, 1998), in particular not in Germany (Franks and Mayer, 1998). For Germany, this lack is typically attributed to bank voting power, complex ownership structures, and political resistance. This chapter shows that control transfers in Germany occur more frequently than often assumed, and that there are some indications characterizing these control transfers as disciplinary.

Since hostile takeovers are rare, we use a broader concept to examine takeover activity, namely the market for large share blocks. While this approach does not distinguish between hostile and friendly takeovers, it does account for partial firm sales. The apparent drawback of analyzing both forms of takeovers in combination is insignificant in light of Schwert (2000). He shows for the US that hostile and friendly takeovers are not distinguishable in economic terms, but negotiations are publicized earlier in hostile transactions. Our approach – tracking block ownership through time to identify changes in corporate control – is supported by Jenkinson and Ljungqvist (2001) who apply a similar methodology to assemble case-study evidence on (hostile) stake building in Germany.

The following analysis addresses two main questions. First, we investigate how frequently corporate ownership changes. This involves tracking the names of all large investors in almost 1,000 listed and non-listed German corporations through the years 1987–1994. Second, we examine both the causes and consequences of control transfers. We extend the literature in several ways. First, we provide large-sample evidence on the causes as well as the consequences of control transfers, and hence complement the work of Denis and Sarin (1999) and Denis and Kruse (2000) who focus on the consequences. In contrast to Bethel et al. (1998) we examine purchases of blocks that are likely to change corporate control, and thus make our analysis less vulnerable to potentially misspecified shareholder types. Second, previous studies focus on the market-based economy of the US, while this study examines a bank-based economy. The German economy is particularly interesting for analyzing changes in ownership because ownership structures are highly complex and therefore perceived to be stable. One reason for this assumption is the widespread use of such forms of organization as pyramids, cross ownership, and large conglomerates (e.g., La Porta et al., 1999). Third, since the majority of corporations in continental Europe and particularly in Germany is not listed on a stock exchange, this study covers listed as well as non-listed firms. Previous studies examining control transfers focus exclusively on listed firms, and so far nothing is known about control transfers in non-listed firms. Fourth, due to the complexity of ownership structures in Germany, analyzing direct share ownership is not sufficient. We therefore examine ultimate ownership of firms. As this approach requires data on individual shareholders, our analysis also accounts for changes *within* shareholder categories, and in this sense extends the work of Denis and Sarin (1999) that is based on changes *between* shareholder categories. This is essential because positive and negative gross changes in a category might offset each other, causing them to be neglected.

The structure of this chapter is as follows: Chapter 4.1 briefly reviews the evidence on the market for large share blocks and draws on the relevant theoretical and empirical literature to formulate a set of hypotheses. Chapter 4.2 describes the data used for this study and defines the concept of control that is applied to identify the ultimate owner. Chapter 4.3 describes the frequency of control transfers in Germany as well as the type of buyers and sellers of control blocks. Chapter 4.4 analyzes the causes and consequences of control transfers and tests the hypotheses put forward in Chapter 4.1. Chapter 4.5 summarizes the main results and discusses some methodological implications.

4.1 Hypotheses

Evidence on the market for large share blocks is accumulating. For Belgium, Renneboog (2000) reports 127 cases in which blocks larger than ten percent are purchased during the years 1989–1994. For a sample of over 1,000 firm years, this implies that on average 12.4% of Belgian firms experienced such a block purchase in any year. For the UK, the corresponding annual rate is 9.0% (Franks et al., 2001). For the US, Bethel et al. (1998) find 244 purchases of blocks larger than five percent during the years 1980–1989. For a sample of almost 3,700 firm years, this translates into an annual rate of 6.6%. For Germany, so far no comparable figure on block trading is available. Franks and Mayer (1994) compare the ownership structures of 171 listed German companies for the years 1988 and 1991. They find that in about a fifth of firms a new major shareholder is in place by 1991. Although their analysis is conducted on the basis of direct ownership and changes in ultimate ownership are neglected, their results suggest that there is a market for large share blocks in Germany. Similarly, recent case-study evidence collected by Jenkinson and Ljungqvist (2001) indicates that control changes in Germany are more frequent than previously assumed. While their study focuses on hostile control transactions and neglects cases without perceived hostility, their methodology – tracking block ownership through time – appears to be crucial to identifying changes in control.

We now turn to the literature on causes and consequences of ownership changes to formulate two sets of hypotheses. The first set focuses on the causes and distinguishes between firm-specific and owner-specific characteristics as well as performance.

Hypothesis 4.1 *Changes in ultimate ownership are less likely for firms with high concentration of ownership.*

Hypothesis 4.2 *Changes in ultimate ownership are more likely for firms with high leverage.*

Hypothesis 4.3 *Changes in ultimate ownership are less likely for firms with complex ownership structures.*

Hypothesis 4.4 *Changes in ultimate ownership are less likely for large firms.*

Hypothesis 4.5 *Changes in ultimate ownership are less likely for firms with high insider ownership.*

Hypothesis 4.6 *Changes in ultimate ownership are more likely for firms with poor performance.*

The first hypothesis (**4.1**) follows Holmström and Tirole (1993) who argue that takeovers require low concentration of ownership and, in turn, high market liquidity because only then are capital markets able to determine the necessity of a takeover. The few cases of hostile takeovers in Germany support Holmström and Tirole because in all cases the shares of the takeover target were widely dispersed. Note that Grossman and Hart (1980) argue to the opposite that some share concentration is required for takeovers to be effective because under dispersed ownership shareholders would prefer to free-ride.

The second hypothesis (**4.2**) is derived from Mitchell and Mulherin (1996) who argue that changes in the firm's growth opportunities, leverage, or firm size could make adjustments in ownership necessary, for example as a result of economic shocks to an industry. Consistent with this view, Zingales (1998) reports that following deregulation in the US trucking industry firms faced increasing leverage, and that this has lead to a higher probability of market exit. We expect leverage to have a similar impact on changes in ownership.

The third and fourth hypothesis consider firm-specific characteristics that might deter changes in ownership. The third hypothesis (**4.3**) focuses on defensive mechanisms implemented against a change in ownership. In the US, defensive mechanisms encompass employee stock ownership plans, anti-takeover charter amendments, and poison pills, as noted by Bethel et al. (1998). In Germany, pyramids (Franks and Mayer, 1995) and cross-holding structures (Wenger and Kaserer, 1998) are likely to hinder ownership changes. The fourth hypothesis (**4.4**) establishes that also the size of a firm can deter changes in ownership. Shleifer and Vishny (1992) argue that the market for corporate control is less liquid as firm size increases. Bethel et al. (1998) and Mulherin and Boone (2000) provide empirical evidence that smaller firms are more likely to become takeover targets.

The fifth hypothesis (**4.5**) emphasizes owner-specific characteristics, in particular the fraction of shares owned by insiders. Jensen and Meckling (1976) argue that incentives of managers and owners are better aligned when managers hold a large fraction of shares. In this case outside investors should have little opportunity to improve on performance. However, managers might also become entrenched when owning large blocks (Fama and Jensen, 1983). Irrespective whether insider ownership is good or bad for shareholders, we expect high insider ownership to reduce the likelihood of a control change. This conjecture is in line with evidence on the US (Barber et al., 1995) and Canada (St-Pierre et al., 1996).

Finally, the sixth hypothesis (**4.6**) focuses on performance. When managers diverge from the interest of shareholders and performance suffers, both the market for corporate control as well as internal control mechanisms could act as disciplining devices (e.g., Jensen, 1988; Shleifer and Vishny, 1997). Denis and Sarin (1999) and Maksimovic and Phillips (2001) provide empirical evidence for the US. Hence, irrespective of the causes of bad performance, we expect that poor performance makes block purchases more likely.

The second set of hypotheses concerns the consequences of ownership changes. We focus on three aspects: governance changes, corporate restructuring, and performance.

Hypothesis 4.7 *Changes in ultimate ownership are followed by increased management turnover.*

Hypothesis 4.8 *Changes in ultimate ownership are followed by increased asset divestitures, employee layoffs, and cost cutting.*

Hypothesis 4.9 *Changes in ultimate ownership are followed by improvements in performance.*

The seventh hypothesis (**4.7**) follows from considerations that takeovers can be disciplinary, and that different management teams compete with each other (Jensen and Ruback, 1983). The empirical evidence suggests that changes in board and ownership structure are strongly related to top executive turnover and prior performance (e.g., Denis and Sarin, 1999, and Kole and Lehn, 1999, for the US; Renneboog, 2000, for Belgium). For Germany, Jenkinson and Ljungqvist (2001) report that following hostile control changes typically incumbent management is removed or resigns.

The eighth hypothesis (**4.8**) is concerned with three different aspects of corporate restructuring as a consequence of a change in ownership: asset divestitures, employee layoffs, and cost cutting. Previous empirical studies find that following changes in ownership asset divestitures increase, the frequency of mergers and acquisitions decreases, and share repurchases increase (e.g., Bethel et al., 1998, and Denis and Sarin, 1999, for the US; Franks and Mayer, 1995, for the UK).

Finally, the ninth hypothesis (**4.9**) establishes that changes in ownership ultimately affect performance. Bethel et al. (1998) show that industry-adjusted operating profitability rises in firms that experience activist block purchases, whereas it falls in firms that do not experience a block purchase. Denis and Kruse (2000) find for a sample of firms that experienced a large performance decline that industry-adjusted operating performance improves significantly in combination with major asset restructuring.

4.2 Data

The sample used for the analysis of the frequency, causes, and consequences of control transfers is a subsample of the German Corporations Database (GCD). Specifically, in a first step, out of the 2,959 firms contained in GCD we eliminate 1,200 firms for which no information on ownership is available. Second, we use only observations from the years 1986–1994 because for the later years in the sample we do not have consistent information on insider ownership, which is required for the analysis of the causes of control transfers (247 firm deletions). Third, since the following analysis examines changes in ownership, we eliminate 566 firms for which only one year of data is available. For most of these 566 firms the year 1994 is the single year. This is due to the fact that Hoppenstedt substantially increased firm coverage in 1994.

In total, the analysis of the frequency of control transfers (Chapter 4.3) is based on data from 946 firms (4,882 firm years) for the years 1987–1994. This sample (in the following, Sample I) includes firms with at least two continuous years of data because changes in ownership must be calculated. The analysis of causes and consequences of control transfers (Chapter 4.4) is based on a subsample and encompasses data from 664 firms (4,433 firm years). This sample (in the following, Sample II) includes firms with at least four continuous years of data because the analysis of consequences of control transfers requires data on the year prior and the two years after change in ownership. In Chapter 4.2.1 we investigate whether dropping firms with fewer continuous years of data introduces a selection bias, particularly which variables are most likely to be affected.

In the following empirical analysis we distinguish between listed and non-listed firms to examine whether the frequency, causes, and consequences of control transfers are different for both types of firms. In contrast, we do not distinguish between private and public firms because they are similar in many regulatory characteristics (e.g., liability status, publication requirements, and taxation). One major difference between private (GmbH) and public corporations (AG) is that in private corporations the general meeting of shareholders can give instructions to management, but not in public corporations. Therefore, management could in principle be under tighter control in GmbH firms. This difference is unlikely to be of major relevance in our sample because ownership concentration is high for both types of firms.

4.2.1 Characteristics of Entering and Exiting Firms

In the following we examine whether our sample systematically excludes some type of firms. For example, if poor performance increased the likelihood of firm failure or takeover, the sample could contain systematically fewer poorly performing firms. This would bias any observed correlation of performance and the likelihood of a control transfer. We choose two approaches to analyze sample composition. First, we check whether Sample II, which is used for the analysis of causes and consequences of control transfers (Chapter 4.4), systematically excludes some type of firms. Second, we examine what kind of firms enter and exit the full sample (Sample I) during the years 1987–1994.

We compare Sample I with Sample II, which contain firms with at least two and at least four continuous years of data, respectively, on some key firm characteristics, separately for listed and non-listed firms (Table 4.1). For nearly all firm characteristics we find no significant differences except for ownership concentration being significantly smaller in Sample II for non-listed firms. This could be due to the fact that Hoppenstedt, the data provider, strongly increased coverage of non-listed subsidiary companies in the early 1990s. As these firms typically show very high ownership concentration, Sample I contains relatively more firms with few observations and high concentration. Next, we compare firms with at least four continuous years of data (Sample II) with firms that have fewer than four observations. Again we find that for non-listed firms ownership concentration is smaller in Sample II. In addition, Sample II contains fewer non-listed firms with a large burden of debt, poor performance, and smaller firm size. For listed firms, we find no systematic difference between the two samples except for firm size, which is larger in Sample II.

Table 4.2 shows whether firms that enter Sample I after 1987, the first year of the sample, or exit before 1994, the last year of the sample, are systematically different from other firms. For firms entering in year t, the comparison group is firms in year t that are in the sample at least since year $t-1$. Vice versa, for firms exiting at the end of year t, the comparison group is firms in year t that are still in the sample in year $t+1$. On average across all sample years, we find that non-listed firms show higher shareholder concentration, a larger burden of debt, and smaller firm size when they enter the sample. In addition, a comparably large fraction of entering non-listed firms reports a contemporaneous earnings loss. Exiting non-listed firms are also smaller in size and more indebted than firms remaining in the sample. For listed firms we find that ownership concentration is larger, firm size is smaller, and performance is better when they enter the sample. Exiting listed firms are smaller in size. All results are qualitatively similar at the median (not reported).

The lesson from this sample composition analysis is that comparing sample averages of shareholder concentration year by year could be misleading because entering firms show higher average concentration than firms already in the sample. Regarding the other characteristics, it is possible that Sample II is somewhat biased towards well-performing firms, however only for non-listed firms. Overall, a systematic bias due to sample attrition appears to be unlikely because, with the exception of firm size, exiting firms are not significantly different from other sample firms. This result could be expected because 60% of sample exits are cases of non-reporting due to name changes, and not due to failure or acquisition.

4.2.2 Concept of Control

A source of dispute in early empirical studies on the relation between ownership and performance has been the definition of corporate control. One approach is to classify companies into either manager-controlled or owner-controlled firms (Short, 1994). This classification is to some extent arbitrary. Using continuous ownership variables based upon the fraction of share ownership or voting rights is a more precise measure of *direct ownership*. However, both approaches do not capture the effects of complex ownership structures. For Germany such analysis of direct ownership is therefore not sufficient. By using the concept of *ultimate ownership* it becomes possible to define corporate control within complex ownership structures. This requires the analysis of control chains throughout several levels and the identification of a most powerful ultimate owner if any such exists. We use the concept of ultimate ownership in this study.

The identification of the ultimate owner for each firm is based upon German corporate law and involves two steps. First, we identify the ultimate owner for each direct shareholder using the following three rules. Rule 1 (strong ownership rule): A chain of control is pursued to the next level if the shareholder being analyzed is owned to 50% or more by a shareholder on the next level, while all other shareholders on the next level own less than 50%. Rule 2 (weak ownership rule): If rule 1 does not apply, a chain of control is pursued to the next level if the shareholder being analyzed is owned to 25% or more by a shareholder on the next level, while all other shareholders on the next level own less than 25%. Rule 3 (stop rule): If neither rule 1 nor rule 2

Table 4.1. Characteristics of firms with different number of observations

	Firms with x continuous years of data		
	$x \geq 2$ (Sample I)	$x < 4$	$x \geq 4$ (Sample II)
Non-listed firms:			
Size of largest block	85.9%**	88.7%**	84.4%
Fraction of dispersed shares	9.3%**	6.9%**	10.5%
Debt-to-assets ratio	39.0%	45.9%***	38.2%
Return on assets (ROA)	0.7%	-4.4%***	0.8%
Return on equity (ROE)	1.3%	-9.5%***	1.0%
Change in ROA	0.0%	-0.9%	-0.2%
Change in ROE	0.2%	-3.6%	-0.4%
Earnings loss	14.1%	29.8%***	12.9%
Sales (in mio. DM)	2,146.7	371.4***	2,369.3
Number of observations	2,422	181	2,012
Listed firms:			
Size of largest block	60.6%	65.9%	60.6%
Fraction of dispersed shares	31.5%	32.1%	31.5%
Debt-to-assets ratio	41.3%	41.8%	41.2%
Return on assets (ROA)	1.4%	1.7%	1.4%
Return on equity (ROE)	1.6%	-4.0%	1.8%
Change in ROA	-0.3%	-1.8%	-0.3%
Change in ROA	-0.8%	-8.9%	-0.6%
Earnings loss	9.3%	11.1%	9.3%
Stock market return	2.4%	-0.8%	2.4%
Sales (in mio. DM)	3,346.9	590.5***	3,392.2
Number of observations	2,460	18	2,421

Notes: Firms with at least four continuous years of data (Sample II, column 3) are compared with firms with at least two continuous years of data (Sample I, column 1), and with firms with less than four continuous years of data (column 2). Firms are compared at the mean of each firm characteristic. For definitions, see Appendix. All performance measures except the loss indicator are corrected for median performance at the two-digit industry level. The test statistics are heteroscedastic t-tests of equal means. *, **, *** indicates significance at the 0.10, 0.05, and 0.01 levels, respectively. The sample comprises 946 firms (Sample I), with 2,460 observations for listed firms and 2,422 observations for non-listed firms.

Table 4.2. Characteristics of entering and exiting firms

	Entry analysis		Exit analysis	
	Entering in year t	In sample at least since year $t-1$	Exiting at end of year t	Still in sample in year $t+1$
Non-listed firms:				
Size of largest block	89.1%	85.7%***	82.1%	84.8%
Fraction of dispersed shares	6.9%	9.5%***	14.8%	10.3%
Debt-to-assets ratio	43.8%	37.9%***	47.2%	37.8%**
Return on assets (ROA)	0.1%	0.8%	-0.4%	1.0%
Return on equity (ROE)	1.7%	1.3%	-3.9%	1.6%
Change in ROA	0.9%	-0.2%*	2.3%	-0.4%
Change in ROE	1.7%	-0.2%	-1.3%	-0.6%
Earnings loss	20.0%	13.0%***	19.3%	12.3%
Sales (in mio. DM)	1,109.3	2,430.3***	798.7	2,334.7***
Number of observations	448	1,842	60	1,842
Listed firms:				
Size of largest block	67.3%	60.8%***	84.0%	60.3%*
Fraction of dispersed shares	26.7%	31.3%**	16.0%	31.6%
Debt-to-assets ratio	41.0%	41.6%	41.1%	41.2%
Return on assets (ROA)	4.6%	1.2%***	0.1%	1.5%
Return on equity (ROE)	6.9%	1.3%***	0.2%	1.8%
Change in ROA	0.4%	-0.3%	4.6%	-0.6%
Change in ROE	0.4%	-0.9%	3.3%	-1.6%
Earnings loss	3.5%	10.1%***	20.0%	8.9%
Stock market return	12.7%	4.5%**	6.7%	4.1%
Sales (in mio. DM)	843.2	3,546.7***	28.6	3,325.3***
Number of observations	171	2,094	5	2,094

Notes: Characteristics of firms entering the sample after 1987, the first year of the sample, or exiting the sample before 1994, the last year of the sample, compared with characteristics of firms that do not enter or exit the sample, separately for non-listed and listed firms. For firms entering in year t, the comparison group is firms in year t that are in the sample at least since year $t-1$. Vice versa, for firms exiting the sample at the end of year t, the comparison group is firms in year t that are still in the sample in year $t+1$. Firms are compared at the mean of each firm characteristic. For definitions, see Appendix. All performance measures except the loss indicator are corrected for median performance at the two-digit industry level. The test statistics are heteroscedastic t-tests of equal means. *, **, *** indicates significance at the 0.10, 0.05, and 0.01 levels, respectively. The sample comprises 946 firms (Sample I), with 2,460 observations for listed firms and 2,422 observations for non-listed firms.

applies, a chain of control is not pursued further. These rules guarantee that no more than one ultimate owner is identified for each direct shareholder. Note that if a shareholder has split his ownership stake in a particular company into several smaller stakes, for example into two blocks of 50% held by two subsidiary firms, we combine these smaller stakes into one single block. We set the first cutoff point at 50% because German law allows an investor owning 50% of all shares to appoint management.[1] The second cutoff point is set at 25% because an investor owning 25% of the shares has the right to veto decisions. In a second step in determining the ultimate owner for each sample firm, we apply the three rules to all direct shareholders. This allows to identify one single shareholder that is in ultimate control. When no single shareholder fulfills the criteria, this firm is seen to have no ultimate owner.

For illustration, consider the example of Dornier Aeronautics GmbH, a non-listed medium-sized firm in the aeronautics industry (Figure 4.1). In the year 1992 it is one hundred percent owned by Dornier GmbH, the *direct* shareholder (level 1). In turn, Dornier GmbH is owned by the Dornier family (42.4%) and by Deutsche Aerospace AG (57.6%)(level 2). This latter firm is part of the Daimler-Benz AG conglomerate structure, being owned with 83.0% by the automobile giant (level 3). Daimler-Benz AG itself is in the hands of Deutsche Bank AG (28.2%), Mercedes Automobil-Holding AG (25.2%), and the Emirate of Kuwait (14%). The rest of the shares is dispersed. Applying our concept of control, we find a continuous chain of majority stakes between Dornier Aeronautics GmbH and Daimler-Benz AG, but several shareholders owning minority stakes larger than 25% in Daimler-Benz AG. Hence, we identify Daimler-Benz AG on the third level in the ownership structure as the *ultimate* owner of Dornier Aeronautics GmbH.

In addition to our concept of control, two main alternatives of how to define ultimate ownership are conceivable. One possibility is to pursue each ownership chain to its end, multiply the individual share blocks along the way, and compare the shareholders at the end of each chain by size of the resulting product of ownership blocks. In the above example this implies that Dornier Aeronautics GmbH would be ultimately owned by the Dornier family (42.4%), Deutsche Bank AG (13.5%), Mercedes Automobil Holding AG (12.0%), the Emirate of Kuwait (6.7%), and many small shareholders. Hence, Dornier Aeronautics GmbH would be seen to have at least four ultimate owners, each controlling Dornier Aeronautics GmbH with a certain probability. Another alternative is to assume that shareholders on higher levels of the ownership structure cannot influence decisions at the base level, for example due to information asymmetries or transaction costs. In this case Dornier GmbH is identified as the single ultimate owner.

[1] A 50% majority is sufficient to dismiss management after their regular period of office. But a majority of 75% is required to dismiss management during its period of office (§103 (1) AktG).

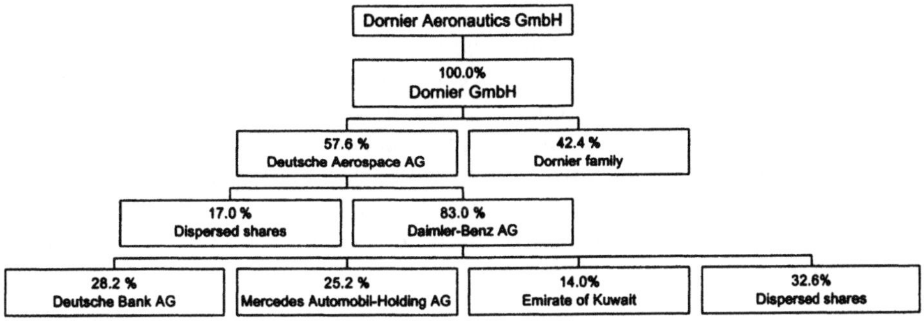

Figure 4.1. Ownership structure of Dornier Aeronautics GmbH (1992)

Both alternatives have weaknesses. For the first alternative, information on the complete control chains of all direct shareholders is required. In most cases this information is available only for the largest shareholders. The second alternative depends on the assumption of complete dilution of control in pyramid structures. The large number of conglomerate firms in Germany with up to six or more layers of ownership suggests that pyramids are attractive forms of organization. Hence, control is unlikely to be fully diluted in pyramids. Our concept of control overcomes these weaknesses and combines advantages of both alternatives: clear identification of one single ultimate owner and the incorporation of complex ownership structures.

Our concept of control could be subject to potential bias because it is based on officially reported ownership rights instead of voting rights.[2] Ownership rights do not need to coincide perfectly with voting rights. There are two main reasons for this. First, shares might have voting caps or carry multiple voting rights. Second, shares that are officially reported as dispersed might be under de facto control of banks because the German system of proxy voting gives banks the right to execute voting rights of deposited shares. Unless shareholders have given instructions, banks can multiply their influence this way. We believe that these weaknesses are unlikely to produce a systematic bias. Although legal during 1987–1994, limitations on voting rights do not seem to be widespread. Gorton and Schmid (2000) report that only 14 of

[2] Note that information on voting rights, as provided by the German Securities Exchange Commission (BAWe) and used in the study of Becht and Böhmer (2002), is preferable to pure ownership information. But this information is available only from 1996 onwards, and the methodology applied by the BAWe to attribute voting rights in complex ownership structures has serious drawbacks, as shown by Becht and Böhmer.

the largest German firms had voting rights restrictions. Hence, in the vast majority of sample firms voting rights do coincide with ownership rights. As for proxy voting, recent evidence suggests that proxy voting is extremely unlikely to enhance German banks' voting power considerably (Edwards and Nibler, 2000). In addition, only few of our sample firms have a widely dispersed shareholder base, which is the precondition for bank voting power based on proxy rights. Hence, proxy voting is unlikely to significantly bias our concept of control. We recognize, however, that investors identified as ultimate owners at higher levels in the ownership structure might also be subject to proxy voting by banks.

4.3 Frequency of Control Transfers

In the following we describe the frequency of control transactions in Germany as well as the type of buyers and sellers of control blocks. We analyze changes in aggregate measures of ownership (Chapter 4.3.1) and changes in individual shareholders (Chapter 4.3.2). We show that ownership structures are not constant over time.

4.3.1 Evidence Based on Aggregate Measures

If concentration of ownership changes over time, this can be a first indication that ownership structures are not constant. Table 4.3 examines this issue for three measures of concentration. We consider the size of the largest block, the sum of the three largest blocks, and the fraction of firms that are under ultimate control according to our concept of control. Table 4.3 reports average concentration over the years 1987–1994.

Table 4.3 shows that ownership concentration is large, irrespective of the measure applied. For listed firms, the average size of the largest block is 60.6%, and for non-listed firms it is even larger with 85.9%. The figure for listed firms closely resembles the figure of 58.9% reported by Becht and Böhmer (2002), which is based on voting rights and calculated as the average for all listed firms in 1996. The similarity of these two figures suggests that the concept of control as applied in this study is indeed a suitable methodological tool to reconstruct voting hierarchies based on information of direct ownership rights. Note also that the two other concentration measures are highly correlated with our measure of control.

Furthermore, Table 4.3 suggests that ownership concentration has been increasing during the years 1987–1994. While the average size of the largest block in listed firms is 53.1% in 1987, it constantly increases to 61.9% in 1994. An analogous increase can be observed for non-listed firms. One reason for increasing average concentration could be that old shareholders or incoming new shareholders purchase shares from other shareholders holding smaller stakes. But as argued in Chapter 4.2.1, this observed increase could

Table 4.3. Ownership concentration

	Non-listed firms			Listed firms		
	BLOCK	*BLOCK3*	*CONTROL*	*BLOCK*	*BLOCK3*	*CONTROL*
1987	78.1%	81.4%	92.4%	53.1%	55.8%	75.4%
1988	82.0%	84.4%	94.0%	57.7%	60.1%	78.0%
1989	83.8%	85.7%	94.1%	59.7%	62.1%	80.0%
1990	84.1%	85.7%	93.8%	60.5%	62.9%	82.4%
1991	84.6%	86.2%	95.1%	61.6%	64.1%	82.0%
1992	87.0%	88.2%	96.3%	62.5%	64.7%	82.4%
1993	88.2%	89.6%	96.3%	63.5%	65.5%	83.8%
1994	90.3%	92.1%	95.8%	61.9%	64.6%	84.2%
Average	85.9%	87.7%	95.0%	60.6%	63.0%	81.5%
Correlation with *CONTROL*	0.51	0.37	1.00	0.61	0.68	1.00

Notes: Ownership concentration calculated as sample average in a given year for the period 1987–1994, separately for non-listed and listed firms. Measures of ownership concentration include the average size of the largest share block (*BLOCK*), the average sum of the three largest share blocks (*BLOCK3*), and the fraction of firms for which an ultimate owner can be identified applying the concept of control (*CONTROL*). The size of the largest block and the sum of the three largest blocks are calculated at the direct level of ownership. The sample comprises 946 firms (Sample I).

also be an artefact because firms entering the sample show, on average, higher concentration than firms already in the sample. The case of ownership concentration illustrates that it can be difficult to infer changes in disaggregate measures from changes in aggregate measures.

Another aggregate figure commonly used to describe ownership structures is the distribution of shares controlled by different shareholder types. Following the empirical literature, we define five shareholder types: individuals, financial firms (banks, insurance companies, and investment funds), non-financial firms, government, as well as dispersed shares. For individuals, we distinguish between directors (insiders) that play a particular role in governing a corporation and individuals not related to the firm. Partnerships are included in the category 'individuals' because in Germany managers of these firms are usually identical with their owners. Hence no additional agency problem exists.

Table 4.4 classifies all direct share blocks, which are assigned to the type of their ultimate owner, into these five ownership categories. For listed firms, we find that individuals (36.8%) and non-financial firms (24%) ultimately control the largest fraction of shares. Financial firms own about nine percent of shares, with banks owning a larger fraction than insurance companies, with 7.3% and 1.8% respectively (not tabled). About 32% of the shares of listed

Table 4.4. Ownership of large share blocks by type of ultimate owner

	Individuals		Fin. firms	Non-fin. firms	Gov.	Disp. shares	Total
	total	insiders					
Non-listed firms	30.7%	12.0%	9.2%	48.6%	4.7%	9.3%	100%
Listed firms	36.8%	22.5%	9.2%	24.0%	1.9%	31.5%	100%

Notes: Ownership of large share blocks by type of ultimate owner as sample average for the period 1987–1994, separately for non-listed and listed firms. For each share block on the direct level of ownership, the type of the ultimate owner is identified applying the concept of control. Second, for each firm the distribution of share blocks across five categories of the ultimate owner is determined, using block size at the direct level. Third, sample distribution of share blocks across categories is calculated as the average across all firm years. The five categories of the ultimate owner are: individuals (families, partnerships (*Personengesellschaften*), foundations), non-financial firms, financial firms (banks, insurance companies, investment funds), government authorities, and dispersed shares (shares not held in a block). Insiders are executive and non-executive directors. The sample comprises 946 firms (Sample I).

firms are not owned by any large shareholder (dispersed), and about 10% for non-listed firms. The role of banks as ultimate owners appears to be limited compared to the central role they are often assumed to play in corporate Germany. But as argued in Chapter 4.2.2, the influence of banks is hard to capture based solely on shares directly owned because the German system of proxy voting potentially enhances their influence. A theoretical upper limit of bank voting power can be calculated by attributing all dispersed shares to banks. For listed firms, according to Table 4.4 this would enable German banks to cast votes for at most about 39% of all shares in listed firms.

Similar to concentration of ownership, a changing distribution of shares across shareholder types could also indicate changes in ownership structure. Examining sample averages year by year we find that the fraction of shares controlled by non-financial firms and individuals increases, for non-listed firms and listed firms respectively. At the same time, the fraction of dispersed shares declines considerably for both listed and non-listed firms. One interpretation could be that dispersed shares are purchased by either individuals or non-financial firms. But as shown in Chapter 4.2.1, entering firms typically have a lower fraction of dispersed shares. Again this suggests that aggregate measures are less useful to determine changes in disaggregate measures.

4.3.2 Evidence Based on Changes in Individual Shareholders

In contrast to evidence based on ownership changes *between* shareholder categories, as discussed in the previous section, this section takes into account ownership changes *within* shareholder categories. With data on individual shareholders it is possible to overcome the weaknesses of evidence based on aggregate measures of ownership, which result from changing sample composition. Applying our concept of control, we identify the ultimate owner of each direct shareholder. Then we compare the names of those ultimate owners year by year and aggregate annual changes in individual shareholders into three categories: (1) the increase of shares held by new shareholders, (2) the increase of shares held by old shareholders, and (3) the decrease of shares held by old shareholders.

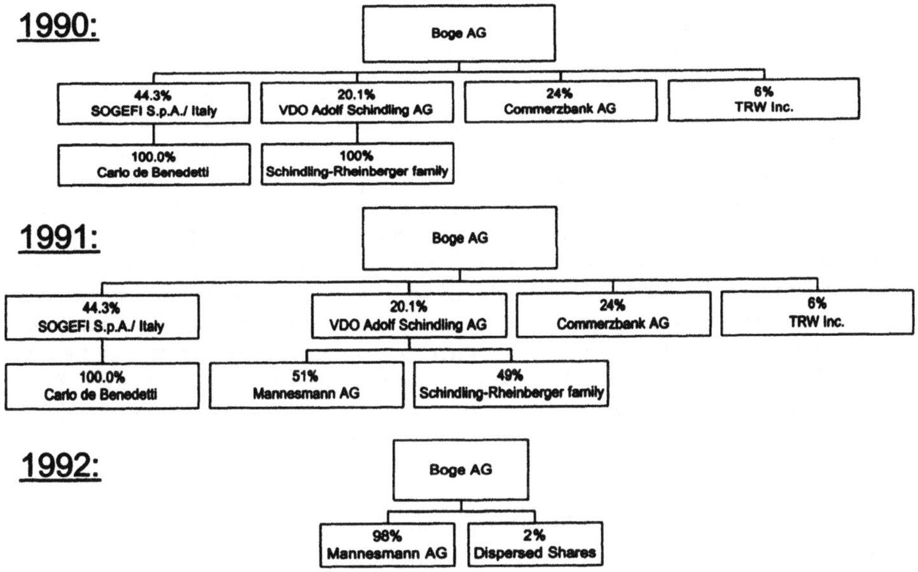

Figure 4.2. Ownership structure of Boge AG (1990–1992)

For better illustration, consider the following example (Figure 4.2). In the year 1990, Boge AG, a large non-listed firm in the rubber industry, is owned by four large shareholders. Applying the concept of control, we identify Carlo de Benedetti as the ultimate owner of Boge AG. In the year 1991, Mannesmann AG becomes the new ultimate owner of VDO Adolf Schindling AG, a direct shareholder of Boge AG. For Boge AG this implies a decrease of 20.1% by an old shareholder (the Schindling-Rheinberger family), and an increase of 20.1% by a new shareholder (Mannesmann AG). Note that de Benedetti remains the ultimate owner of Boge AG. In the year 1992, Mannesmann AG acquires almost all shares of Boge AG, becoming its new ultimate owner. This implies a decrease of 74.3% by old shareholders, and an increase of 80.4% by an old shareholder.

Table 4.5. Purchases and sales of large share blocks

	Non-listed firms			Listed firms		
	Increase new shrh.	Increase old shrh.	Decrease old shrh.	Increase new shrh.	Increase old shrh.	Decrease old shrh.
1987	6.9%	0.8%	7.5%	7.7%	1.6%	7.7%
1988	3.9%	1.3%	3.9%	2.7%	1.5%	3.3%
1989	7.7%	1.3%	8.0%	5.6%	1.8%	5.6%
1990	7.4%	0.8%	8.6%	5.0%	1.7%	6.4%
1991	1.6%	1.1%	2.0%	4.8%	1.6%	5.0%
1992	4.3%	1.4%	4.6%	2.6%	1.7%	4.1%
1993	1.2%	0.7%	1.7%	3.1%	1.3%	3.1%
1994	6.8%	1.4%	6.5%	5.3%	1.3%	8.8%
Average	4.9%	1.1%	5.2%	4.4%	1.5%	5.4%

Notes: Average fraction of shares purchased by new shareholders (columns 1 and 4), purchased by old shareholders (columns 2 and 5), and sold by old shareholders (column 3 and 6) in any given year for the period 1987–1994, separately for non-listed and listed firms. First, the ultimate owner of each direct share block is identified. Second, the names of those ultimate owners are compared year by year and annual changes in individual shareholders are aggregated into the three categories. Third, for each of the three measures the average across all firm years is determined. The sample comprises 946 firms (Sample I).

Table 4.5 shows that in listed firms, on average in any given year, 4.4% of shares are purchased by new shareholders during 1987–1994. Old shareholders increase their investment by 1.5%, and old shareholders decrease their investment by 5.4%.[3] For non-listed firms, average figures are very similar. Statistically, the difference between both types of firms is not significant. Hence, there is a significant market for large share blocks in Germany, both for listed and non-listed firms.

An interesting feature of this market is that there is large variation over time (Table 4.5). During the period of observation, boom times of large block trading are the years 1987, 1989, 1990, and 1994. This variation is reflected both in increases by new shareholders and decreases by old shareholders, and both for listed and non-listed firms. Therefore it is unlikely to be driven by variation in the fraction of dispersed shares. One reason for increased transaction activity is privatization. In 1990, the year of German reunification,

[3] The sum of increases of old and new shareholders does not need to be equal to the decrease of old shareholders because free-floating shares are not counted as held by a blockholder.

privatization of formerly state-owned enterprises accounts for about ten percent of all transactions. But also the purchase of large conglomerates with many subsidiaries is important. When Feldmühle Nobel AG was acquired by VEBA AG in a hostile takeover during the year 1989, VEBA AG also became the ultimate owner of another four non-listed firms in our sample. And when Metallgesellschaft AG came into trouble in 1993, it had to sell five subsidiaries contained in the sample to other industrial companies.

In the remaining part of this section we analyze these block transactions in depth. First, we look at their frequency and the size of traded blocks. Second, we examine block trading with respect to the identity of block traders. The sample encompasses 2,422 firm years for non-listed firms and 2,460 firm years for listed firms. This is the total number of cases in which block trading could occur. For listed firms, in 258 cases (10.5% on average in any given year) we observe that a block is purchased by a new shareholder. For non-listed firms, the respective rate of block purchases is lower with 7.3%. Table 4.6 shows the size distribution of blocks purchased by new shareholders. For listed firms, the purchased block is equal or exceeds 50% in 107 cases (41.5%). In 62 cases, the new shareholder purchases 25% or more but less than 50%. In sum this means that in 169 cases (65.5%) an incoming shareholder acquires a stake of at least 25%. This strongly suggests that new shareholders come in *because* they want to take over control of the respective firm.

Table 4.6. Size distribution of blocks purchased by new shareholders

	Size of purchased block							
	[5%; 10%[		[10%; 25%[		[25%; 50%[		[50%; 100%]	
	total	%	total	%	total	%	total	%
Non-listed firms	6	3.4%	24	13.5%	21	11.8%	125	70.2%
Listed firms	11	4.3%	74	28.7%	62	24.0%	107	41.5%

Notes: Size distribution of blocks that are purchased by a new shareholder for the period 1987–1994, separately for non-listed and listed firms. Block size is observed at the direct level of ownership, block ownership is determined at the ultimate level, applying the concept of control. Therefore, purchases by new shareholders refer to changes in ultimate ownership of direct share blocks. The total number of block purchases by new shareholders is 178 for non-listed firms and 258 for listed firms. Columns 1, 3, 5, and 7 disaggregate these purchases into four size classes. Columns 2, 4, 6, and 8 relate the disaggregate number of blocks to the number of all block purchases by new shareholders. The sample comprises 946 firms (Sample I).

To put these results into perspective, we compare the frequency of block purchases with results from previous studies. For listed firms, we find that a new shareholder purchases a block larger than ten percent in 9.9% of sample firms, on average in any given year. This rate of block purchases compares to 12.4% for Belgium (Renneboog, 2000) and 9.0% for the UK (Franks et al., 2001). For the US, Bethel at al. (1998) report a rate of 6.6% for blocks larger than five percent. Hence, the frequency of block transfers in Germany is similar to other countries. For non-listed firms, the respective annual rate is 7.0%; however, no comparable figures from other countries are available.

As exemplified by the case of Boge AG (Figure 4.2), the transfer of a large block (partial firm sale) does not need to be associated with a transfer of control over the entire firm. An example of this is a new shareholder purchasing a large block, while the majority of shares remains in the hands of the ultimate owner. To identify transfers of control we check for name changes of the ultimate owner. We find that a change in control takes place in 205 cases in listed firms (8.3% on average in any given year), and in 146 cases in non-listed firms (6.0%).[4] Hence, the frequency of control transfers is considerably higher than suggested by the average size of blocks traded (Table 4.5), but lower than suggested by the number of blocks traded. We conclude that not all block transfers lead to control transfers, but that a large part does.

To see whether a particular shareholder type dominates control transfers we examine the transaction partners more closely. For listed firms, we find that most control blocks are sold by non-financial firms (33.2%) and individuals (29.3%). In turn, the largest number of control blocks is purchased by non-financial firms (41.5%) and individuals (25.9%). Compared to the fraction of listed firms under ultimate ownership of non-financial firms (28.6%) and individuals (42.4%), it becomes clear that non-financial firms trade control blocks more often than would be expected by their frequency as ultimate owners. In comparison with all other shareholder types, non-financial firms are the most active traders of control blocks. For non-listed firms, non-financial firms buy an even larger fraction of control blocks (56.8%), more than three times the fraction individuals purchase.

4.4 Causes and Consequences of Control Transfers

In the following we analyze the causes and consequences of changes in ultimate ownership. The aim is to test the hypotheses lined out in Chapter 4.1. All results are based on bivariate analyses, and any causal interpretation we give to correlations between variables is in the sense of Granger (1969).

To identify the causes and consequences of control transfers, we compare firms that experience a change in ultimate ownership with firms that do not experience such a change in any of the sample years, based on various firm characteristics. Specifically, we calculate the mean of each firm characteristic for the year of control change (year 0) as well as for the two years preceding

[4] Overall, 73.2% of sample firms do not experience any change in control. For about 20% of firms the ultimate owner changes once, for about six percent twice. Hence, several consecutive changes in control are not very likely.

(year -1, year -2) or following this change (year 1, year 2). Our benchmark are firms that do not experience a control transfer in any of the sample years, or more exactly, the characteristics' average over all sample years for these firms.[5] The analysis is based on Sample II, which contains firms with at least four continuous years of data.

4.4.1 Causes of Control Transfers

To examine the causes of control transfers, we compare firms on measures of ownership structure, capital structure, size, and performance. Tables 4.7 and 4.8 investigate the differences between firms with (columns 2 and 4) and without (columns 1 and 3) a change in control, separately for listed and non-listed firms. Three consecutive years are considered: the year in which the change in ultimate ownership occurs (year 0), and the two years prior to this change (year -1 and year -2).

Table 4.7 shows that firms experiencing a change in control differ significantly from firms not experiencing such a change on a range of characteristics. These differences are observed for listed as well as non-listed firms; often it is only the level of the respective firm characteristic that differs between both types of firms. We find that ownership concentration is significantly smaller for firms in which the ultimate owner changes. For listed firms, one year prior to the change in control the average size of the largest block is 50.7%, but 62.7% in firms without a transfer of corporate control. For non-listed firms, the difference in ownership concentration is also significant, but the average size of the largest block is much larger. Similarly, we find that changes in control are less likely to occur for firms that are under control of an ultimate owner than for firms that are not under control of an ultimate owner. This is strong empirical support for **Hypothesis 4.1**: Changes in ultimate ownership are less likely for firms with high ownership concentration.

We also find strong support for **Hypothesis 4.2** that highly leveraged firms are more likely to experience a change in control. Listed as well as non-listed firms for which we observe a change in ultimate ownership show a significantly larger burden of debt than other firms. This result is robust when interest coverage or the borrowing ratio are used as alternative measures of leverage. Regarding complexity of ownership, the results in Table 4.7 indicate that the level at which the ultimate owner is located is important. For non-listed firms, this level is significantly lower prior to a change in ultimate ownership. Therefore non-listed firms controlled through pyramids are less likely to experience a change in control. In turn, for listed firms the level of control is significantly higher after the change. This suggests that listed firms tend to be controlled through a pyramid after a change in control. To

[5] All results are qualitatively similar when we compare firms at the characteristics' median instead.

Table 4.7. Causes of control transfers

		Non-listed firms		Listed firms	
		No change in control	Change in control	No change in control	Change in control
Largest block	year -2		69.4%***		50.2%***
	year -1		70.8%***		50.7%***
	year 0	87.5%	76.5%***	62.7%	55.1%***
Debt-to-assets ratio	year -2		40.9%*		44.5%***
	year -1		41.9%**		46.0%***
	year 0	36.9%	41.9%**	39.9%	45.1%***
Level of control	year -2		1.60***		1.39
	year -1		1.70*		1.40
	year 0	1.86	2.00	1.41	1.68***
Sales (in mio. DM)	year -2		1,541.7**		1,975.4***
	year -1		1,592.5**		2,042.7***
	year 0	2,404.1	1,557.6**	4,030.3	2,245.0***
Insider ownership	year -2		12.6%		14.6%***
	year -1		10.3%		12.2%***
	year 0	13.5%	5.4%***	27.3%	9.7%***
Number of observations		1,391	621	1,443	978

Notes: Characteristics of firms that experience a change in ultimate ownership (control) in year 0 (columns 2 and 4), compared with characteristics of firms that do not experience such a change in any year (columns 1 and 3), separately for non-listed and listed firms. Firms are compared at the mean of each firm characteristic. For firms with a change in control, statistics are calculated for the two years preceding the change (year -1 and year -2) and the year of change (year 0). For other firms, statistics refer to the whole period of observation. For definitions, see Appendix. The test statistics are heteroscedastic t-tests of equal means. *, **, *** indicates significance at the 0.10, 0.05, and 0.01 levels, respectively. The sample comprises 664 firms (Sample II).

investigate how changes in ownership are related to cross ownership, we define a variable indicating whether a sample firm is ultimately controlled by a firm belonging to the well-known web of financial and non-financial German firms, similar to Wenger and Kaserer (1998). This web consists of the five largest commercial German banks, two large insurance companies, as well as large non-financial firms such as Linde AG, Siemens AG, and VIAG AG. The analysis shows that firms experiencing a change in ultimate ownership are less likely to be under control of a web firm (not tabled), but the difference is not statistically significant. Summarizing, there is evidence supporting **Hypothesis 4.3** that complex ownership structures make a change in control less likely, but only for non-listed firms. In turn, listed firms tend to become integrated in pyramids after a change in ownership.

Table 4.8. Industry-adjusted performance as cause of control transfers

		Non-listed firms		Listed firms	
		No change in control	Change in control	No change in control	Change in control
Return-on-assets	year -2		1.3%		1.3%
	year -1		0.3%		0.8%
	year 0	0.9%	-1.0%	1.8%	0.9%
Return-on-equity	year -2		1.7%		2.8%
	year -1		-0.3%		2.7%
	year 0	1.4%	-4.6%**	2.1%	0.1%
Change in ROA	year -2		-0.7%		-1.8%*
	year -1		-1.4%		-0.4%
	year 0	-0.1%	-2.2%*	-0.4%	0.0%
Change in ROE	year -2		-0.3%		-3.4%
	year -1		-2.3%		-0.9%
	year 0	-0.2%	-5.8%**	-0.6%	-3.0%
Earnings loss	year -2		6.2%**		9.9%
	year -1		12.4%		13.7%**
	year 0	13.8%	15.5%	8.0%	11.8%*
Stock market return	year -2				0.1%
	year -1				13.3%***
	year 0			1.8%	7.1%
Number of observations		1,391	621	1,443	978

Notes: Mean industry-adjusted performance of firms that experience a change in ultimate ownership (control) in year 0 (columns 2 and 4), compared with performance of firms that do not experience such a change in any year (columns 1 and 3), separately for non-listed and listed firms. For firms with a change in control, statistics are calculated for the two years preceding the change (year -1 and year -2) and the year of change (year 0). For other firms, statistics refer to the whole period of observation. For definitions, see Appendix. All performance measures except the loss indicator are corrected for median performance at the two-digit industry level. The test statistics are heteroscedastic t-tests of equal means. *, **, *** indicates significance at the 0.10, 0.05, and 0.01 levels, respectively. The sample comprises 664 firms (Sample II).

Larger firms, whether listed or not, are significantly less likely to be exposed to a change in ultimate ownership (Table 4.7). For example, we find that listed firms in which the ultimate owner does not change are about 80% larger in terms of sales than listed firms experiencing a change in control. Analogous differences are found when using total assets or the number of employees as measures of firm size. This is strong support for **Hypothesis 4.4.** Concerning the role of insider ownership, insiders (executive and non-executive directors) own a significantly lower fraction of shares in listed firms that experience a change in control. In addition, insider ownership falls considerably in listed as well as non-listed firms when ultimate ownership changes. For example, in non-listed firms it drops from an average of 10.3% to 5.4%. A Wald test shows that this difference is statistically significant at the 0.10 level. This indicates that insiders tend to sell out in control transactions. Hence, for listed firms there is strong evidence supporting **Hypothesis 4.5**: Changes in ultimate ownership are less likely when insider ownership is high.

As a last cause of control changes we consider performance. To check for robustness we examine several measures of performance: return on assets (ROA), return on equity (ROE), the change in ROA, the change in ROE, the fraction of firms reporting an earnings loss, and annual stock market return. All measures except the loss indicator are corrected for median performance at the two-digit industry level.[6]

Table 4.8 suggests that poor performance is not related to changes in ultimate ownership. Only listed firms that report an earnings loss are significantly more likely to experience a change in control. For non-listed firms we do not find evidence that performance is particularly poor before a change in control occurs. Accounting returns appear to be somewhat lower one year preceding the change; however, the difference in industry-adjusted performance to firms without a change in control is insignificant. Only in the year of control change performance of non-listed is significantly smaller. One reason for this lack of evidence regarding performance can be that our sample contains systematically fewer poorly performing non-listed firms (see Chapter 4.2.1). If poor performance makes a change in control more likely and these firms disappear from the sample due to a takeover, this will bias any observed relation between performance and the likelihood for a change in control towards zero. In summary, our data confirm **Hypothesis 4.6**, but only for listed firms with very poor performance. This result does not necessarily stand in contrast to our finding that stock market returns are significantly higher one year before control changes. To the contrary, this might indicate that control transfers are anticipated and perceived as value-enhancing events.

4.4.2 Consequences of Control Transfers

In the following we analyze the consequences of control transfers. Again, we compare firms that experience a change in ultimate ownership with firms that do not experience such a change in any of the sample years. Subsequently, we investigate the effects on governance changes, corporate restructuring, and on performance.

---

[6] We also calculated performance relative to median returns in the same accounting year. For non-listed firms, the obtained results suggest a stronger effect of poor performance on changes in ultimate ownership than the results reported in Table 4.8.

Governance Changes and Corporate Restructuring Table 4.9 describes how management turnover, asset divestitures, employment growth, and labor costs evolve in firms that experience a change in control. All figures are calculated for the year of ultimate ownership change (year 0), the two following years (year 1 and year 2), and the year prior to the change (year -1).

For listed and non-listed firms we observe a strong increase in management turnover. For example, for listed firms that experience a change in control CEO turnover rates more than double from 10.2% in the year preceding the change to 21.1% in the year of change (Table 4.9). This turnover rate is significantly above average CEO turnover in listed firms without a change in ultimate ownership. For non-listed firms we find a similar increase in CEO turnover following the control change. The increase in management turnover is consistent with Denis and Sarin (1999) who find that US firms experiencing large increases or decreases in insider ownership show CEO turnover rates of 15%-20%; in contrast, small changes in ownership are associated with turnover rates of only 8%. Hence, a CEO turnover rate of 14%, which we find for German listed firms not experiencing a change in control, is comparatively high. Partially this difference might be explained by the fact that our turnover data include CEOs leaving the board voluntarily. Unfortunately, for Germany no consistent data are available on voluntary or forced management resignation.

Similar to CEO turnover, the replacement rate of executive directors increases considerably following control transfers (Table 4.9). For the supervisory board, which in Germany is separated from the management board, we find turnover rates for the chairman and the other board members (not tabled) that are above those reported for the management board. These findings strongly support **Hypothesis 4.7** that changes in ultimate ownership are followed by increases in management (and supervisory) board turnover.

Asset divestitures also increase in control transfers; this increase is significant for sales of fixed assets, but only for listed firms (Table 4.9). Specifically, for listed firms we find that sales rates of fixed assets increase from 6.9% in year -1 to 8.8% in year 0. The difference in the rate of asset sales to firms without a change in control is significant at the 0.05 level. For non-listed firms, we also observe an increase in sales of fixed and financial assets, but the difference to firms without a change in ultimate ownership is insignificant. Concerning employment, we find that in the second year after the control transfer the average growth rate of employment is negative for listed and non-listed firms, but the difference in growth rates between firms with and without a change in control is significant only for listed firms. Hence, employee layoffs increase, but not before two years after the change in control. This time lag suggests that adjustment costs play an important role in reorganizing a firm.

Whereas there is evidence for asset divestitures and layoffs, we find no evidence of cost cutting. On the contrary, labor costs per employee do not

Table 4.9. Governance changes and corporate restructuring following control transfers

		Non-listed firms		Listed firms	
		No change in control	Change in control	No change in control	Change in control
Turnover of CEO	year -1		12.8%		10.2%
	year 0	14.2%	17.9%	14.0%	21.1%**
	year 1		25.6%**		19.5%*
	year 2		20.5%		21.1%**
Turnover of exec. directors	year -1		11.2%		10.9%
	year 0	11.5%	20.6%***	11.9%	19.6%***
	year 1		23.4%***		15.8%*
	year 2		16.2%		16.5%**
Sales of fixed assets	year -1		6.0%		6.9%
	year 0	6.6%	5.2%*	6.2%	8.8%**
	year 1		8.5%		7.4%
	year 2		5.8%		7.3%
Sales of fin. assets	year -1		12.1%		16.5%
	year 0	14.8%	16.7%	16.2%	20.0%
	year 1		13.8%		18.6%
	year 2		17.7%		17.4%
Growth rate of employment	year -1		-0.1%		4.6%
	year 0	-1.3%	-3.2%	4.6%	5.5%
	year 1		1.1%		1.1%
	year 2		-3.2%		-2.0%***
Growth rate of labor costs	year -1		3.3%**		4.6%
	year 0	6.4%	4.9%	4.6%	4.3%
	year 1		13.6%**		10.9%**
	year 2		6.8%		4.3%
Number of observations		1,391	621	1,443	978

Notes: Characteristics of firms that experience a change in ultimate ownership (control) in year 0 (columns 2 and 4), compared with characteristics of firms that do not experience such a change in any year (columns 1 and 3), separately for non-listed and listed firms. Firms are compared at the mean of each firm characteristic. For firms with a change in control, statistics are calculated for the year preceding the change (year -1), the year of change (year 0), and the two years following the change (year 1 and year 2). For other firms, statistics refer to the whole period of observation. For definitions, see Appendix. The test statistics are heteroscedastic t-tests of equal means. *, **, *** indicates significance at the 0.10, 0.05, and 0.01 levels, respectively. The sample comprises 664 firms (Sample II).

Table 4.10. Industry-adjusted performance following poor performance

Performance measure		Relative to zero		Relative to performance of firms without a change in control	
		Non-listed firms	Listed firms	Non-listed firms	Listed firms
Return-on-assets	year -1	-5.0%***	-4.8%***	0.9%	0.0%
	year 0	-4.9%***	-3.4%	-0.7%	-0.7%
	year 1	-2.3%*	-2.7%***	1.4%	-0.4%
	year 2	-2.3%*	0.4%	0.7%	2.6%
Return-on-equity	year -1	-10.6%***	-10.6%***	0.2%	-1.3%
	year 0	-11.3%***	-10.2%**	-3.0%	-4.3%
	year 1	-4.0%*	-6.9%*	2.7%	-1.6%
	year 2	-2.3%	-3.1%	3.7%	2.5%
Change in ROA	year -1	-5.3%***	-4.3%***	-0.6%	-0.1%
	year 0	-0.6%	1.2%	-1.1%	1.3%
	year 1	3.3%*	-0.3%	3.8%**	-0.4%
	year 2	0.0%	1.1%	-0.5%	1.1%
Change in ROE	year -1	-9.1%***	-8.9%***	0.6%	-0.8%
	year 0	-0.8%	-1.2%	-1.7%	-1.3%
	year 1	6.3%	3.3%	6.4%	2.4%
	year 2	1.4%	3.5%	0.2%	3.8%
Stock market return	year -1		-22.7%***		1.8%
	year 0		-1.5%		-4.6%
	year 1		-7.0%		-15.4%
	year 2		0.5%		1.6%
Number of observations		104	116	104	116

Notes: Mean industry-adjusted performance of firms that perform poorly in year -1 and that experience a change in ultimate ownership (control) in year 0, but not in years -1, 1, and 2, relative to zero (columns 1 and 2). Mean industry-adjusted performance of firms that perform poorly in year -1 and that experience a change in control in year 0, but not in years -1, 1, and 2, relative to mean industry-adjusted performance of firms that perform poorly in year -1 and do not experience such a change in any year (columns 3 and 4). Poor performance is defined as negative industry-adjusted performance. The statistics are calculated separately for non-listed and listed firms. For definitions, see Appendix. All performance measures are corrected for median performance at the two-digit industry level. The test statistics are t-tests of being equal to zero (columns 1 and 2) and heteroscedastic t-tests of equal means (columns 3 and 4). *, **, *** indicates significance at the 0.10, 0.05, and 0.01 levels, respectively. The sample comprises 55 firms from Sample II for which the above conditions hold.

decline, but increase after a change in ultimate ownership. This suggests that the new owner is working to improve incentives for employees. Overall, the empirical evidence on corporate restructuring supports **Hypothesis 4.8**, but only for listed firms.

Effects on Performance As a last consequence we examine the impact of control changes on performance. If there is any impact, then it should be most visible for firms that previously experienced a decline in performance. The analysis proceeds in two steps. First, we compare firms that perform worse than their industry peers in year -1 and experience a change in control in year 0, with median industry performance. Table 4.10 reports the difference in performance, starting with the year of poor performance (year -1) through the three following years (columns 1 and 2). For robustness, various performance measures are used. We recognize that requiring four continuous years of data potentially induces a selection bias. As shown in Chapter 4.2.2, this does not cause a selection bias for listed firms. For non-listed firms, our sample contains systematically fewer poorly performing firms; but this should bias any observed relation between control transfer and performance improvement towards zero.

In the second step of analysis, we compare firms that perform worse than their industry peers in year -1 and experience a change in control in year 0, with those that also perform worse than their industry peers in year -1 but do *not* experience such a change in any year. The reason is that selecting only poorly performing firms to examine performance improvements could induce a second type of selection bias, particularly if there is mean reversion in our performance measures. If this is the case, performance should improve irrespective whether followed by a change in control or not. Table 4.10 reports the difference in performance, starting with the year of poor performance (year -1) through the three following years (columns 3 and 4). Poor performance is defined as the respective measure being below its median in the same two-digit industry in year -1.

Table 4.10 suggests that performance of listed and non-listed poorly performing firms adjusts to the industry benchmark after they experience a change in control. For example, we find that industry-adjusted return on assets, which by definition is negative in year -1 (-4.8%), improves to 0.4% in the second year after the change in control. Comparing the levels of performance in year 2 and in year -1 we ascertain that performance improves significantly (difference in levels not reported). We find analogous results using alternative measures of performance.

The observed improvement in performance does not necessarily have to be caused by a change in control. As noted above, it might be due to mean reversion. Table 4.10 shows that for firms performing poorly in year -1 and experiencing a control transfer in year 0 the improvement in performance is stronger than for firms performing poorly in year -1 without a subsequent control transfer. However, this difference in performance improvement is insignificant. Hence, after taking into account potential bias resulting from mean reversion, we do not find evidence that performance improves particularly following control transfers. This result holds for listed as well as non-listed firms. We must reject **Hypothesis 4.9**. Note, however, that major improvements in performance might become visible only three or more years after a change in control. Unfortunately, our data set is too small for this exercise because requiring five or more continuous years of data would leave too few observations.

4.5 Summary and Lessons

This chapter sheds light on the market for corporate control in Germany. It provides evidence on the size of this market, as well as the causes and consequences of control transfers. We find that Germany has an active market for large share blocks. For listed firms, a new shareholder purchases a block larger than ten percent in 9.9% of sample firms, on average through the years 1987–1994. This rate of block purchases compares to 12.4% for Belgium (Renneboog, 2000) and 9.0% for the UK (Franks et al., 2001). For the US, Bethel et al. (1998) report a rate of 6.6% for blocks larger than five percent. Hence, the frequency of block trades in Germany is similar to other countries. For non-listed firms, the respective rate is 7.0%; no comparable figures from other countries are available. The vast majority of block trades leads to changes in ultimate ownership (control transfers). Taking into account only block trades that lead to a control transfer, we find annual rates of 8.3% for listed firms and 6.0% for non-listed firms. The most active traders of control blocks are non-financial firms and to a lesser extent individuals.

We find that control transfers are more likely for firms with high leverage, but less likely for larger firms and firms with high concentration of ownership. In addition, high insider ownership and complex ownership structures make control transfers less likely for listed and non-listed firms, respectively. Our finding regarding insider ownership is consistent with evidence from the US (Barber et al., 1995) and Canada (St-Pierre et al., 1996) that high director ownership is associated with an increase in resistance to ownership changes. In contrast, our findings regarding performance indicate that the German market for corporate control works differently compared with the US. Case-study evidence collected by Denis and Sarin (1999) suggests that poor performance is often the impetus for the purchase of large blocks. For Germany we find that control changes are related to poor performance as well, but only when performance is very poor and only for listed firms. This suggests that changes in ownership tend to occur when the firm's regular governance mechanisms (such as board control) fail.

Changes in ultimate ownership are followed by increased management and supervisory board turnover. For listed firms, asset divestitures and employee layoffs increase after a change in control. In contrast, there is no evidence of cost cutting as labor costs per employee tend to increase after control transfers. Regarding management turnover, our results are consistent with evidence from Belgium (Renneboog, 2000) and the US (Denis and Sarin, 1999). Concerning asset restructuring, a similar impact has been reported for the US (Bethel et al., 1998; Denis and Sarin, 1999; Denis and Kruse, 2000). Our results have implications for the speed of organizational change. Kole and Lehn (1999) show for the US airline industry that internal governance structures adjust gradually after deregulation. In contrast, we find that CEO turnover occurs rapidly after a change in ownership. Hence, changes in external governance structures serve as a catalyst for organizational adaptation.

In contrast, we do not find evidence that control changes are followed by improvements in performance, irrespective whether we measure performance by accounting- or market-based returns. This result is at odds with evidence from the US where performance improves after major changes in ownership (Bethel et al., 1998; Denis and Kruse, 2000).

Our results have implications for the design of future empirical studies. First, we find that important causes and consequences of control transfers are different for listed and non-listed firms. Specifically, complex ownership structures limit control changes for non-listed firms. This indicates that empirical studies focusing on listed firms tend to underestimate the impact of ownership complexity on control transfers. Regarding restructuring, we cannot find evidence of asset divestitures or layoffs for non-listed firms. This indicates that studies focusing on listed firms tend to overestimate the impact of control transfers on restructuring. Our finding that control transfers are preceded by poor performance only for listed firms suggests that factors other than performance motivate ownership changes in non-listed firms. Whether this is so for other countries as well, or which factors this could be are open questions. The main lesson is that empirical analyses should consider listed as well as non-listed firms because important aspects of the control transfer process work differently.

Second, we find that ownership structures are not stable over time. As argued in Chapter 2, this implies that using cross-section data on ownership is not sufficient to explain variation in performance because any unobserved variation in ownership will be included in the error term. But correlation of the error term with (observed) cross-section data on ownership will cause coefficients to be biased and inconsistent. Likewise, explaining firm performance without data on ownership, but instead applying fixed-effect models to account for unobserved firm heterogeneity will also result in biased and inconsistent coefficients because unobserved (ownership) variables are *not* fixed over time. Hence, results of previous studies using either cross sections of ownership data or no ownership data are likely to be biased.

5 Determinants of Acquisition and Failure

This chapter is an extended and adapted version of Köke (2001b). It examines the determinants of acquisition and failure of German corporations. Both issues have recently attracted the increased attention of researchers and policy makers alike. In Germany, but also in other continental European countries the number of insolvencies continued to rise or stagnated at high levels. At the same time, in the past decade we have seen an upsurge in merger and acquisitions activity, both within and across the borders. In Germany and in other continental European countries, hostile takeovers are rare (Franks and Mayer, 1998). But as shown in Chapter 4, similarly to the US block trades occur more frequently than tender offers. Especially German policy makers often argue that acquisitions occur to the disadvantage of shareholders and other stakeholders. A recent example is the takeover of Mannesmann by the British telecom company Vodafone that provoked intense discussions on the merits of acquisitions.

At first sight, acquisition and failure of firms might appear as two distinct phenomena. However, we would argue that they are closely related and hence should be analyzed in combination. One reason is that the causes of corporate failure and control transfers are similar. Poor performance (Altman, 1968; Denis and Sarin, 1999; Maksimovic and Phillips, 2001), high financial pressure (Powell, 1997; Zingales, 1998), or small firm size (Bethel et al., 1998; Harhoff et al., 1998; Mulherin and Boone, 2000) are identified as factors that make failure as well as control transfers more likely. Hence, examining one form of sample exit, but disregarding the other is likely to create a sample selection problem which could lead to biased estimation results. Another reason supporting a joint analysis is that bankruptcy and takeover are the two most important sources of sample attrition in panel analyses. Hence, any attempt to correct for sample attrition should consider factors leading to failure and acquisition simultaneously.

Using a sample of almost 1,700 listed and non-listed German corporations through the years 1986–1995, the following analysis examines which firm-specific characteristics explain corporate failure and acquisition. We also investigate to what extent the length of the forward-looking time horizon matters for the usefulness of these explanatory variables, and whether different shareholder types react differently to poor performance, as suggested by theoretical considerations. There are a number of novel elements that this analysis adds to the literature. First, we examine corporate acquisition and failure simultaneously. To our knowledge no previous study on Germany does that – with the exception of Heiss and Köke (2001) who investigate control changes and firm failure with a technically more refined econometric method than the present analysis. Second, based on changes in *ultimate* ownership (Chapter 4.2.2) we investigate the impact of different types of shareholders on the likelihood of acquisition and failure. Third, in contrast to Harhoff et al. (1998) and other studies on firm failure in Germany, this analysis incorporates financial information which is typically used in bankruptcy models (Scott, 1981) and in merger models (Powell, 1997). Fourth, we use a much larger sample than previous corporate governance studies for Germany, both in terms of the number of firms and in terms of industry coverage.[1] Finally, in contrast to standard bankruptcy and merger models we do not only focus on the year prior to exit because this would introduce a selection bias, as argued by Shumway (2001). Rather we consider different forward-looking time horizons from one year to four or more years.

The following analysis uses a relatively simple multinomial logit approach to model the determinants of survival, acquisition, and failure. Heiss and Köke (2001) show that using a mixed multinomial logit model, which takes into account unobserved firm heterogeneity and allows for a more involved correlation structure between the outcomes, leads to qualitatively similar results.

The structure of this chapter is as follows: Chapter 5.1 provides a short overview to the theoretical and empirical literature on the determinants of acquisition and failure as well as a discussion of the role of different types of selling shareholders in control transactions. The literature is condensed into a set of hypotheses which are tested in the empirical analysis. Chapter 5.2 shortly explains the procedure applied to select the data from the German Corporations Database (GCD). Chapter 5.3 presents detailed descriptive evidence on the industry distribution of firms that fail or are acquired and on important firm-specific characteristics of these firms. Chapter 5.4 examines the determinants of survival, acquisition, and failure within a multinomial logit framework. Chapter 5.5 summarizes the main results and discusses some methodological implications.

---

[1] Related studies for Germany use larger samples (Harhoff et al., 1998; Wagner, 1999; Almus, 2000). But these analyses focus on small firms and exclude all cases of acquisitions.

5.1 Hypotheses

To structure our empirical analysis of firm survival, acquisition, and failure, we formulate a set of hypotheses building on the theoretical and empirical literature. We expect that acquisition and failure are affected as follows:

Hypothesis 5.1 *Acquisition and failure are more likely for firms with poor performance.*

Hypothesis 5.2 *Acquisition and failure are more likely for firms with high leverage.*

Hypothesis 5.3 *Acquisition is less likely for firms with very high and very low concentration of ownership. Failure is less likely for firms with high concentration of ownership.*

Hypothesis 5.4 *Acquisition and failure are less likely for firms with complex ownership structure.*

Hypothesis 5.5 *A poorly performing firm is less likely to be sold when owned by a private shareholder than when owned by a corporate shareholder, but most likely when no dominant shareholder exists. And a poorly performing firm is less likely to fail when owned by a corporate shareholder or the government than when owned by a private shareholder.*

Hypothesis 5.6 *Acquisition and failure are more likely for firms that undergo severe restructuring.*

Hypothesis 5.7 *Acquisition and failure are less likely for large firms.*

The current theoretical view of control transfers is largely shaped by two conflicting effects of blockholder control (Kahan, 1993; Bebchuk, 1994). On the one hand, transferring control to a more effective management team could improve efficiency. On the other hand, the acquirer's primary motive may be to loot the firm to the disadvantage of small shareholders. The first hypothesis (**5.1**) is based on empirical evidence. For the US, Barcley and Holderness (1991) find that block trades lead to efficiency gains. Bethel et al. (1998) find that block trades are followed by significant operational changes, increased CEO turnover, and improvements in profitability. Denis and Sarin (1999) and Maksimovic and Phillips (2001) show that poorly performing firms in the US are more likely to become takeover targets. For Germany, the results from Chapter 4 suggest that the impact of poor performance on the likelihood of control transfers is weak. Note, however, that these results are based on bivariate analyses. Concerning firm failure, a number of studies suggest that poor performance is an important factor (see, e.g., Altman, 1968; Powell, 1997; Astebro and Winter, 2001).

The second hypothesis (**5.2**) recognizes that also the capital structure can be a determinant of failure or changes in ownership. Mitchell and Mulherin

(1996) argue that economic shocks to an industry can alter the allocation of resources within the firm. In turn, changes in the firm's growth opportunities, leverage, or firm size could make adjustments in ownership necessary. Consistent with this view, Zingales (1998) reports that following deregulation in the US trucking industry in 1977 firms were confronted with increasing leverage, and that this has lead to a higher probability of market exit. Other empirical studies on firm failure confirm this role of financial pressure (Altman, 1968; Powell, 1997).

The third hypothesis (**5.3**) focuses on the impact of ownership concentration. Grossman and Hart (1980) argue that a precondition for hostile takeovers to be effective is concentrated share ownership because under a dispersed ownership structure shareholders would prefer to free-ride. In consequence, no takeover would take place in widely held firms. Burkart et al. (2000) show that the incumbent and new controlling shareholder prefer to trade the block rather than sell shares to the public and, in a second step, accumulate those dispersed shares because they anticipate the free-riding behavior of small shareholders in tender offers. Hence, an ex ante larger concentration of shares should make block transfers more likely. In contrast, Holmström and Tirole (1993) argue that takeovers require low concentration of ownership and, in turn, high market liquidity because only then are capital markets able to determine the necessity of a takeover. However, the significant number of non-hostile control transfers in Germany indicates that block trades occur also in the presence of large share concentration (Chapter 4). In sum, we expect the costs of a takeover to be the largest for both very high and very low concentration of share ownership.

The implication of share concentration for firm failure is less ambiguous. Higher share concentration implies that the scope for agency conflicts is reduced, and hence large shareholders can alleviate the agency problem via better monitoring (Shleifer and Vishny, 1986). We expect that the likelihood of failure shrinks with ownership concentration.

The fourth hypothesis (**5.4**) considers the role of a different aspect of ownership, namely the complexity of ownership. If a firm is part of a pyramid, management could be more likely to resist control sales because selling parts of a conglomerate would imply a loss of organizational capital. Likewise, pyramids can manifest managerial empires when they are of value to managers (Franks and Mayer, 1995), and cross ownership can provide target management with an effective anti-takeover device against unwelcome raiders (Bebchuk et al., 2000). Similarly, failures might be less likely for firms that are part of pyramids or are controlled by cross-owned shareholders when these organizational structures reduce informational asymmetries or when empire building prevents management from closing down firms in mature industries (Jensen, 1986).

The fifth hypothesis (**5.5**) examines the role of different types of owners. If performance is poor, we expect that firms owned by a private shareholder are less likely to be sold than firms owned by a corporate shareholder. One reason is that private shareholders are often deeply involved in the respective firm besides their monetary investment, for example because they are members of the founding family. Therefore, for individuals performance is unlikely to provide an impetus for selling as strong as for corporate shareholders. In contrast, we expect that poorly performing firms which do not have a dominant shareholder are more likely to be sold to a strong private or corporate shareholder because a dominant shareholder should be able to fix governance problems.

In turn, if a firm performs poorly, corporate shareholders might be better able to rescue the firm because they are typically less wealth-constrained than private shareholders. Lamont (1997) shows for the US oil industry that internal capital markets are often used to transfer cash flow between divisions. Hence, we expect that firms controlled by a large financial or non-financial corporate shareholder, but also firms controlled by the government, are less likely to fail because – in case of financial trouble – they should have better access to credit extensions or other forms of capital infusions.

The sixth hypothesis (**5.6**) considers restructuring activity and its relation to acquisition and failure. If a firm starts a restructuring program, for example by laying off employees or selling assets after financial difficulties became obvious, then restructuring could serve as an indicator that the firm has been or still is in the need of reorganization. Almus (2000) provides evidence for small German firms that failing firms show stagnation or reductions in employment already several years before final failure. Hence, ongoing restructuring activity could represent either first indicators of failure or difficulties that need to be solved by a new owner of the distressed firm.

Finally, the seventh hypothesis (**5.7**) follows Shleifer and Vishny (1992) who argue that the market for corporate control becomes less liquid as firm size increases. Hence, size could deter changes in control. Likewise, wealth constraints on the side of the buyer can make acquisitions of large firms less likely. Bethel et al. (1998) and Mulherin and Boone (2000) provide empirical evidence that smaller firms are more likely to become takeover targets. If firms are very large and if these firms get into financial trouble, this might give management the opportunity to be eligible for help from outside creditors or the government. A recent example is the case of Holzmann AG, a large German construction conglomerate. After having come into severe financial difficulties, creditors agreed – under the lead of German chancellor Schröder – to extend existing credits to Holzmann AG by another two billion DM.

5.2 Data and Frequency of Exit

The sample used for the analysis of survival, acquisition, and failure is a subsample of GCD. Specifically, in a first step, out of the 2,959 firms contained in GCD we eliminate 1,200 firms for which no information on ownership is available. Second, we use only observations from the years 1986–1996 because 1996 is the last year for which information on the survival status is available (see Chapter 3.1) (115 firm deletions). Third, since the following analysis uses information on the year before an acquisition or failure occurs, we eliminate 109 firms for which GCD contains only one year of data. Fourth, missing values on important firm characteristics require to drop 71 firms. This leaves a preliminary sample of 1,464 firms.

To construct the final sample required for this analysis we proceed in three steps. First, we add information on the firms' survival status which is contained in GCD. For 241 firms, balance sheet data end before 1996, the final year of the sample. These firms represent potential cases of acquisition or failure in the year ahead. Second, applying the concept of control developed in Chapter 4.2.2, we calculate changes in ultimate ownership to identify further acquisitions. Taken together, firm exit can occur in two forms: (1) failure or acquisition, reflected in an interrupted time series of balance sheet data and information on acquisition or failure in the year following the last year of balance sheet data, and (2) acquisition, reflected in an ongoing time series of balance sheet data but a change in ultimate ownership. Applying this definition of exit to our sample, the number of 1,464 firms increases to 1,676 firms because we treat firms before and after an acquisition as two distinct entities. Of course, the number of observations (6,541 firm years) remains constant. We apply this procedure in order not to use firm years in which an earlier control transfer takes place because the information content of these observations might be contaminated. Note that this approach assumes independence of the so-defined distinct firms over time. This potential drawback appears to be small, given that several consecutive changes in ownership do not occur often.[2] In a third step, we eliminate six firms that shut down operations but did not declare bankruptcy because the determinants of voluntary and forced exit are eventually different. This leaves a final sample of 1,670 firms (6,515 firm years). Since the last year for which the survival status can be observed is 1996, and since the present analysis focuses on the years prior to a change in control or failure, the sample used for the analysis covers the years 1986–1995.

Note that we consider only cases in which a new owner acquires control, either from the dominant shareholder or from previously dispersed shares. We do not consider cases in which an initially concentrated control block is dissolved because this analysis focuses on true acquisitions of control. Mello and Parsons (1998) argue that the market for dispersed shares is distinct from the market for control blocks. For empirical evidence that the market for shares is segmented along this line, see Hanley and Wilhelm (1995).

---

[2] For 1,103 firms (75.3 percent), ultimate ownership remains constant during the full sample period. For 309 firms (21.1 percent), the ultimate owner changes once, for 45 firms (3.1 percent) twice, and for 7 firms (0.5 percent) three times.

Table 5.1 shows how many firms exit from the sample in any one year, together with the reason for exit. In addition, Table 5.1 provides information in which year the time series of surviving firms end. Out of 1,670 firms the largest majority (73.1%) survives until the year 1996. For most surviving firms time series data end in the year 1996. A few surviving firms, though, have shorter time series, ending the earliest in 1988. A small fraction of firms (1.9%) declares bankruptcy, and a quarter of firms is acquired by another entity. Most cases of failure take place in the year 1995. Likewise, the rate of acquisitions is the highest during the years 1994–1996. One explanation for these high rates of market exit could be that the German economy went through a major recession in the mid 1990s.

Table 5.1. Number of firms by reason and year of exit

Year of sample exit	Survival	Failure	Acquisition	Total
1987	0	0	3	3
1988	2	0	19	21
1989	2	0	45	47
1990	3	1	38	42
1991	4	1	22	27
1992	3	3	34	40
1993	10	6	19	35
1994	19	1	52	72
1995	68	16	54	138
1996	1,110	3	132	1,245
Total	1,221	31	418	1,670
In percent	73.1%	1.9%	25.0%	100.0%

Notes: Number of firms that exit the sample in a given year due to failure or acquisition (reported in columns *failure* and *acquisition*, respectively). Firms that leave the sample but survive (reported in column *survival*) exit simply due to an interrupted balance sheet data time series. Only those firms are classified as surviving which do not experience failure or acquisition within one year. The last year for which information on the survival status was collected is 1996.

The empirical analysis in Chapters 5.3 and 5.4 is based on a full sample (6,515 firm years) and three subsamples (Table 5.2). In the full sample, for each firm year included it is known whether the respective firm still exists in the following year (survival), declares bankruptcy (failure), or is taken over by another entity (acquisition). Hence, the forward-looking time horizon is one year. In the three subsamples, the number of observations is reduced because the forward-looking time horizon is extended to two years (5,331 firm years), three years (4,049 firm years), and four or more years (3,283 firm years), respectively. The subsamples include only those observations for which information on the exit status is available for the next two, three, and four or more years. Table 5.2 summarizes the number of observations used in the empirical analysis, separately for a varying number of years looking ahead (time horizon).

Table 5.2. Number of observations by time horizon

Time horizon	Survival	Failure	Acquisition	Total
within 1 year	6,066	31	418	6,515
within 2 years	4,605	54	672	5,331
within 3 years	3,321	75	653	4,049
within 4 years +	2,228	139	916	3,283

Notes: Number of firms in a given year that survive, fail, or are acquired within the next year, the next two years, the next three years, or the next for or more years, respectively.

5.3 Preliminary Evidence

In the following, we present detailed descriptive statistics on firm-specific characteristics which are likely to determine failure and acquisition. Our intention is to provide some preliminary evidence on the validity of the hypotheses discussed in Chapter 5.1. In addition, we compare different measures of firm-specific characteristics to identify measures that could be useful to explain failure and acquisition in the multivariate analysis of Chapter 5.4. In Chapter 5.3.1, we look whether there is significant industry clustering of firms that survive, fail, or are acquired. In Chapters 5.3.2-5.3.5 we present descriptive evidence on various firm-specific characteristics such as performance, capital structure, ownership structure, restructuring activity, and firm size. Chapter 5.3.6 briefly summarizes which measures turn out to be helpful as explanatory variables.

5.3.1 Industry Distribution

Table 5.3 shows the industry pattern of surviving, failing, and acquired firms, based on the full sample of 1,670 firms. The largest fraction of sample firms operates in wholesale trade (12.4 percent), machinery (11.3 percent), chemicals (8.6 percent), and food (7.7 percent).

Industries with a comparatively large fraction of failing firms are textiles, clothing, machinery, construction of other vehicles (in particular shipyards), as well as furniture, jewelry, and toys. All these industries can be regarded as mature industries in which German firms lost competitiveness since years. For acquisitions, we find comparatively high rates of takeover activity for the industries of ore mining, rock and stone mining, paper, metals, and again textiles as well as furniture, jewelry, and toys.

These simple statistics provide a first indication that the determinants of firm failure and acquisition are likely to be different because industry clustering for failures is different from industry clustering for acquisitions. Secondly, these figures suggest that both, firm failure and acquisition, have a strong industry-specific component. In consequence, the following descriptive analysis differentiates between these two reasons for exit. For the regression analysis in Chapter 5.4 this calls for some kind of industry adjustment, for example by including industry dummies or by correcting firm-specific variables with the respective industry benchmark.

5.3.2 Performance

Table 5.4 shows how average performance of surviving firms compares to average performance of failing and acquired firms.[3] The statistics are calculated for different time horizons, ranging from looking one year ahead to looking four or more years ahead. The reason for calculating firm-specific characteristics for different time horizons is that ex ante it is unknown whether a particular firm fails within the next year or not, within the next two years or not, and so on. In a realistic situation, it is typically more interesting, for example from the perspective of a banker, whether a firm survives the next x years or not (Astebro and Winter, 2001). Knowing when exactly within these x years a firm fails is a more complicated problem and presumably only second order to a banker. All performance measures are industry-adjusted in the sense that they represent the difference to median performance at the two-digit industry level.[4] Productivity is corrected for mean productivity in the same two-digit industry. Annual stock market return is adjusted for performance of the DAFOX, which is the size-weighted return of all German stocks.

Table 5.4 indicates that performance of failing firms is significantly worse than performance of surviving firms, irrespective whether based on accounting measures such as return on assets (ROA), return on equity (ROE), return on sales (ROS), or whether based on total factor productivity or stock market return. Interestingly, performance of failing firms is also significantly worse than performance of surviving firms, irrespective which time horizon is used. For example, industry-adjusted total factor productivity of firms that fail within a time window of the next three years (-35.2 percent) is significantly worse than productivity of firms that survive at least three more years

[3] Results calculated for median performance are very similar (see Köke, 2001b). Median results are also similar for the other firm-specific characteristics discussed below, if not stated otherwise.

[4] We also compared accounting performance without industry-adjustment. The obtained results were similar in quality and in relative magnitude.

Table 5.3. Survival and exit of firms by industry

Industry (Two-digit NACE code)	Survival	Failure	Acquisition	Firms
Coal mining (10)	100.0%	0.0%	0.0%	8
Oil and gas extraction (11)	100.0%	0.0%	0.0%	17
Ore mining (13)	50.0%	0.0%	50.0%	4
Rock and stone mining (14)	50.0%	0.0%	50.0%	12
Food (15)	76.6%	1.6%	21.9%	128
Tobacco (16)	100.0%	0.0%	0.0%	7
Textiles (17)	39.1%	10.9%	50.0%	46
Clothing (18)	68.8%	6.3%	25.0%	16
Leather (19)	66.7%	0.0%	33.3%	6
Wood (20)	100.0%	0.0%	0.0%	5
Paper (21)	47.2%	2.8%	50.0%	36
Publishing and printing (22)	87.5%	0.0%	12.5%	16
Coal and oil processing (23)	85.7%	0.0%	14.3%	21
Chemicals (24)	84.6%	0.0%	15.4%	143
Rubber and plastic products (25)	74.2%	0.0%	25.8%	62
Rock, stone, glass (26)	61.7%	1.7%	36.7%	60
Metals (27)	59.5%	1.4%	39.2%	74
Metal products (28)	63.4%	2.8%	33.8%	71
Machinery (29)	70.7%	4.8%	24.5%	188
Equ. for data processing (30)	73.7%	2.6%	23.7%	38
Equ. for power generation (31)	74.0%	2.0%	24.0%	50
Equ. for broadcasting and TV (32)	78.0%	0.0%	22.0%	50
Medical and optical instruments (33)	74.2%	0.0%	25.8%	31
Cars and car parts (34)	72.0%	2.0%	26.0%	50
Other vehicles (35)	69.8%	4.7%	25.6%	43
Furniture, jewelry, toys (36)	46.2%	7.7%	46.2%	13
Recycling (37)	66.7%	0.0%	33.3%	3
Construction (45)	85.1%	1.4%	13.5%	74
Trade of cars and car parts (50)	81.0%	0.0%	19.0%	21
Wholesale trade (51)	79.7%	0.5%	19.8%	207
Retail trade (52)	79.4%	0.0%	20.6%	34
Hotel and restaurant (55)	66.7%	0.0%	33.3%	9
Diversified holding companies (74)	71.7%	0.8%	27.6%	127
Average	73.1%	1.9%	25.0%	1,670

Notes: Fraction of firms by industry that survive, are acquired, or fail at a one-year horizon. Fractions of firms add to 100 percent by industry.

(-5.8 percent). The only difference between the four time horizons is that the market-based measures, annual stock market returns and the market-to-book ratio, of failing firms are not significantly different from those of surviving firms with a time window of one or two years.

Table 5.4. Industry-adjusted performance as determinant of exit

	Survival	Failure	Acquisition	Obs.
Return on assets				
within 4 years +	2.1%	-3.0%***	0.6%***	3,283
within 3 years	1.4%	-4.9%***	0.2%**	4,049
within 2 years	1.2%	-5.2%***	-1.0%***	5,331
within 1 year	0.9%	-9.3%***	-0.5%**	6,515
Return on equity				
within 4 years +	3.3%	-5.5%***	1.2%**	3,283
within 3 years	2.4%	-11.5%***	1.0%	4,049
within 2 years	2.8%	-14.7%***	-2.7%***	5,331
within 1 year	2.4%	-28.7%***	-1.5%**	6,515
Return on sales				
within 4 years +	5.4%	-2.5%***	2.3%***	3,137
within 3 years	4.4%	-5.9%***	1.2%***	3,869
within 2 years	4.1%	-6.3%***	1.0%***	5,111
within 1 year	3.6%	-8.9%***	2.6%	6,259
Total factor productivity				
within 4 years +	-4.2%	-36.1%***	-14.9%***	2,918
within 3 years	-5.8%	-35.2%***	-9.0%	3,590
within 2 years	-1.7%	-42.2%***	-9.0%**	4,756
within 1 year	0.6%	-39.2%***	-8.3%**	5,851
Annual stock market return				
within 4 years +	1.6%	-13.0%***	2.0%	1,343
within 3 years	0.0%	-18.6%**	-1.5%	1,611
within 2 years	0.2%	-29.9%***	-1.1%	1,865
within 1 year	-1.9%	-23.0%	-1.8%	2,106
Market-to-book-ratio				
within 4 years +	19.5%	6.5%***	30.8%**	1,198
within 3 years	21.7%	4.5%*	19.8%	1,443
within 2 years	21.0%	60.5%	15.6%	1,670
within 1 year	19.4%	67.1%	13.5%	1,891

Notes: Mean industry-adjusted performance of firms that survive or exit within the next one to four or more years. The test statistics are heteroskedastic t-tests of equal means (columns 1 vs. 2, and 1 vs. 3). *, **, *** indicates significance at the 10, 5, and 1-percent levels, respectively. For definitions, see Appendix.

Concerning acquired firms, Table 5.4 shows that they perform significantly worse than surviving firms, when performance is based on accounting measures and productivity, but not when based on market measures. In general, performance of failing firms is several times worse than performance of acquired firms. For example, firms that fail within one year show an average industry-adjusted ROA of -9.3 percent, but firms that are acquired an industry-adjusted ROA of -0.5 percent. With a time of horizon of four years and above, the difference in performance between failing and acquired firms is significantly different from zero at the one-percent level, irrespective of the performance measure chosen (difference not reported).

5.3.3 Capital Structure

Table 5.5 shows how the average capital structure of surviving firms compares to the average capital structure of failing and acquired firms. Similar to Table 5.4, the statistics are reported for different time horizons, ranging from looking one year ahead to looking four or more years ahead.

Firms that fail face significantly higher financial pressure than firms that survive, irrespective which time horizon we choose and irrespective whether we look at interest coverage or the debt-to-assets ratio (Table 5.5). For example, firms that fail within one year have an average debt-to-assets ratio of 61 percent, compared with a ratio of about 42 percent for firms that survive the following year. Similarly, average interest coverage is considerably lower for failing firms than for surviving firms. When looking at median interest coverage (not reported), we find an analogous difference; in addition, median interest coverage is well below the value of two, a level by analysts typically regarded as an indicator of financial distress.

The picture for other measures of financial pressure is less clear. When using the quick ratio, defined as short-term assets less inventory, normalized by short-term liabilities, failing firms are significantly less liquid than surviving firms. Results look weaker when using the working capital ratio, defined as short-term assets less short-term liabilities, normalized by total assets, or when using the ratio of cash flow to assets. But in general, most measures indicate that failing firms face higher financial pressure than surviving firms.

Analogous results are found for acquired firms. The debt-to-assets ratio is significantly higher, and the other capital structure measures except interest coverage are significantly lower compared with surviving firms. However, when looking at median interest coverage, we also find a significant difference here (not reported). For the debt-to-assets ratio and interest coverage, the difference between failing and acquired firms is significantly different from zero at the one-percent level, but generally not for the other measures (difference not reported).

Table 5.5. Capital structure as determinant of exit

	Survival	Failure	Acquisition	Obs.
Debt-to-assets ratio				
within 4 years +	39.2%	51.4%***	41.9%***	3,283
within 3 years	39.8%	52.7%***	43.5%***	4,049
within 2 years	41.2%	56.0%***	46.2%***	5,331
within 1 year	42.3%	61.0%***	46.2%***	6,515
Interest coverage				
within 4 years +	78.4	0.7***	124.5*	3,245
within 3 years	80.4	16.6***	93.4	4,000
within 2 years	89.2	26.0***	72.8	5,259
within 1 year	99.5	24.7**	71.0	6,428
Working capital ratio				
within 4 years +	31.7%	27.6%**	29.1%***	3,283
within 3 years	31.1%	28.0%	28.7%**	4,049
within 2 years	30.4%	26.9%	28.2%**	5,331
within 1 year	30.0%	24.8%	28.8%	6,515
Quick ratio				
within 4 years +	2.26	1.76***	2.12*	2,587
within 3 years	2.23	1.63**	2.15	3,183
within 2 years	2.22	1.40***	2.06*	4,121
within 1 year	2.19	1.45***	2.11	4,998
Cash flow to assets				
within 4 years +	-8.8%	-11.6%	-11.2%***	2,955
within 3 years	-9.5%	-15.4%*	-13.4%***	3,587
within 2 years	-10.4%	-14.9%	-14.9%***	4,770
within 1 year	-11.1%	-17.6%	-13.7%**	5,879

Notes: Mean values of capital structure measures, calculated for firms that survive or exit within the next one to four or more years. The test statistics are heteroskedastic t-tests of equal means (columns 1 vs. 2, and 1 vs. 3). *, **, *** indicates significance at the 10, 5, and 1-percent levels, respectively. For definitions, see Appendix.

5.3.4 Ownership Structure

Three facets of a firm's ownership structure are analyzed in the following: concentration of ownership, complexity of ownership, and the type of the shareholder that is in ultimate control. First, Table 5.6 describes how ownership concentration differs between firms that survive, fail, or are acquired. In analogy to the tables in Chapters 5.3.2 and 5.3.3, mean statistics are reported for different time horizons, ranging from looking one year ahead to looking four or more years ahead.

Table 5.6 shows that ownership concentration of failing or acquired firms is significantly below ownership concentration of surviving firms. For exam-

Table 5.6. Ownership concentration as determinant of exit

	Survival	Failure	Acquisition	Obs.
Ownership concentration (Herfindahl index)				
within 4 years +	64.9%	46.2%***	55.5%***	3.283
within 3 years	64.5%	49.9%***	55.8%***	4,049
within 2 years	66.5%	50.8%***	59.6%***	5,331
within 1 year	67.6%	51.2%**	60.4%***	6,515

Notes: Mean values of ownership concentration, calculated for firms that survive or exit within the next one to four or more years. The test statistics are heteroskedastic t-tests of equal means (columns 1 vs. 2, and 1 vs. 3). *, **, *** indicates significance at the 10, 5, and 1-percent levels, respectively. For definitions, see Appendix.

ple, concentration as measured by the Herfindahl index is, on average, 51.2 percent for firms one year before they fail, 60.4 percent for firms one year before they are acquired, but 67.6 percent for firms that survive the following year. The difference to surviving firms is highly significant, irrespective of the time horizon considered. For a time horizon of four or more years, the difference in ownership concentration between failures and acquisitions is also significant at the one-percent level (difference not reported).

Table 5.7 differs from Tables 5.4-5.6 because the variables used to describe the complexity of ownership and the type of firms' ultimate owner are dummy variables. Table 5.7 reports the fraction of firms at a given time horizon for which the respective ownership characteristic is true.

The first two variables in Table 5.7 describe pyramids and cross ownership, two elements of the ownership structure that can increase its complexity. We find that a significantly smaller fraction of failing firms is part of a pyramid compared with surviving firms. For example, 22.6 percent of firms that fail within one year are part of a pyramid structure, compared to more than 50 percent of firms that survive at least one more year. Likewise, failing firms are also less likely to be controlled by an owner which is part of the web of large financial and non-financial German companies (Adams, 1994; Wenger and Kaserer, 1998). In fact, the fraction of failing firms that are cross-owned is zero, irrespective of the time horizon considered. For firms that are acquired, the fraction of firms being part of a pyramid or controlled by a cross-owned shareholder is significantly lower than among surviving firms, but only for a time horizon of four or more years. In sum, the results on the complexity of ownership strongly suggest that pyramids and cross ownership can help avert firm failure and, to a weaker extent, also acquisition by another entity.

The next five variables in Table 5.7 describe the type of the ultimate owner. There are five types of shareholders: private, financial, non-financial, government, and dispersed. In the latter case, no single dominant shareholder can be identified when applying the concept of control (Chapter 4.2.2). Table 5.7 shows that the largest fraction of failing firms is controlled by a large pri-

Table 5.7. Ownership type as determinant of exit

	Survival	Failure	Acquisition	Obs.
Fraction of firms being part of pyramid				
within 4 years +	43.7%	23.0%***	36.7%***	3,283
within 3 years	43.3%	29.3%**	43.6%	4,049
within 2 years	47.5%	25.9%***	48.8%	5,331
within 1 year	50.6%	22.6%***	50.5%	6,515
Fraction of firms controlled by cross-owned firm				
within 4 years +	9.0%	0.0%***	4.8%***	3,283
within 3 years	8.1%	0.0%**	6.6%	4,049
within 2 years	8.1%	0.0%**	6.8%	5,331
within 1 year	8.0%	0.0%*	5.7%*	6,515
Type of ultimate owner: individuals				
within 4 years +	40.3%	68.3%***	30.3%***	3,283
within 3 years	39.4%	64.0%***	28.8%***	4,049
within 2 years	36.1%	63.0%***	28.4%***	5,331
within 1 year	33.8%	54.8%**	25.8%***	6,515
Type of ultimate owner: financial firm				
within 4 years +	10.1%	0.0%***	6.0%***	3,283
within 3 years	9.2%	0.0%***	7.8%	4,049
within 2 years	8.8%	0.0%**	7.1%	5,331
within 1 year	8.5%	3.2%	6.2%*	6,515
Type of ultimate owner: non-financial firm				
within 4 years +	35.8%	17.3%***	40.2%**	3,283
within 3 years	37.2%	16.0%***	38.4%	4,049
within 2 years	39.8%	18.5%***	39.3%	5,331
within 1 year	41.1%	25.8%*	40.2%	6,515
Type of ultimate owner: dispersed shares				
within 4 years +	10.3%	10.8%	22.7%***	3,283
within 3 years	11.0%	16.0%	23.7%***	4,049
within 2 years	11.2%	14.8%	20.8%***	5,331
within 1 year	11.5%	12.9%	21.3%***	6,515
Type of ultimate owner: government				
within 4 years +	3.5%	3.6%	0.8%***	3,283
within 3 years	3.2%	4.0%	1.2%***	4,049
within 2 years	4.1%	3.7%	4.3%	5,331
within 1 year	5.0%	3.2%	6.5%	6,515

Notes: Fraction of firms for which ownership characteristic is true, calculated for firms that survive or exit within the next one to four or more years. The test statistics are calculated as two-sided t-tests on the equality of proportions (columns 1 vs. 2, and 1 vs. 3). *, **, *** indicates significance at the 10, 5, and 1-percent levels, respectively. For definitions, see Appendix.

vate owner. This fraction is significantly higher than the fraction of surviving firms under private control. In turn, a comparatively low fraction of failing firms is controlled by a financial or a non-financial firm. For example, 17.3 percent of firms that are ultimately owned by a financial institution such as a bank, an insurance company, or a mutual fund, fail within the next four or more years. The respective fraction of firms that survive four or more years is more than two times higher (35.8 percent). We also find that a significantly larger fraction of firms with no dominant owner (dispersed) are acquired than survive. In turn, a comparatively low fraction of firms are acquired that are under the control of a large private owner. Finally, there is some evidence that the likelihood to be acquired is lower than the likelihood to survive for firms under control of a financial firm, and higher for firms under control of a non-financial firm. In sum, the results discussed in this subsection suggest that not only concentration of shares matters. Also the complexity of indirect ownership structures and the type of the ultimate owner appear to be relevant for whether a firm is likely to fail or to be acquired.

5.3.5 Restructuring and Firm Size

As a last set of potential determinants of failure and acquisition we consider restructuring activity and firm size. Table 5.8 is structured in analogy to Tables 5.4-5.6 and shows mean statistics calculated for different time horizons, ranging from looking one year ahead to looking four or more years ahead, separately for firms that survive, fail, or are acquired.

Restructuring activity, if measured by the annual growth rate of employment, is more extensive in failing firms than in surviving firms. For example, firms that fail within one year cut employment by 11.2 percent, but firms that survive at least one more year increase employment by 1.9 percent. Likewise, firms that are acquired show decreasing employment. But the growth rates of employment for acquired and surviving firms are significantly different only at the median (not reported), not at the mean. However, failing and acquired firms are significantly different in terms of employment growth at the one-percent level, both at the mean and at the median. When restructuring is measured by the fraction of fixed assets sold per year, there is also evidence that restructuring activity is more extensive in failing firms because assets are sold at a higher rate compared with surviving firms. In contrast, sales of financial assets are, at least at the median, significantly lower in firms that are about to experience an acquisition compared with surviving firms. One interpretation for this could be that firms to be acquired suffer from low liquidity. This is consistent with our finding that firms to be acquired have significantly lower cash-to-assets ratios than surviving firms. Hence, acquisitions do not appear to be (primarily) driven by free-cash-flow considerations (Jensen, 1986).

Finally, firm size also appears to be relevant. Firms that survive at least one more year show average total assets of about 1,800 million DM. This

Table 5.8. Restructuring and firm size as determinants of exit

	Survival	Failure	Acquisition	Obs.
Sales of fixed assets				
within 4 years +	6.4%	7.6%	6.3%	3,065
within 3 years	6.5%	10.3%*	6.6%	3,712
within 2 years	7.0%	10.4%	7.2%	4,902
within 1 year	7.1%	7.3%	8.1%	6,015
Sales of financial assets				
within 4 years +	15.5%	16.2%	13.8%*	2,994
within 3 years	15.7%	16.7%	14.6%	3,610
within 2 years	15.8%	17.9%	14.7%	4,668
within 1 year	15.9%	18.3%	16.0%	5,644
Growth rate of employment				
within 4 years +	4.9%	-3.3%***	3.6%	2,772
within 3 years	3.7%	-7.3%***	1.9%	3,400
within 2 years	2.4%	-7.2%**	-0.6%***	4,412
within 1 year	1.9%	-11.2%***	-0.4%	5,496
Total assets in million DM				
within 4 years +	2,514	454.4***	1,068.0***	3,283
within 3 years	2,213	495.6***	1,017.0***	4,049
within 2 years	1,967	501.1***	821.7***	5,331
within 1 year	1,847	419.8***	776.9***	6,515

Notes: Mean values of restructuring and firm size measures, calculated for firms that survive or exit within the next one to four or more years. The test statistics are heteroskedastic *t*-tests of equal means (columns 1 vs. 2, and 1 vs. 3). *, **, *** indicates significance at the 10, 5, and 1-percent levels, respectively. For definitions, see Appendix.

compares to total assets of about 420 million DM for firms that fail, and about 780 million DM for firms that are acquired within one year. These differences are found across all four time horizons, and also for other measures of firm size such as total sales and the number of employees (not reported). Generally, the difference between failing and acquired firms is significant at the one-percent level (difference not reported). In sum, firms that are acquired are approximately half as large as surviving firms, and firms that fail are about half as large as acquired firms. This indicates that firm size can reduce the likelihood of acquisition and failure.

5.3.6 Summary

The literature review in Chapter 5.1 suggests that performance, capital structure, ownership structure, as well as firm size and restructuring activity are important determinants of acquisition and failure of firms. In general, this is confirmed by the descriptive evidence presented in Chapters 5.3.2-5.3.5. However, the descriptive evidence also suggests that the power of firm characteristics to explain failure and acquisition depends on the specific measure chosen. For performance, accounting measures such as industry-adjusted ROA as well as industry-adjusted total factor productivity seem to be the most helpful. For capital structure, the debt-to-assets ratio and interest coverage look promising, and for restructuring activity and firm size, the growth rate of employment and the natural logarithm of total assets, respectively. Finally, the preliminary evidence on ownership structure suggests that not only concentration of shares is relevant. In addition, information on the complexity of ownership, as reflected in pyramids and cross ownership, and information on the type of the ultimately controlling shareholder should enter any model that attempts to explain corporate failure or acquisition.

5.4 Estimation Results

The evidence presented in Chapter 5.3 gives a first indication which firm-specific characteristics are likely to be the most useful to explain failure and acquisition. Now we employ these measures in an econometric framework which considers all potential determinants simultaneously. This approach allows to identify the effect of each variable under ceteris paribus conditions.

We analyze the determinants of corporate acquisition and failure as a discrete choice problem. There are three potential outcomes: *survival*, *failure*, and *acquisition*. For its computational simplicity we choose to estimate this discrete choice problem using a multinomial logit model (MNL). The MNL model uses one outcome, in the present case the most frequent outcome *survival*, as the reference. Any parameter estimate represents the effect of the particular explanatory variable on the outcome *acquisition* or *failure* relative to the reference outcome *survival*.

Subsequently, we analyze the role of performance, capital structure, concentration and complexity of ownership, restructuring activity, and firm size in Chapter 5.4.1, and the role of different types of owners in Chapter 5.4.2. Throughout these analyses we choose a time horizon of four or more years for analysis. The reason is that models with a shorter time horizon explain not only whether a firm fails or is acquired, but also more precisely when it fails. As discussed in Chapter 5.3.2, for example from the perspective of a banker it should be more important whether a firm fails or not. When exactly bankruptcy occurs should be of secondary relevance (Astebro and Winter, 2001). Therefore we argue that models with a longer time horizon are more appropriate to analyze the determinants of survival, acquisition, and failure. However, models with a longer time horizon have the disadvantage that they require longer time series of data. As described in Chapter 5.2, this significantly reduces the number of observations compared to models with a one-year time horizon. Note that the advantage of an overall larger number of observations (by using a shorter time horizon) comes at the cost of a significantly smaller number of observations for firms that experience exit. In any case, in Chapter 5.4.3 we test the sensitivity of our results, in particular with respect to the length of the time horizon and to alternative measures of important firm-specific characteristics.

5.4.1 Performance, Capital Structure, Ownership Concentration

Table 5.9 shows the results from estimating multinomial models, explaining acquisition and failure of firms within a time horizon of four or more years. In Model (1), firm performance (industry-adjusted ROA) and the capital structure (debt-to-assets ratio) enter the model as explanatory variables. We also include the natural logarithm of total assets as a measure of firm size, two-digit industry dummies (not reported), a dummy indicating whether a firm is listed, and a dummy for the legal form of the company, which is one for a GmbH (private corporation) and zero for an AG (public corporation).

Model (1) suggests that – within the next four or more years – firms are more likely to fail or to be acquired when performance is poor (Table 5.9). This finding is consistent with evidence from the US (Powell, 1997; Denis and Sarin, 1999; Maksimovic and Phillips, 2001; Astebro and Winter, 2001). Hence, we find support for **Hypothesis 5.1**, both for acquisition and failure. A Wald test reveals that the impact of performance is larger for the outcome failure than for the outcome acquisition (significant at the one-percent level). This indicates that the likelihood of failure increases relative to the likelihood of acquisition when performance worsens further. Similarly, we find that firms with high financial pressure are more likely to be acquired and even more likely to fail. This is consistent with evidence provided by Powell (1997) and Zingales (1998). This supports **Hypothesis 5.2**, both for acquisition and failure. Firm size has a significantly negative impact on the likelihood of acquisition and failure, with the respective coefficient again being larger for failure than for acquisition (significant at the one-percent level). This confirms that firm size works as a kind of takeover deterrent (Bethel et al., 1998; Mulherin and Boone, 2000), but also as a shelter against failure. Hence, we find support for **Hypothesis 5.7**, both for acquisition and failure.

In Model (2) of Table 5.9 we add variables that describe concentration of ownership, the complexity of ownership, and the intensity of restructuring activity. Since theoretical considerations in Chapter 5.1 suggest a non-linear impact of ownership concentration on the likelihood of acquisition, both the Herfindahl index and its square are included. As expected, we cannot confirm a non-linear impact of concentration on failure. The likelihood of failure decreases linearly with share concentration. This supports **Hypothesis 5.3** regarding the impact of share concentration on failure. In contrast, we find weak evidence for a non-linear impact of ownership concentration on the likelihood of acquisition. Interpreting both coefficients for the Herfindahl index as parameters of a second order polynomial and taking the first derivative, we find that this curve is downward-sloping for most firms. This means that firms with a higher concentration of ownership are less likely to be purchased. Concerning the complexity of ownership, we find that firms which are part of a pyramid or are ultimately controlled by a cross-owned shareholder are less likely to fail.[5] We also find that cross ownership makes firms less likely to be purchased, but we do not find evidence that pyramid structures hinder acquisitions. Hence, the evidence confirms **Hypothesis 5.4** regarding failure, but only partially for acquisition. There is also evidence that firms with lower growth rates of employment are more likely to fail. This is consistent with empirical work on small German firms (Almus, 2000), and therefore with **Hypothesis 5.6**. For acquisitions, we also find evidence on this restructuring effect, but it is weaker than for failing firms.

In Model (3) of Table 5.9 we examine the effect of ownership concentration more closely. In this specification, we interact the Herfindahl index and its square with a dummy variable ($CONTROL$), which is one for firms that are under control of an ultimate owner, and zero for firms without such an owner. The reason is that the impact of shareholder concentration on the likelihood of control transfer or failure could be different for both types of firms, as argued in Chapter 5.1. Table 5.9 shows that for acquisitions this difference exists. For firms under tight control ($CONTROL = 1$), the curve described by the estimated coefficients for Herfindahl and its square has a minimum at about 0.73. Since for most firms under tight control the Herfindahl index is around or below this point, this implies that ownership concentration has a negative impact on the likelihood of acquisition. This finding is consistent with Holmström and Tirole (1993) who predict that takeovers are more likely when share concentration is low. However, for firms under loose control ($CONTROL = 0$) this curve has a maximum at about 0.31. For many firms under loose control the Herfindahl index is considerably above or below this point. Hence, the marginal effect of shareholder concentration is positive for firms with a highly dispersed ownership structure. This finding supports Burkart et al. (2000) who argue that block trades should be more likely when shares are sufficiently concentrated. In sum, we can confirm **Hypothesis 5.3** for the case of acquisition as well, and we are able to formulate this concentration effect more precisely: Acquisitions become more likely for firms with a highly dispersed ownership structure when concentration increases, but acquisitions become less likely when the shares are owned by less than three or four equally large shareholders.

5.4.2 Shareholder Types

As suggested by theoretical considerations in Chapter 5.1 and by our preliminary evidence in Chapter 5.3, the type of the initial owner can also play an

[5] Note that we cannot assign a standard error to the coefficient of cross ownership for the failure model because essentially no cross-owned firm fails.

important role for acquisition or failure of a firm. In particular, we expect that the impact of performance on the probability of acquisition or failure varies with the type of the dominant shareholder. And this difference in impact should be particularly pronounced in cases of poor performance. To address this issue we interact the type of owner with a dummy variable, Π, that indicates whether industry-adjusted return on assets (ROA) is below zero or not. In analogy to Chapter 5.3, there are five types of shareholders: private, non-financial, financial, government, and dispersed shares. In Table 5.10, we choose non-financial firms as the reference category because it is the most populated. Therefore, the interaction coefficients measure the difference in the impact of poor performance on the probability of failure or acquisition between non-financial firms and the other types of controlling shareholders.

For better comparison with the results from Chapter 5.4.1, we first ignore any difference in the impact of performance, depending on the type of shareholder (Model (1) of Table 5.10). We find that firms which perform worse than the industry benchmark are more likely to be acquired and even more likely to fail. This result is consistent with evidence from Table 5.9.

In Model (2) of Table 5.10 we interact shareholder types with the dummy Π that indicates poor performance. For the moment we neglect shareholder concentration as an explanatory variable because firms with low concentration typically belong to the ownership category 'dispersed'; thus, the type of shareholder should already capture information on concentration. The results show that for non-financial firms as dominant shareholders the impact of performance on the likelihood of failure is not statistically different from zero. But in case of poor performance the likelihood of failure is significantly lower when financial firms such as banks or insurance companies are the major shareholders. In contrast, in case of poor performance the likelihood of failure is significantly higher when the shares are dispersed. Concerning acquisitions we find that non-financial owners are more likely to sell a firm when industry-adjusted performance is negative. However, private and financial shareholders behave differently. As the results from Model (2) of Table 5.10 show, the coefficients for private owners and financial owners, which are the sum of the coefficients of non-financial owners and the respective interaction term, are negative.[6] This implies that these two types of shareholders are less likely to sell when performance is poor.[7] In contrast, firms with no dominant owner are more likely to be sold.

As expected, when including the polynomial for shareholder concentration we observe that the impact of dispersed shares changes (Model (3) in Table 5.10). Its effect on the likelihood of failure becomes insignificant, and

[6] A Wald test confirms that the sum of coefficients is significantly different from zero (at the one-percent level), for private and financial shareholders.

[7] A Wald test shows that the resulting coefficients of private and financial shareholders are not significantly different.

Table 5.9. MNL results: four-year time horizon, without type of owner

	Model (1)		Model (2)		Model (3)	
	Failure	Acquisition	Failure	Acquisition	Failure	Acquisition
Intercept	2.219	1.477***	3.388**	2.517***	3.273**	2.498***
	(0.116)	(0.003)	(0.029)	(0.000)	(0.034)	(0.000)
Ind.-adj. ROA	-4.559***	-1.635***	-4.353***	-1.687***	-4.364***	-1.698***
	(0.002)	(0.001)	(0.009)	(0.003)	(0.007)	(0.003)
Debt ratio	2.568***	0.542***	3.161***	0.781***	3.165***	0.820***
	(0.000)	(0.016)	(0.000)	(0.003)	(0.000)	(0.002)
Herfindahl			-3.002*	-1.688***	5.920	6.474***
			(0.053)	(0.006)	(0.334)	(0.006)
Herfindahl* Control					-8.416	-7.956***
					(0.133)	(0.000)
Herfindahl^2			0.636	0.998*	-30.882*	-10.590**
			(0.608)	(0.061)	(0.089)	(0.039)
Herfindahl^2* Control					31.130*	11.612**
					(0.082)	(0.019)
Pyramid			-0.551**	-0.059	-0.577**	-0.084
			(0.027)	(0.569)	(0.019)	(0.424)
Cross own.			-32.626	-0.729***	-35.617	-0.678***
			(n.a.)	(0.001)	(n.a.)	(0.003)
Growth rate of empl.			-1.717**	-0.325*	-1.722**	-0.341*
			(0.048)	(0.082)	(0.046)	(0.067)
log (assets)	-0.209***	-0.134***	-0.179**	-0.147***	-0.178**	-0.156***
	(0.003)	(0.000)	(0.015)	(0.000)	(0.014)	(0.000)
Listed	-3.529***	-0.023	-4.188***	-0.332***	-4.199***	-0.322***
	(0.000)	(0.807)	(0.000)	(0.004)	(0.000)	(0.006)
GmbH	-1.755***	-0.746***	-1.471***	-0.876***	-1.439***	-0.939***
	(0.000)	(0.000)	(0.001)	(0.000)	(0.001)	(0.000)
Number of obs.		3,283		2,772		2,772
Log likelihood		-2081.8		-1706.1		-1688.4

Notes: Estimates of multinomial logit models relating the difference in probability for the outcome survival vs. failure and survival vs. acquisition to industry-adjusted performance, capital structure, ownership structure, restructuring activity, and firm size. The forward-looking time horizon is four or more years. All regressions include two-digit industry dummies (not reported). The p-values (reported in parentheses) are based on robust standard errors, which are calculated using the White/Huber sandwich estimator for the variance-covariance matrix. *, **, *** indicates significance at the 10, 5, and 1-percent levels, respectively. For definitions, see Appendix.

Table 5.10. MNL results: four-year time horizon, with type of owner

Performance Π	Industry-adjusted return on assets					
	Model (1)		Model (2)		Model (3)	
	Failure	Acquisition	Failure	Acquisition	Failure	Acquisition
Intercept	1.524	1.283**	1.647	1.847***	2.822*	2.182***
	(0.277)	(0.027)	(0.243)	(0.002)	(0.068)	(0.001)
$\Pi < 0$	0.467**	0.297***	-0.089	0.385***	0.023	0.416***
	(0.038)	(0.002)	(0.810)	(0.003)	(0.951)	(0.002)
$\Pi < 0$ and			0.468	-0.560***	0.124	-0.578***
priv. owner			(0.228)	(0.002)	(0.768)	(0.001)
$\Pi < 0$ and			-34.123***	-0.932**	-29.432***	-0.957**
fin. owner			(0.000)	(0.015)	(0.000)	(0.012)
$\Pi < 0$ and			1.714***	0.954***	0.619	0.808***
disp. owners			(0.000)	(0.000)	(0.227)	(0.000)
$\Pi < 0$ and			1.048	-1.127*	0.944	-1.135**
gov. owner			(0.144)	(0.054)	(0.146)	(0.048)
Debt ratio	3.591***	0.781***	3.537***	0.840***	3.337***	0.851***
	(0.000)	(0.003)	(0.000)	(0.001)	(0.000)	(0.001)
Herfindahl					-2.577	-0.382
					(0.108)	(0.566)
Herfindahl^2					0.330	0.086
					(0.793)	(0.879)
Pyramid	-0.738***	-0.117	-0.776***	-0.033	-0.524**	-0.014
	(0.002)	(0.259)	(0.002)	(0.751)	(0.046)	(0.892)
Cross own.	-34.093	-0.744***	-38.351	-0.500*	-32.936	-0.492*
	(n.a.)	(0.001)	(n.a.)	(0.059)	(n.a.)	(0.064)
Growth rate	-1.558*	-0.342*	-1.607**	-0.360*	-2.016**	-0.360*
of empl.	(0.057)	(0.068)	(0.048)	(0.053)	(0.015)	(0.053)
log (assets)	-0.170**	-0.122***	-0.173**	-0.149***	-0.162**	-0.155***
	(0.017)	(0.000)	(0.015)	(0.000)	(0.029)	(0.000)
Listed	-3.827***	-0.188*	-3.884***	-0.267**	-4.109***	-0.332***
	(0.000)	(0.075)	(0.000)	(0.012)	(0.000)	(0.004)
GmbH	-2.143***	-0.949***	-1.958***	-1.004***	-1.519***	-0.978***
	(0.000)	(0.000)	(0.000)	(0.000)	(0.001)	(0.000)
Number of obs.		2,772		2,772		2,772
Log likelihood		-1700.7		-1700.7		-1685.6

Notes: Estimates of multinomial logit models relating the difference in probability for the outcome survival vs. failure and survival vs. acquisition to industry-adjusted performance, capital structure, ownership structure, restructuring activity, and firm size. In contrast to Table 5.9, performance Π is a dummy which is one when the continuous measure of industry-adjusted performance is negative, zero otherwise. And performance is interacted with shareholder types, with non-financial firms as owners being the reference category. The forward-looking time horizon is four or more years. All regressions include two-digit industry dummies (not reported). The p-values (reported in parentheses) are based on robust standard errors, which are calculated using the White/Huber sandwich estimator for the variance-covariance matrix. *, **, *** indicates significance at the 10, 5, and 1-percent levels, respectively. For definitions, see Appendix.

the effect on the likelihood of acquisition is slightly smaller in magnitude. The other coefficients, in particular those of the other interaction terms, remain qualitatively unaffected. In summary, we find strong evidence that different types of owners react differently to poor performance. We find support for **Hypothesis 5.5** regarding acquisitions that private shareholders are less likely to sell poorly performing firms, but that firms without a dominant shareholder are more likely to be sold. In addition, financial owners appear to behave similar to private owners. However, we do not find support for **Hypothesis 5.5** regarding failure. When performance is poor, only firms under control of a financial firm are less likely to fail, but there is no difference in the reaction to performance between other shareholder types. All other coefficients reported in Table 5.10 point in the same direction as the coefficients reported in Table 5.9. Hence, we do not comment on them further.

5.4.3 Sensitivity of Results

To check the sensitivity of our main findings we conduct a range of robustness tests. As mentioned above, one concern is the length of the forward-looking time horizon chosen for the analysis. Tables 5.11 and 5.12 address this issue. Taking the full model for a specification without different types of shareholder categories as the reference (Model (3) from Table 5.9), the sensitivity analysis reveals that most coefficients do not change qualitatively when the time horizon is shortened to three, two, or one year (Table 5.11). Hence, our main results from Section 5.9 remain valid. However, in a few cases coefficients, which are significant in the four-years-or-above model, turn insignificant in models with a shorter time horizon. For failure, ownership concentration and firm size loose their explanatory power. And for acquisition, cross ownership as one measure of the complexity of ownership, and the growth rate of employment, our measure of restructuring activity, turn insignificant in models with shorter time horizons. Table 5.11 shows that mainly coefficients for the outcome failure become insignificant. This effect can be explained by the much smaller number of observations on failure for shorter time horizons.

For the models taking into account different types of owners, we use Model (3) from Table 5.10 as the reference (Table 5.12). The sensitivity analysis shows that, irrespective of the length of the time horizon, poor performance provides an impetus to sell when a non-financial firm is the dominant owner. The robustness check confirms that, in general, private owners and financial firms are significantly less likely to sell in case of poor performance compared with non-financial firms, and dispersed shareholders are more likely. These results are in line with our main findings from Chapter 5.4.2. For time horizons of one to three years we cannot confirm the finding that the government is less likely to sell than non-financial firms when performance is poor. Concerning failure, for a one-year time horizon we find that financial owners are significantly more likely to sell poorly performing firms, not less likely as suggested by the models with a longer time horizon. One interpretation of this result could be that financial firms generally help avoid firm failure, for example by extending credit lines. But when failure seems unavoidable, they force a troubled firm into bankruptcy, potentially to recover outstanding loans.

Next, we test whether our results depend on the choice of the performance measure. Tables 5.13 and 5.14 address this issue. First, we analyze the robustness of results for a model that does not distinguish between different shareholder types (Chapter 5.4.1). The reference model is Model (3) from Table 5.9. We find that including industry-adjusted return on sales as alternative performance measure leaves the results qualitatively unaffected. When we add industry-adjusted total factor productivity instead, we find a significantly negative impact of productivity on the likelihood of failure. At the same time, the coefficients for our measures of restructuring and firm size turn insignificant. However, our findings regarding the impact of poor performance, financial pressure, and complexity of ownership on the likelihood of failure and acquisition, as well as the non-linear impact of concentration on the likelihood of acquisition remain valid. In contrast, when we add market-adjusted stock market return instead, we find that a range of coefficients turn insignificant, for example those measuring the impact of poor performance and financial pressure on the likelihood of failure, others become significantly different from zero. Since this measure is only available for listed firms, the number of observations is reduced considerably. But selecting only listed firms could induce selection bias, if non-listed firms are systematically different from listed firms. Therefore, the results from this check of robustness are questionable.

Second, we analyze whether our findings on the reaction of different shareholder types to poor performance (Chapter 5.4.2) depend on the performance measure chosen. Taking Model (3) from Table 5.10 as the reference, we obtain basically the same results when using return on sales or total factor productivity instead of return on assets as measures of performance (Table 5.14). There are two exceptions: Non-financial owners are not more likely to sell when productivity is low, and firms under control of the government are more likely to fail than firms under control of a non-financial shareholder. When we choose stock market return as our measure of performance, again a range of coefficients change qualitatively. But as discussed above, choosing this performance measure could create a sample selection problem.

Finally, we re-estimate the full model (Model (3) in Table 5.9) by adding alternative measures of financial pressure, such as interest coverage, the ratio of short-term assets less short-term liabilities divided by total assets (working capital ratio), or the ratio of cash flow to assets (Table 5.15). The coefficients of these new variables are not or only weakly significant, and our main findings remain valid. Likewise, adding alternative measures of restructuring, such as sales of fixed or financial assets, or an alternative measure of firm size, the natural logarithm of total sales, leaves our results virtually unaf-

Table 5.11. Robustness tests: different time horizons, without type of owner

Time horizon	Four or more years		Three years		Two years		One year	
	Failure	Acquisition	Failure	Acquisition	Failure	Acquisition	Failure	Acquisition
Ind.-adj.	-4.364***	-1.698***	-3.887***	-1.474**	-4.396**	-1.620***	-5.652***	-0.670
ROA	(0.007)	(0.003)	(0.007)	(0.014)	(0.011)	(0.003)	(0.003)	(0.279)
Debt ratio	3.165***	0.820***	3.390***	1.242***	3.152***	0.909***	3.819***	0.686**
	(0.000)	(0.002)	(0.000)	(0.000)	(0.001)	(0.000)	(0.006)	(0.016)
Herfindahl	5.920	6.474***	18.925**	6.165***	12.390	7.278***	6.288	6.241**
	(0.334)	(0.006)	(0.015)	(0.005)	(0.262)	(0.001)	(0.682)	(0.013)
Herfindahl*	-8.416	-7.956***	-21.220***	-9.135***	-13.577	-9.641***	-6.494	-7.863***
Control	(0.133)	(0.000)	(0.002)	(0.005)	(0.167)	(0.000)	(0.620)	(0.000)
Herfindahl^2	-30.882*	-10.590**	-60.373**	-11.348**	-43.236	-15.842***	-21.693	-13.730**
	(0.089)	(0.039)	(0.012)	(0.020)	(0.193)	(0.001)	(0.573)	(0.016)
Herfindahl^2*	31.130*	11.612**	60.774***	13.569***	43.012	17.533***	21.117	14.763***
Control	(0.082)	(0.019)	(0.009)	(0.004)	(0.185)	(0.000)	(0.567)	(0.007)
Pyramid	-0.577**	-0.084	-0.343	0.121	-0.833**	0.081	-1.045**	-0.029
	(0.019)	(0.424)	(0.287)	(0.261)	(0.013)	(0.445)	(0.018)	(0.823)
Cross ownership	-35.617	-0.678***	-36.712	-0.039	-45.925	0.037	-33.664	-0.117
	(n.a.)	(0.003)	(n.a.)	(0.849)	(n.a.)	(0.844)	(n.a.)	(0.628)
Growth rate	-1.722**	-0.341*	-2.358***	-0.322	-2.163	-0.418**	-2.974***	-0.377
of employment	(0.046)	(0.067)	(0.003)	(0.117)	(0.134)	(0.036)	(0.006)	(0.168)
log (assets)	-0.178**	-0.156***	-0.104	-0.136***	-0.123	-0.142***	-0.131	-0.091***
	(0.014)	(0.000)	(0.251)	(0.000)	(0.192)	(0.000)	(0.348)	(0.006)
Number of obs.		2,772		3,400		4,412		5,496
Log likelihood		-1688.4		-1630.1		-1774.8		-1370.4

Notes: Estimates of multinomial logit models relating the difference in probability for the outcome survival vs. failure and survival vs. acquisition to various firm characteristics. The forward-looking time horizon varies between one and four or more years. All regressions include an intercept, a dummy for listed firms, a dummy for GmbH firms, and two-digit industry dummies (not reported). The p-values (reported in parentheses) are based on robust standard errors, which are calculated using the White/Huber sandwich estimator for the variance-covariance matrix. *, **, *** indicates significance at the 10, 5, and 1-percent levels, respectively. Similar remarks apply to Tables 5.12–5.16.

Table 5.12. Robustness tests: different time horizons, with type of owner

Time horizon	Four years		Three years		Two years		One year	
	Failure	Acquisition	Failure	Acquisition	Failure	Acquisition	Failure	Acquisition
$\Pi < 0$	0.023	0.416***	-0.323	0.431***	-0.056	0.413***	0.364	0.308**
	(0.951)	(0.002)	(0.516)	(0.002)	(0.908)	(0.001)	(0.544)	(0.044)
$\Pi < 0$ and priv. owner	0.124	-0.578***	0.960**	-0.374**	0.751*	-0.369**	0.241	-0.448**
	(0.768)	(0.001)	(0.050)	(0.038)	(0.097)	(0.031)	(0.679)	(0.039)
$\Pi < 0$ and fin. owner	-29.432***	-0.957**	-31.853***	-1.030***	-30.613***	-0.900***	1.968**	-0.619
	(0.000)	(0.012)	(0.000)	(0.006)	(0.000)	(0.008)	(0.021)	(0.159)
$\Pi < 0$ and disp. owners	0.619	0.808***	1.897***	0.456**	0.696	0.460**	-0.159	0.234
	(0.227)	(0.000)	(0.002)	(0.043)	(0.316)	(0.032)	(0.878)	(0.363)
$\Pi < 0$ and gov. owner	0.944	-1.135**	1.302	-0.632	0.451	-0.026	0.575	0.207
	(0.146)	(0.048)	(0.122)	(0.154)	(0.656)	(0.931)	(0.562)	(0.516)
Debt ratio	3.337***	0.851***	3.243***	1.153***	3.252***	0.871***	4.188***	0.668**
	(0.000)	(0.001)	(0.000)	(0.000)	(0.001)	(0.000)	(0.004)	(0.018)
Herfindahl	-2.577	-0.382	-2.017	-2.214***	-1.916	-1.854***	-0.789	-1.315
	(0.108)	(0.566)	(0.317)	(0.001)	(0.415)	(0.008)	(0.840)	(0.119)
Herfindahl^2	0.330	0.086	0.297	1.450**	0.321	1.160**	-0.321	0.652
	(0.793)	(0.879)	(0.850)	(0.013)	(0.862)	(0.044)	(0.917)	(0.354)
Pyramid	-0.524**	-0.014	-0.406	0.187*	-0.803**	0.124	-1.009**	-0.009
	(0.046)	(0.892)	(0.229)	(0.084)	(0.025)	(0.242)	(0.030)	(0.944)
Cross ownership	-32.936	-0.492*	-36.241	0.198	-32.970	0.293	-32.982	0.021
	(n.a.)	(0.064)	(n.a.)	(0.413)	(n.a.)	(0.190)	(n.a.)	(0.943)
Growth rate of employment	-2.016**	-0.360*	-2.550***	-0.320	-2.405*	-0.413**	-3.405***	-0.359
	(0.015)	(0.053)	(0.002)	(0.114)	(0.077)	(0.036)	(0.001)	(0.187)
log (assets)	-0.162**	-0.155***	-0.102	-0.137***	-0.088	-0.149***	-0.132	-0.100***
	(0.029)	(0.000)	(0.268)	(0.000)	(0.350)	(0.000)	(0.392)	(0.003)
Number of obs.		2,772		3,400		4,412		5,496
Log likelihood		-1685.6		-1639.6		-1783.3		-1375.4

Notes: Performance Π is a dummy which is one when the continuous measure of industry-adjusted performance is negative, zero otherwise. And performance is interacted with shareholder types, with non-financial firms as owners being the reference category.

Table 5.13. Robustness tests: different performance measures, without type of owner

	Model (1)		Model (2)		Model (3)		Model (4)	
	Failure	Acquisition	Failure	Acquisition	Failure	Acquisition	Failure	Acquisition
Industry-adjusted	-4.364***	-1.698***	-4.044**	-1.682***	-3.803**	-1.626***	0.068	-2.144**
return on assets	(0.007)	(0.003)	(0.044)	(0.008)	(0.034)	(0.007)	(0.982)	(0.041)
Industry-adjusted			-0.447	-0.161				
return on sales			(0.714)	(0.499)				
Industry-adjusted total					-0.728***	-0.108		
factor productivity					(0.002)	(0.219)		
Market-adjusted stock							-1.316*	0.096
market return							(0.070)	(0.744)
Debt ratio	3.165***	0.820***	3.269***	1.041***	3.539***	1.097***	-0.245	-0.698
	(0.000)	(0.002)	(0.000)	(0.000)	(0.000)	(0.000)	(0.868)	(0.144)
Herfindahl	5.920	6.474***	9.898	5.471**	11.413	5.855**	-6.277	12.720***
	(0.334)	(0.006)	(0.161)	(0.023)	(0.112)	(0.017)	(0.820)	(0.000)
Herfindahl*	-8.416	-7.956***	-12.450*	-7.111***	-13.346**	-7.445***	-2.829	-16.378***
Control	(0.133)	(0.000)	(0.057)	(0.001)	(0.044)	(0.001)	(0.920)	(0.000)
Herfindahl^2	-30.882*	-10.590**	-45.002**	-8.394	-49.217**	-9.783*	-9.675	-24.273***
	(0.089)	(0.039)	(0.047)	(0.105)	(0.033)	(0.066)	(0.955)	(0.010)
Herfindahl^2*	31.130*	11.612**	45.272**	9.616*	49.131**	10.976**	19.623	27.925***
Control	(0.082)	(0.019)	(0.042)	(0.054)	(0.030)	(0.033)	(0.910)	(0.002)
Pyramid	-0.577**	-0.084	-0.629**	-0.059	-0.657**	-0.057	-2.008***	0.342**
	(0.019)	(0.424)	(0.013)	(0.576)	(0.011)	(0.595)	(0.009)	(0.042)
Cross ownership	-35.617	-0.678***	-38.548	-0.688***	-36.570	-0.713***	-46.306	-1.229***
	(n.a.)	(0.003)	(n.a.)	(0.003)	(n.a.)	(0.002)	(n.a.)	(0.007)
Growth rate	-1.722**	-0.341*	-1.471*	-0.401**	-0.950	-0.393*	-0.514	0.024
of employment	(0.046)	(0.067)	(0.095)	(0.047)	(0.228)	(0.053)	(0.609)	(0.932)
log (assets)	-0.178**	-0.156***	-0.176**	-0.162***	-0.079	-0.144***	-0.451***	-0.149***
	(0.014)	(0.000)	(0.017)	(0.000)	(0.325)	(0.000)	(0.007)	(0.001)
Number of obs.		2,772		2,711		2,664		1,212
Log likelihood		-1688.4		-1646.1		-1615.7		-643.5

Table 5.14. Robustness tests: different performance measures, with type of owner

Performance Π	Return on assets		Return on sales		Total factor productivity		Stock market return	
	Failure	Acquisition	Failure	Acquisition	Failure	Acquisition	Failure	Acquisition
$\Pi < 0$	0.023	0.416***	0.244	0.353***	0.107	0.116	-1.285*	0.277
	(0.951)	(0.002)	(0.477)	(0.007)	(0.797)	(0.410)	(0.057)	(0.194)
$\Pi < 0$ and	0.124	-0.578***	0.694*	-0.413**	0.212	-0.431***	2.078***	-0.862***
priv. owner	(0.768)	(0.001)	(0.072)	(0.018)	(0.551)	(0.003)	(0.006)	(0.002)
$\Pi < 0$ and	-29.432***	-0.957**	-36.716***	-0.741**	-44.121	-0.485*	-32.152***	-1.130**
fin. owner	(0.000)	(0.012)	(0.000)	(0.033)	(n.a.)	(0.092)	(0.000)	(0.025)
$\Pi < 0$ and	0.619	0.808***	0.731	0.694***	0.780	0.447**	1.362	0.109
disp. owners	(0.227)	(0.000)	(0.177)	(0.003)	(0.123)	(0.045)	(0.161)	(0.725)
$\Pi < 0$ and	0.944	-1.135**	1.130*	-1.281**	1.286**	-1.161	-33.811***	-0.587
gov. owner	(0.146)	(0.048)	(0.073)	(0.035)	(0.034)	(0.147)	(0.000)	(0.336)
Debt ratio	3.337***	0.851***	3.188***	1.044***	3.836***	1.211***	-0.351	-0.284
	(0.000)	(0.001)	(0.000)	(0.000)	(0.000)	(0.000)	(0.788)	(0.544)
Herfindahl	-2.577	-0.382	-3.289**	-0.835	-1.900	-0.837	-8.579**	-4.005***
	(0.108)	(0.566)	(0.043)	(0.209)	(0.287)	(0.233)	(0.013)	(0.000)
Herfindahl^2	0.330	0.086	0.962	0.495	-0.140	0.489	9.290***	3.702***
	(0.793)	(0.879)	(0.460)	(0.382)	(0.920)	(0.410)	(0.010)	(0.000)
Pyramid	-0.524**	-0.014	-0.650**	-0.015	-0.564**	-0.013	-2.010**	0.402**
	(0.046)	(0.892)	(0.016)	(0.889)	(0.037)	(0.901)	(0.012)	(0.017)
Cross ownership	-32.936	-0.492*	-37.925	-0.600**	-45.862	-0.672***	-40.148	-1.150**
	(n.a.)	(0.064)	(n.a.)	(0.015)	(n.a.)	(0.009)	(n.a.)	(0.013)
Growth rate	-2.016**	-0.360*	-1.465*	-0.408**	-1.442*	-0.442**	-0.744	0.104
of employment	(0.015)	(0.053)	(0.056)	(0.037)	(0.056)	(0.037)	(0.457)	(0.719)
log (assets)	-0.162**	-0.155***	-0.152**	-0.148***	-0.156**	-0.163***	-0.333**	-0.144***
	(0.029)	(0.000)	(0.035)	(0.000)	(0.044)	(0.000)	(0.017)	(0.002)
Number of obs.		2,772		2,711		2,664		1,212
Log likelihood		-1685.6		-1645.0		-1627.0		-656.1

Table 5.15. Robustness tests: different measures of capital structure, without type of owner

	Model (1)		Model (2)		Model (3)		Model (4)	
	Failure	Acquisition	Failure	Acquisition	Failure	Acquisition	Failure	Acquisition
Industry-adjusted	-4.364***	-1.698***	-2.986*	-1.982***	-4.351***	-1.636***	-4.428**	-1.635***
return on assets	(0.007)	(0.003)	(0.074)	(0.001)	(0.008)	(0.005)	(0.015)	(0.006)
Debt ratio	3.165***	0.820***	3.120***	0.913***	2.927***	0.446	3.532***	0.819***
	(0.000)	(0.002)	(0.000)	(0.001)	(0.000)	(0.172)	(0.000)	(0.003)
Interest coverage			-0.016**	0.000				
			(0.022)	(0.451)				
Working capital ratio					-0.439	-0.701**		
					(0.592)	(0.038)		
Cash flow to assets							0.337	-0.196
							(0.667)	(0.508)
Herfindahl	5.920	6.474***	6.841	6.348***	5.855	6.330***	6.634	6.707***
	(0.334)	(0.006)	(0.294)	(0.007)	(0.341)	(0.008)	(0.295)	(0.006)
Herfindahl*	-8.416	-7.956***	-9.838	-8.035***	-8.336	-7.836***	-8.423	-8.227***
Control	(0.133)	(0.000)	(0.103)	(0.000)	(0.139)	(0.000)	(0.144)	(0.000)
$Herfindahl^2$	-30.882*	-10.590**	-35.870*	-10.627**	-30.582*	-10.233**	-31.596*	-11.751**
	(0.089)	(0.039)	(0.079)	(0.037)	(0.092)	(0.045)	(0.088)	(0.027)
$Herfindahl^2$*	31.130*	11.612**	36.391*	11.831**	30.826*	11.281**	31.241*	12.805**
Control	(0.082)	(0.019)	(0.070)	(0.016)	(0.085)	(0.022)	(0.086)	(0.012)
Pyramid	-0.577**	-0.084	-0.560**	-0.057	-0.581**	-0.092	-0.611**	-0.079
	(0.019)	(0.424)	(0.025)	(0.591)	(0.018)	(0.381)	(0.017)	(0.455)
Cross ownership	-35.617	-0.678***	-34.544	-0.680***	-45.602	-0.674***	-46.565	-0.682***
	(n.a.)	(0.003)	(n.a.)	(0.003)	(n.a.)	(0.003)	(n.a.)	(0.003)
Growth rate	-1.722**	-0.341*	-1.485*	-0.309*	-1.719**	-0.350*	-1.245	-0.317
of employment	(0.046)	(0.067)	(0.066)	(0.098)	(0.049)	(0.061)	(0.135)	(0.120)
log (assets)	-0.178**	-0.156***	-0.185**	-0.155***	-0.178**	-0.156***	-0.176**	-0.152***
	(0.014)	(0.000)	(0.011)	(0.000)	(0.017)	(0.000)	(0.019)	(0.000)
Number of obs.		2,772		2,752		2,772		2,708
Log likelihood		-1688.4		-1665.1		-1686.1		-1646.4

Table 5.16. Robustness tests: different measures of restructuring and firm size, without type of owner

	Model (1)		Model (2)		Model (3)		Model (4)	
	Failure	Acquisition	Failure	Acquisition	Failure	Acquisition	Failure	Acquisition
Industry-adjusted return on assets	-4.364***	-1.698***	-4.259**	-1.560***	-5.021***	-2.107***	-4.956***	-1.835***
	(0.007)	(0.003)	(0.010)	(0.009)	(0.002)	(0.001)	(0.005)	(0.002)
Debt ratio	3.165***	0.820***	3.053***	0.802***	3.203***	0.795***	3.318***	1.044***
	(0.000)	(0.002)	(0.000)	(0.003)	(0.000)	(0.004)	(0.000)	(0.000)
Herfindahl	5.920	6.474***	4.220	6.765***	5.367	6.126**	10.036	5.488**
	(0.334)	(0.006)	(0.478)	(0.005)	(0.397)	(0.013)	(0.159)	(0.022)
Herfindahl* Control	-8.416	-7.956***	-7.106	-8.493***	-8.682	-8.376***	-12.493*	-7.118***
	(0.133)	(0.000)	(0.194)	(0.000)	(0.131)	(0.000)	(0.060)	(0.001)
Herfindahl^2	-30.882*	-10.590**	-25.094	-11.938**	-30.510	-10.823**	-45.430**	-8.409
	(0.089)	(0.039)	(0.134)	(0.024)	(0.107)	(0.043)	(0.047)	(0.104)
Herfindahl^{2}* Control	31.130*	11.612**	25.722	13.168***	31.486*	12.513**	45.536**	9.621*
	(0.082)	(0.019)	(0.118)	(0.010)	(0.090)	(0.015)	(0.043)	(0.054)
Pyramid	-0.577**	-0.084	-0.585**	-0.081	-0.550**	-0.066	-0.591**	-0.062
	(0.019)	(0.424)	(0.022)	(0.448)	(0.025)	(0.547)	(0.017)	(0.557)
Cross ownership	-35.617	-0.678***	-39.575	-0.621***	-38.645	-0.569**	-46.527	-0.687***
	(n.a.)	(0.003)	(n.a.)	(0.008)	(n.a.)	(0.013)	(n.a.)	(0.003)
Growth rate of employment	-1.722**	-0.341*	-1.528*	-0.358*	-1.782**	-0.368*	-1.667*	-0.394**
	(0.046)	(0.067)	(0.079)	(0.080)	(0.050)	(0.073)	(0.065)	(0.049)
Sales of fixed assets			1.815	-0.277				
			(0.116)	(0.558)				
Sales of financial assets					0.648	-0.555**		
					(0.151)	(0.021)		
log (assets)	-0.178**	-0.156***	-0.185**	-0.158***	-0.235***	-0.173***	-0.517**	-0.173**
	(0.014)	(0.000)	(0.012)	(0.000)	(0.002)	(0.000)	(0.028)	(0.034)
log (sales)							0.341	0.011
							(0.125)	(0.888)
Number of obs.		2,772		2,685		2,593		2,711
Log likelihood		-1688.4		-1631.7		-1552.9		-1645.2

fected (Table 5.16). In summary, we are confident that our main findings as presented in Chapters 5.4.1 and 5.4.2 are generally not sensitive to alternative specifications of explanatory variables or different time horizons.

5.5 Summary and Lessons

This chapter analyzes the determinants of corporate survival, acquisition, and failure in Germany. In particular, we identify which firm-specific characteristics are helpful to explain corporate acquisition and failure, and which measures of these characteristics have the highest explanatory power. We also examine to what extent the length of the forward-looking time horizon affects the usefulness of our explanatory variables.

Evidence based on bivariate analyses identifies the following firm-specific characteristics as useful to explain acquisition and failure, with suitable measures of these characteristics reported in parentheses: performance (industry-adjusted return on assets or industry-adjusted total factor productivity), capital structure (debt-to-assets ratio), ownership concentration (Herfindahl index), ownership complexity (cross ownership and pyramids), restructuring activity (growth rate of employment), and firm size (total assets or total sales). In addition, detailed information on the type of the ultimately controlling shareholder turns out to be important. Regarding the length of the time horizon, we find that it does not significantly affect our main findings. However, for models with a time horizon shorter than four years, firm size and ownership concentration loose their explanatory power concerning failure. In turn, in models that explain acquisition, cross ownership and the growth rate of employment become less important.

Results from multinomial models simultaneously explaining survival, acquisition, and failure show that firms are more likely to fail or to be acquired when performance is poor or financial pressure is high. This is consistent with other studies (Altman, 1968; Powell, 1997; Denis and Sarin, 1999; Maksimovic and Phillips, 2001). Note that the documented relation between poor performance and the likelihood of a control transfer is much stronger compared with the weak relation found in the bivariate analysis of Chapter 4. Firm size and cross ownership act as a kind of takeover deterrent. These findings are in line with theoretical predictions (Shleifer and Vishny, 1992; Bebchuk et al., 2000). Similarly, larger firms and firms that are part of pyramid structures or are controlled by a cross-owned shareholder are also less likely to fail. In addition, we show that the likelihood of failure decreases when ownership concentration increases. This could be explained with large shareholders alleviating the agency problem via better monitoring (Shleifer and Vishny, 1986). In contrast, the impact of ownership concentration on the likelihood of acquisition is non-linear. More precisely, for firms with a highly dispersed ownership structure the likelihood of acquisition increases with share concentration, but it decreases when concentration exceeds a particular level. Firms with three or four equally large shareholders are the most likely to be acquired. One interpretation for the positive impact of concentration on the likelihood of acquisition is that shareholders prefer to trade a large block than first to sell to the public and, in a second step, to acquire those dispersed shares (Burkart et al., 2000). Only when concentration becomes too large, capital markets are not any longer able to determine the necessity of a takeover (Holmström and Tirole, 1993). This makes takeovers less likely for firms without a sufficiently dispersed ownership structure. Finally, there is strong evidence that different shareholder types react differently to poor performance. Private and financial owners (such as banks and insurance companies) are less likely than non-financial owners (such as industrial and trade companies) to sell poorly performing firms. In turn, firms without a dominant shareholder are more likely to be sold (to a large blockholder) when performance is poor. And poorly performing firms are less likely to fail when under control of a financial firm.

Our findings have implications for the design of empirical studies explaining corporate failure or acquisition. First, we find that acquisition and failure tend to be influenced by common factors. This implies that they should be examined in combination. Models explaining failure but not taking into account the second form of sample exit, acquisition (see, e.g., Harhoff et al., 1998; Almus, 2000), or vice versa, are likely to suffer from a sample selection problem. This could bias estimation results (Börsch-Supan and Köke, 2002), in particular because acquisition and failure are important reasons for sample attrition. Second, we find that the industry distribution is significantly different for failure and acquisitions. This calls for some kind of industry adjustment in the empirical analysis, for example by including industry dummies or by correcting some variables for their industry benchmark. Third, a range of firm-specific characteristics are helpful to explain failure and acquisition. Analyses leaving out some of these measures are potentially subject to the classical omitted variables problem. Finally, care should be taken when selecting measures for firm-specific characteristics because some measures perform much better than others in the analysis of firm exit.

Finally, our results imply that the market for corporate control cannot a priori be regarded as disadvantageous to target firm's shareholders because typically poorly performing firms are acquisition targets. Rather, our results are consistent with the view that control transfers allow to improve efficiency. If the new owner achieves to solve performance problems, for example by restructuring the respective firm, this could increase corporate value and thus benefit the economy as a whole (Jensen, 1988). However, such a beneficial impact of control transfers still needs to be examined in further analyses, particularly because the evidence in Chapter 4 does not indicate significant performance improvements in the aftermath of control transfers.

6 Corporate Governance, Market Discipline, and Productivity Growth

This chapter is a revised and adapted version of Köke (2001a). It examines the role of corporate governance and market discipline for total factor productivity growth. Understanding the determinants of productivity growth is important. According to Börsch-Supan (1999), Germany and France have lagged the US in terms of total factor productivity by around 20% throughout the entire period of 1970–1995. Researchers and policy makers alike recently recognize productivity as a major determinant of future generations' welfare. The corresponding interest in the sources of productivity is likely to increase as countries move away from pay-as-you-go financing into partially or fully funded pension systems: While total factor productivity is equally important for the (internal) rate of return under both types of pension systems, greater use of capital markets under a funded system could improve corporate governance and ultimately spur productivity growth, as argued by Börsch-Supan and Winter (1999). Hence, good corporate governance could help reduce the transition burden associated with a change in the pension scheme.

In a recent survey, Bartelsman and Doms (2000) identify four factors that are likely to influence productivity growth at the micro level: (1) government regulation altering the incentives for innovating, market entry, and gaining market share; (2) managerial ability and firm ownership determining the firm's choices on technology and inputs; (3) technology and human capital affecting efficiency in production; and (4) (international) competition on product markets making firms learn faster about new technologies. This study focuses on corporate governance and product market competition (and their interaction) as two important determinants of managerial behavior. Corporate governance is understood and measured as the system of firm's ownership structure, capital structure, and board structure.[1]

Empirical work on corporate governance, competition, and their relation to productivity is accumulating. Studies examining the role of competition include Green and Mayes (1991) and Nickell (1996) for the UK, Klette (1999) for Norway, Bottasso and Sembenelli (2001) for Italy, and Caves (1992),

---

[1] For theoretical analyses on the role of ownership structure, see Shleifer and Vishny (1986), on the role of capital structure, see Jensen (1986), and on the role of competition, see Hart (1983). We discuss these theoretical arguments in Chapter 6.1.

Porter (1992), and Börsch-Supan (1999) for a range of industrialized countries. Studies investigating the role of ownership structure encompass Nickell et al. (1997) for the UK and Januszewski et al. (2002) for Germany, and a study on the role of capital structure is Nickell and Nicolitsas (1999). Another strand of literature investigates different corporate governance mechanisms, such as the structure of the board (e.g., Yermack, 1996); however, empirical studies on board structure typically examine the impact on firm value or some accounting measure, but not the impact on productivity. A study that examines the impact of corporate governance (shareholder control and financial pressure), product market competition, and their interactions on productivity growth in UK firms is Nickell et al. (1997). Januszewski et al. (2002) conduct a similar analysis for German firms but they neglect the role of creditors. In contrast to the UK, lending relationships in Germany are often characterized as long-term and comparatively stable, ensuring lending even to ailing firms (Mayer, 1988). Recently, this German 'housebank' system has been criticized as too inflexible in times of rapid economic change. Hence, new evidence on creditors' governance role is desirable.

Using a panel of 841 German manufacturing firms through the years 1986–1996, this study analyzes the impact of five corporate governance mechanisms (ownership concentration, ownership complexity, type of owner, financial pressure, and board size), product market competition, and their interactions on productivity growth. The following analysis adds to the literature on four important respects: First, we consider a larger range of governance mechanisms and their relation to productivity growth than previous studies. Second, to our knowledge this study is the first to examine the impact of financial pressure (from creditors) on productivity growth for a continental European country. Due to the methodological similarity, our results are directly comparable to those of Nickell et al. (1997) obtained for the UK. Third, we explicitly address potential endogeneity of our explanatory variables by using the GMM instrumental variables technique developed by Arellano and Bond (1991). This method is now standard in panel econometrics. However, it is not yet widely applied in studies on corporate governance with the exceptions of Nickell et al. (1997) and Januszewski et al. (2002). Finally, the data set used in this study is much larger than data sets used in previous work on corporate governance in Germany (e.g., Cable, 1985; Gorton and Schmid, 2000; Becht and Böhmer, 2002; Januszewski et al., 2002).

The structure of this chapter is as follows: Chapter 6.1 briefly reviews the literature on corporate governance and market discipline, and how these monitoring mechanisms are related to productivity growth. The aim is to formulate a set of testable hypotheses. Chapter 6.2 describes the data sources used and how corporate governance and market discipline are measured. Chapter 6.3 gives some preliminary evidence on the relation of corporate governance and market discipline to productivity growth. Chapter 6.4 presents an empirical model of productivity growth and details on the GMM estimation procedure. Chapter 6.5 contains the estimation results. Chapter 6.6 summarizes the main results and discusses some methodological implications.

6.1 Hypotheses

The classical problem of corporate governance is the separation of ownership and control. The literature on corporate governance discusses a variety of mechanisms that are supposed to alleviate this agency conflict. A common feature of all mechanisms is that they aim to align the interests of managers and owners of a firm (Shleifer and Vishny, 1997). In the following, we discuss mechanisms covered extensively in the literature and deduct hypotheses that are to be tested in the empirical analysis.[2] We distinguish between the firm's ownership structure, capital structure, board structure, and product market competition.

We expect that productivity growth is affected as follows:

Hypothesis 6.1 *Concentrated ownership increases productivity growth.*

Hypothesis 6.2 *The impact of ownership concentration is stronger when a firm is owned by a non-financial firm as a large blockholder, but weaker when a firm is owned by a large private or public blockholder.*

Hypothesis 6.3 *Complex ownership decreases productivity growth.*

Hypothesis 6.4 *A large fraction of bank debt increases productivity growth.*

Hypothesis 6.5 *The impact of bank debt is stronger when performance is poor.*

Hypothesis 6.6 *Small board size increases productivity growth.*

Hypothesis 6.7 *Intense product market competition increases productivity growth.*

The first hypothesis (**6.1**) follows Shleifer and Vishny (1986) who argue that a large block provides the owner with an incentive to collect information and to monitor management. A large blockholder also has enough voting control to put pressure on management. In contrast, in firms with a dispersed shareholder structure free-riding behavior should make monitoring too costly (Grossman and Hart, 1980). The evidence on monitoring by blockholders indicates that large shareholders indeed play an active role in corporate governance. For Japan, Kaplan and Minton (1994) find that poorly

---

[2] Note that in the literature, particularly in studies on financial economics, the goal is typically not to explain productivity but some other measure of firm performance. Therefore, results from empirical studies discussed below are sometimes not directly comparable.

performing management is more likely to be replaced by a large blockholder. For Germany, Franks and Mayer (2001) find little association of ownership concentration with managerial disciplining. In contrast, Januszewski et al. (2002) show that ownership concentration is positively related to productivity growth.

The second hypothesis (**6.2**) is concerned with the type of the controlling blockholder. Pound (1988) notes that institutional investors such as banks should be effective monitors because they have frequent business contacts to their clients; on the other hand, these investors might become entrenched and support incumbent management. Therefore, investment or pension funds could be better monitors than banks or insurers. Similarly, non-financial firms as blockholders can be effective monitors when their investment is strategic; when operating in the same industry, information asymmetries are lower. In contrast, private blockholders typically have only limited access to monitoring competency within their family. For the US, the evidence on the role of institutional investors is mixed (Black, 1998). For Belgium, Renneboog (2000) finds that industrial companies resort to disciplinary action when performance is poor. For Germany, focusing on accounting-based measures of performance Edwards and Nibler (2000) cannot find evidence that the role of banks is different from that of other large corporate shareholders. In contrast, Gorton and Schmid (2000) find a positive impact. Focusing on productivity growth, Januszewski et al. (2002) find that financial institutions as blockholders are harmful for productivity growth.

The third hypothesis (**6.3**) addresses the role of ownership complexity for corporate monitoring. Franks and Mayer (1995) note that cross holdings can exclude small investors from the control over management. Bebchuk et al. (2000) add that pyramids and cross ownership function as anti-takeover devices, and therefore shelter management from capital market pressure. Ownership structures are particularly complex in continental Europe and Japan (La Porta et al., 1999). For Germany, Franks and Mayer (2001) cannot find evidence that managerial disciplining is smaller in firms controlled by pyramids, and Januszewski et al. (2002) cannot find evidence that productivity growth is lower for firms controlled by cross-held blockholders.

The fourth hypothesis (**6.4**) focuses on the firm's capital structure and its effect on performance. Jensen (1986) argues that debt financing reduces free cash flow and therefore has a disciplinary effect on management. Management can use high leverage to signal credibly that they maximize profits. Likewise, any disciplinary impact creditors have on management should be the greatest when a large fraction of debt is bank debt. Previous evidence indicates that high gearing has a positive impact on performance (see Cable, 1985, for Germany; Nickell and Nicolitsas, 1999, for the UK; and Renneboog, 2000, for Belgium).

The fifth hypothesis (**6.5**) recognizes that creditors are concerned about avoiding failure of the provided loans, but much less concerned about monitoring their client firms to ensure that they maximize profits (Stiglitz, 1985). Therefore, we expect banks to interfere in particular when performance is poor and when they are in a strong creditor position, i.e. when a large proportion of debt is bank debt. Similar arguments are put forward by Mayer (1988). He shows that institutionalized lending relationships, as exemplified by the German housebank system (see Edwards and Fischer, 1994, for a detailed discussion), reduce information asymmetries, and as a consequence allow for (new) long-term lending even in times of financial difficulties.

The sixth hypothesis (**6.6**) follows Jensen (1993) who argues that smaller boards control more effectively and therefore have a positive impact on performance. For the US, Yermack (1996) confirms that board size is negatively correlated with firm value. In Germany with its two-tier board structure, a supervisory board is required by law for public corporations, and in some cases also for private corporations. The number of supervisory board members is also regulated by law, with a minimum of three and a maximum of 21 members, depending on firm size and industry; for details, see Hopt (1997). But since firm's discretion is low regarding the size of the board, any empirical relation is likely to be weak.

Finally, the seventh hypothesis (**6.7**) recognizes that even in the presence of weak internal monitoring, fierce product market competition may act to align managers' goals with the aim of efficient production; Allen and Gale (2000) provide a review. For example, Hart (1983) shows that an increase in product market competition reduces managerial slack. Other theoretical studies show that competition has no or a positive impact on agency costs. The empirical evidence is less ambiguous. Green and Mayes (1991), Caves (1992), Nickell et al. (1997), Bottasso and Sembenelli (2001), and Januszewski et al. (2002) document that increased product market competition is associated with higher productivity or higher productivity growth. In a recent study with Norwegian establishment-level data, Klette (1999) provides evidence for the positive relationship between price-cost margins, as a measure for product market competition, scale economies, and productivity.

6.2 Data and Measurement Issues

The sample used for the analysis of corporate governance, market discipline, and their relation to productivity growth is a subsample of the German Corporations Database (GCD). Specifically, in a first step, out of the 2,959 firms contained in GCD we eliminate 1,200 firms for which no information on ownership is available. Second, we use only information from the years 1986–1996 because 1996 is the last year for which information on the survival status is available (115 firm deletions). Third, we drop 486 firms which do not operate primarily in manufacturing industries because our measure of total factor productivity is not readily applicable to non-manufacturing industries such as trade or construction. Fourth, the dynamic panel estimator, which we apply in the empirical analysis, requires at least three continuous years of data. Therefore, we drop another 158 firms for which we have less than three years of continuous data. Finally, 159 firms are eliminated due to missing values on key variables needed for the empirical analysis. The final sample consists of 841 firms (5,329 firm years).

Sample attrition is a concern since it might result in selection biases. To test for a potential selection bias, we analyze information on firms' survival status as contained in GCD. We find that 91 out of 146 firms that exit the sample before 1996 still existed in 1996 without a change in ultimate ownership – they simply changed their name or stopped reporting due to reasons determined within the firm. In 29 cases, operation was shut down due to liquidation or bankruptcy. In 24 cases, a firm had been taken over by another entity. And in two cases operation was shut down voluntarily. Hence, the majority of firm exits from the sample is not related to firm failure or acquisition.[3]

6.2.1 Measuring Corporate Governance

To measure corporate governance, the following analysis uses data on ownership structure, capital structure, and board structure. The Appendix explains in detail how these measures are constructed. In the following we provide some descriptive statistics.

Our main measure of ownership is $CONTROL$, a dummy that indicates whether a firm has an ultimately controlling owner or not. As in Chapter 4 we find that ownership is highly concentrated. Examining ownership at the ultimate level, we identify a controlling owner for, on average, 89.2% of sample firms during the years 1986–96. Measuring concentration at the direct level of ownership by the size of the largest block ($BLOCK$) and the Herfindahl index ($HERF$), concentration is also very high. For example, the largest block is 75.7% at the mean and 90.0% at the median. Both $BLOCK$ and $HERF$ are highly correlated with $CONTROL$. Hence, collinearity problems would be likely when using all three measures simultaneously in the empirical analysis. The degree of ownership complexity in large German firms makes $CONTROL$ a more appealing measure of ownership concentration. Therefore, $CONTROL$ is our preferred measure.

In addition, we measure ownership complexity ($CROSS$, $PYRAMID$) and we identify the type of the ultimate owner for each sample firm ($TYPE$). The largest fraction of firms is ultimately controlled by a non-financial firm (41.7%) or a private owner (36.7%). Only 4.4% of sample firms are ultimately controlled by a bank, and 2.3% are controlled by other financial institutions. Note that actual voting power of banks might be greater in practice when

[3] See Chapter 4.2.1 for a more detailed analysis of selection, entry, and attrition biases in a panel of firms that is very similar to the one used here.

banks make use of proxy voting. However, recent evidence suggests that proxy voting is extremely unlikely to significantly enhance bank voting power (Edwards and Nibler, 2000). Government agencies control 4.1% of firms, and 10.8% of firms have dispersed ownership. Regarding ownership complexity, 7.5% of sample firms are controlled by a firm that belongs to the well-known web of German industrial and financial conglomerates (Wenger and Kaserer, 1998), and 50.2% of sample firms are controlled through a pyramid with at least one intermediate firm between the ultimate owner and the sample firm.

Regarding capital structure, the main measure used in this chapter is the ratio of bank debt to total debt ($BANK$). On average, 27.4% of the total debt burden consists of bank debt. As additional measures we use the ratio of total debt to total assets ($DEBT$), the ratio of total debt to book value of total equity ($LEVERAGE$), and the ratio of operating earnings to interest payments ($COVERAGE$). Our measure of board structure is an indicator whether the number of directors on the supervisory board is equal to the legally specified minimum or whether it is greater ($SMALL$). As discussed in detail in the Appendix, this minimum number depends on industry and firm size, but also on other firm characteristics which are not observable to the researcher. Since not all sample firms have a supervisory board, we also use an indicator whether such a board exists ($BOARD$). In our sample, 74.3% of firms have a supervisory board, and in 76.4% of firms the supervisory board consists of the legally specified minimum number of directors.

6.2.2 Measuring Market Discipline

To measure market discipline we use data on product market competition. The main variable used to measure competition is the firm's rents from production ($RENT$), which can be interpreted as an ex post measure of market power.[4] The motivation for using this measure is that firms operating in less competitive markets should be able to sell their products well above marginal cost, and therefore earn higher rents after covering their expenses (on capital, labor, and materials). For definition of this measure, see Appendix. In addition to firm-specific rents we use the market share of the six largest suppliers ($CR6$) and the respective Herfindahl index (HHI), both measured at the four-digit industry level, as proxy variables for competition. As a proxy for competition from abroad we use the ratio of imports to total market size (i.e., the sum of domestic production and imports), measured at the two-digit industry level ($IMPORT$).

There are two important caveats with respect to all measures of competition used here. First, we acknowledge that these variables do not reflect some important facets of competition, namely potential entry and firm conduct.

[4] In Chapter 6.5.2 we use two average measures of rent instead – one averaged over time, the other averaged across the respective industry – to address endogeneity issues.

Second, as we do not have firm-specific data on market shares, we can only assign companies to their primary four-digit industry group, but we cannot adjust Herfindahl indices and concentration ratios using firms' market shares.

To illustrate these measures of competition, Table 6.1 describes the intensity of competition using all of these measures, separately for the 22 two-digit manufacturing industries contained in the sample. We find that German manufacturing firms earned rents of about 28% during the years 1986–1996. On average, the six largest suppliers cover about 47% of the domestic market, and imports make up for about one fourth of the total market. Table 6.1 also indicates some remarkable differences between industries. Imports represent a large fraction of the total market in clothing, leather, equipment for data processing, and other vehicles (e.g., ships). The market share of the six largest suppliers is low in clothing, wood, publishing and printing, and metal products; in turn, concentration is extremely high in tobacco. Correspondingly, industries with low *RENT* are textiles, metals, and other vehicles. As we could expect, *RENT* is negatively correlated with industry concentration and import penetration. However, this correlation is weak. This implies that the empirical analysis should include firm-level as well as industry-level measures of competition.

6.3 Preliminary Evidence

We begin our empirical analysis with some suggestive evidence based on a simple measure of productivity growth. In a first step, we estimate a standard two-factor Cobb-Douglas production function with value added as the dependent variable, labor and capital as independent variables (i.e., we indirectly account for materials as third input factor), and we interpret the residuals from this static regression as a measure of relative firm productivity (i.e., relative to the regression mean).[5] The concept of relative productivity has a long tradition in applied productivity analysis; see Doms et al. (1995) for an application. In a second step, we calculate the first difference of the predicted residuals to obtain a measure of productivity growth.

To get a first impression of the effects of corporate governance and market discipline on productivity growth, we split the sample into two groups: firms with positive and negative productivity growth. In Table 6.2, we report means of some key measures of corporate governance and market discipline for both splits. One reason for considering growth instead of levels of productivity is that some of our variables for corporate governance and market discipline should be highly endogenous to the level of productivity. Since productivity growth is less persistent than productivity levels, the endogeneity problem

---

[5] To estimate this production function using OLS, we also include time and two-digit industry dummies; see Table 6.2.

Table 6.1. Firm- and industry-specific measures of competition

	Firm level	Industry level			Obs.
	RENT	CR6	HHI	IMPORT	
Food	45.8%	33.1%	4.2%	18.7%	676
Tobacco	48.6%	97.8%	20.3%	10.2%	55
Textiles	16.7%	45.2%	6.2%	46.4%	228
Clothing	55.2%	20.6%	1.4%	61.2%	84
Leather	46.7%	33.3%	3.2%	63.2%	24
Wood	36.0%	19.6%	1.6%	24.0%	30
Paper	30.1%	47.8%	6.7%	27.7%	168
Publishing, printing	30.9%	23.6%	1.9%	5.5%	57
Coal, oil processing	41.1%	81.8%	14.9%	38.4%	63
Chemicals	39.1%	60.1%	10.6%	26.1%	564
Rubber/plastic products	28.4%	34.2%	3.8%	19.6%	318
Rock, stone, glass	30.1%	51.9%	8.5%	17.6%	326
Metals	10.9%	56.7%	10.9%	26.2%	308
Metal products	27.6%	25.7%	2.7%	14.8%	280
Machinery	20.2%	37.9%	5.0%	16.7%	941
Equ. for data processing	27.3%	80.7%	23.5%	60.2%	191
Equ. for power generation	21.6%	42.6%	6.5%	31.1%	230
Equ. for broadcasting and TV	23.0%	60.5%	12.6%	48.4%	188
Medical and optical instr.	20.2%	41.2%	6.7%	33.6%	124
Cars, car parts	26.8%	67.5%	12.7%	20.8%	246
Other vehicles	2.6%	67.7%	19.2%	59.7%	163
Furniture, jewelry, toys	38.5%	32.4%	3.4%	25.7%	65
Average	28.4%	46.6%	7.9%	26.1%	5,329
Correlation with RENT	1.000	-0.034	-0.028	-0.067	-

Notes: Firm- and industry-specific measures of competition, separately by two-digit industry. Measures of competition include the ratio of total operating surplus less costs of capital to value added (*RENT*), the market share of the six largest suppliers (*CR6*), the Herfindahl index of producer concentration (*HHI*), and the ratio of imports to total market size (*IMPORT*). The sample comprises 841 firms.

may be less severe if lagged values of corporate governance and market discipline are used; see also the discussion in Nickell (1996). In the econometric analysis reported below, we use productivity growth as dependent variable and address the potential endogeneity by using an instrumental variables approach. Here we simply use all variables that are supposed to explain productivity growth with a one year lag. Taking into account that corporate governance and market discipline might affect productivity growth in the long run rather than in the short run, we report results for three different forward-looking time horizons: zero years, two years, and four years. For example, for a time horizon of two years we calculate productivity growth as the average of productivity growth in year t, year $t+1$, and year $t+2$.

We find strong support for **Hypothesis 6.1** that firms under concentrated ownership show higher productivity growth (Table 6.2). For our measure of ownership concentration at the direct level, $BLOCK$, this result holds irrespective whether we consider short- or long-run productivity growth. But for our measure of concentration at the ultimate level, $CONTROL$, this holds only for long-run productivity growth, a five-year average. Regarding the type of ultimate owner, a significantly larger fraction of firms under control of a private owner belongs to the group of firms with lower productivity growth. This suggests that productivity in privately-controlled firms tends to grow more slowly. Vice versa, productivity grows faster in firms under control of a non-financial firm; this supports **Hypothesis 6.2**. In addition, productivity growth is higher in firms controlled through a pyramid. We find no indication that cross ownership has an adverse impact on productivity growth.

Regarding our measures of capital structure, there is weak evidence that firms are more productive when a large fraction of total debt is bank debt and when the total burden of debt is high. This implies that financial pressure from creditors appears to play some role in disciplining management. This notion is supported by the results on two measures of performance: firms tend to show significantly higher productivity growth when industry-adjusted return on assets is low or when operating income (EBITDA) is negative. Hence, the preliminary evidence supports **Hypotheses 6.4** and **6.5**. Regarding board size, we do not find evidence that productivity grows faster in firms with small boards.

Moreover, Table 6.2 indicates that firms facing intense competition show higher productivity growth. Both of our industry-level measures of competition, the market share of the six largest suppliers ($CR6$) and the Herfindahl index of producer concentration (HHI), are significantly lower for firms with high productivity growth. The same holds for our measure of firm-level competition ($RENT$). Since all three measures are inverse measures of competition, this finding supports **Hypothesis 6.7**. This result holds irrespective of whether we consider short-run or long-run productivity growth.[6]

In summary, the preliminary evidence suggests that in German manufacturing some elements of corporate governance, such as ownership concentration and bank debt, as well as market discipline reflected by product market competition, are positively related to productivity growth. However, this descriptive analysis is purely bivariate and ignores all potential endogeneity problems. In the remainder of this paper, we address these problems in a dynamic model of productivity growth estimated with an instrumental variables technique.

---

[6] This result also holds when $RENT$ is measured relative to total sales instead of value added, when $RENT$ is measured as the average over two consecutive years, or when $RENT$ is measured as average rent within each three-digit industry.

Table 6.2. Bivariate analysis of corporate governance, market discipline, and productivity growth

Forward-looking horizon	0 years		2 years		4 years	
Performance	negative	positive	negative	positive	negative	positive
Owner concentr. (*BLOCK*)	73.7%**	75.4%	69.3%***	72.6%	65.4%***	71.7%
Ultimate owner (*CONTROL*)	88.9%	89.0%	87.6%	88.0%	84.3%*	87.5%
Owner (*TYPE* = private)	39.4%*	37.0%	43.2%	40.4%	43.4%	40.3%
Owner (*TYPE* = financial firm)	6.6%	6.6%	7.0%	5.8%	7.0%	5.5%
Owner (*TYPE* = non-fin. firm)	39.8%	40.9%	35.2%**	39.6%	31.6%***	39.9%
Owner (*TYPE* = government)	3.0%**	4.5%	2.2%	2.2%	2.3%	1.8%
Cross ownership (*CROSS*)	7.8%	7.1%	7.0%	7.2%	6.7%	6.7%
Pyramid (*PYRAMID*)	45.6%***	50.4%	40.0%	42.5%	36.0%**	40.6%
Bank debt (*BANK*)	28.7%	27.8%	29.8%*	31.5%	31.1%	29.5%
Debt ratio (*DEBT*)	40.8%*	41.8%	39.6%	40.7%	39.2%	39.4%
Ind.-adj. return on assets (*ROA*)	4.7%***	-0.5%	4.7%***	-0.3%	4.4%***	0.6%
Financial distress (*LOSS*)	1.2%	1.4%	0.4%**	1.1%	0.3%	0.9%
Small board (*SMALL*)	75.2%	77.1%	76.8%	75.3%	75.7%	74.8%
Industry concentration (*CR6*)	47.6%**	46.2%	50.1%*	48.5%	50.1%	48.5%
Industry concentration (*HHI*)	8.3%***	7.6%	8.9%**	8.3%	8.7%	8.3%
Rent (*RENT*)	32.0%***	26.2%	32.0%***	26.9%	30.4%***	27.6%
Number of obs.	1,493	1,481	1,087	905	622	504

Notes: Bivariate analysis of corporate governance and market discipline and their relation to productivity growth. Productivity growth is approximated by the first difference in the residuals from pooled OLS estimation of a two-factor Cobb-Douglas production function including time and two-digit industry dummies. Productivity growth is measured at three forward-looking time horizons: zero years (residual in year t), two years (average of residuals in years t through $t+2$), and four years (average of residuals in years t through $t+4$). All other variables are observed in year $t-1$. The test statistics are heteroskedastic t-tests of equal means. *, **, *** indicates significance at the 0.10, 0.05, and 0.01 levels, respectively. For definitions, see Appendix.

6.4 Empirical Model of Productivity Growth

In the following we derive an empirical model of productivity growth from the firm's production function, modelling explicitly the sources of total factor productivity. Specifically, we model the *level* of total factor productivity as a function of the firm's cumulated experience with corporate governance and market discipline. We therefore assume that productivity is shaped by the compound effect of past conditions under which the firm operated, such as intense product market competition or tight shareholder control. For vivid evidence on the compound effect of competition on productivity differentials between industrialized nations, see Porter (1992).

The starting point of our model is a Cobb-Douglas production function with two factor inputs,

$$Y_{it} = {L_{it}}^{\beta_L} {K_{it}}^{\beta_K} A_{it} \,, \tag{6.1}$$

where Y_{it} is value added, L_{it} is labor, K_{it} is capital, and A_{it} is a measure of total factor productivity for firm i in year t. Since we use value added as the output measure, which is defined as total sales less materials costs, we implicitly allow for materials as a third input.

As we are interested in the determinants of total factor productivity growth, we transform the production function (6.1) into a regression equation in several steps. First, we take logs and include lagged output besides the inputs of capital and labor, using a weight λ. This expansion takes into account potential persistence in output. We also include a fixed firm effect, α_i, to allow for unobserved firm heterogeneity. Since output can have a stochastic component, we add an error term, ϵ_{it}, which is assumed to be serially uncorrelated over time. This yields our basic log-linear empirical production function, with small letters denoting logs:

$$y_{it} = \lambda y_{it-1} + (1-\lambda)\beta_L l_{it} + (1-\lambda)\beta_K k_{it} + (1-\lambda) a_{it} + \alpha_i + \epsilon_{it} \,. \tag{6.2}$$

Second, taking first differences eliminates the fixed firm effect α_i. We obtain the differenced growth version of the Cobb-Douglas production function in (6.1):

$$\Delta y_{it} = \lambda \Delta y_{it-1} + (1-\lambda)\beta_L \Delta l_{it} + (1-\lambda)\beta_K \Delta k_{it} + \Delta a_{it} + \Delta\epsilon_{it} \,. \tag{6.3}$$

Finally, we specify the sources of productivity growth by using the level of corporate governance and product market competition in year $t-1$. Employing these variables in *levels* to explain productivity *growth* is appropriate here because we assume that the *level* of total factor productivity is influenced by the *compound* effect of all past states of corporate governance and competition. Specifically, we specify productivity growth with our variables of interest, which follow from the hypotheses derived in Chapter 6.1. These variables include measures of ownership structure ($CONTROL$, $CROSS$, $TYPE$), capital structure ($BANK$), financial distress ($LOSS$), board structure ($SMALL$), and product market competition ($RENT$). Note that all of these variables enter with a one-year lag. To take into account cyclical effects on productivity growth, we add a contemporaneous industry-specific proxy variable that measures capacity utilization ($CYCLE$), and time effects μ_t to filter out productivity shocks. To control for growth effects related to firm size but unrelated to corporate governance and market discipline, we include lagged total assets ($ASSET$). Thus, productivity growth is modeled as

$$\begin{aligned} \Delta a_{it} = {} & (\mu_t - \mu_{t-1}) + \gamma_1 CYCLE_{it} + \gamma_2 ASSET_{it-1} \\ & + \beta_1 CONTROL_{it-1} + \beta_2 CROSS_{it-1} + \beta_3 TYPE_{it-1} \\ & + \beta_4 BANK_{it-1} + \beta_5 LOSS_{it-1} \\ & + \beta_6 SMALL_{it-1} \\ & + \beta_7 RENT_{it-1} \, . \end{aligned} \tag{6.4}$$

The empirical model of productivity growth is given by (6.3) together with (6.4). The structure of this model corresponds to the differenced panel model with lagged endogenous variables considered by Arellano and Bond (1991). They propose a generalized method of moments (GMM) estimator that allows to exploit lags of the lagged dependent variable as well as lags of the explanatory variables as instruments. In our application, using this approach addresses the potential endogeneity problems with respect to the corporate governance and market discipline variables that enter the right-hand side of equation (6.3).[7]

Arellano and Bond (1991) show that endogenous variables lagged two or more periods are valid instruments, provided there is no serial correlation in the time-varying component of the error terms in equation (6.2); we test this condition for all specifications. The instruments we use are y_{it-j} for $j \geq 2$, and second lags of $CONTROL$, $DEBT$, $CR6$ and $ASSET$.[8] We test for

---

[7] An alternative estimation approach for dynamic panel data models is the standard instrumental variables (IV) estimator proposed by Anderson and Hsiao (1981). However, since we have modeled the influence of corporate governance and market discipline on productivity *growth* using the parameterization in equation (6.4), the Anderson-Hsiao IV estimator is not readily applicable in our setting.

[8] We also experimented with additional instruments, using all time-varying measures of ownership structure or competition. However, our main results did not change qualitatively; see Chapter 6.5.2.

instrument validity using a Sargan test of over-identifying restrictions.[9] We report those tests together with the estimation results and standard errors that are robust with respect to general heteroskedasticity in the next section.

While the Arellano-Bond approach can in principle deal with potential endogeneity problems in our application, there is a caveat. Blundell and Bond (1998) show that in autoregressive models with persistent series the first-difference estimator can be subject to finite sample bias as a result of weak instruments. They argue that this bias could be greatly reduced by estimating a model with equations in both levels and first differences. We do not apply such a GMM system estimation procedure here because, as discussed above, we assume that the *level* of corporate governance and market discipline influences productivity *growth*. This suggests to use a first-difference estimator. This approach also has the advantage that we do not have to compare levels of productivity across firms and industries, but only changes in productivity. The disadvantage of potential finite sample bias remains, although our sample is much larger compared with those used for previous studies.

6.5 Estimation Results

In the following we examine the effects of corporate governance and market discipline on productivity growth. Chapter 6.5.1 presents estimation results for our empirical model of productivity growth. All regressions are estimated using the GMM method developed by Arellano and Bond (1991). First, we look at the impact of corporate governance (Table 6.3), then we investigate additional effects of market discipline and their interactions with corporate governance (Table 6.4). Chapter 6.5.2 examines the sensitivity of our main findings.

6.5.1 Effects of Corporate Governance and Market Discipline

Starting with the analysis of firms' corporate governance, we hardly find any significant effect on productivity growth. Model (1) in Table 6.3 shows that ownership structure, measured either by ownership concentration, type of owner, or ownership complexity, is not significantly related to productivity growth. Hence, we do not find support for **Hypotheses 6.1**, **6.2**, nor **6.3.**[10] Note that this result contradicts the descriptive evidence from Chapter

[9] Following Arellano and Bond (1991), we use the two-step version of the GMM estimator for obtaining the Sargan test statistic, while coefficient estimates are based on the one-step version. Arellano and Bond report that the one-step Sargan test is sensitive to heteroskedasticity, tending to over-reject the null.

[10] When we use $PYRAMID$ instead as a measure of ownership complexity, we still do not find a significant relation.

6.3, where firms' ownership structure appears to be related to productivity growth. Note also that we obtain this result as long as not taking into account product market competition. As shown below, interacting corporate governance and competition changes this result.

Examining capital structure in Model (2), we find that the fraction of bank debt is positively related to productivity growth. This suggests that firms in which banks are potentially more influential are subject to tighter discipline, resulting in higher productivity growth. Hence, banks as creditors appear to perform a monitoring function; this supports **Hypothesis 6.4**.

Taking into account that banks' influence should be particularly strong when the borrower's performance is poor, Model (3) additionally includes an indicator of financial distress ($LOSS$) and interacts bank debt and this measure of poor performance. We find that bank debt alone does not show any significant impact on productivity growth any longer. But the interaction of poor performance and bank debt is significantly positive. This suggests that a large fraction of bank debt has a disciplinary effect, but only when performance is poor. This result supports **Hypothesis 6.5**.

Turning to the third main element of governance, the board structure, we cannot confirm that board size is significantly related to productivity growth (**Hypothesis 6.6**). Controlling for the fact that not all sample firms have a supervisory board ($BOARD$), our indicator for small board size ($SMALL$) is positive but insignificant. As mentioned in Chapter 6.1, this result could be expected because in Germany the size of supervisory boards is tightly regulated by law, prescribing minimum and maximum numbers of directors. Hence, firm's discretion is low regarding the size of the board. Therefore, in the subsequent analysis we do not consider board size any longer.

Table 6.4 additionally considers the impact of product market competition and its interaction with corporate governance. We do not include variables measuring ownership complexity and the type of the ultimate owner any longer because we could not find evidence that they affect productivity growth (Table 6.3).[11] Note that the magnitude of the input coefficient on labor is hardly affected, and the input coefficient on capital remains insignificant. As in Table 6.3, the latter result is likely due to measurement error in capital stock, a common problem in productivity analysis. Note also that the coefficient on bank debt remains significantly positive.

The main result from Table 6.4 is that intense product market competition has a positive impact on productivity growth, but only in the presence of a strong ultimate shareholder. Model (5) shows that firms for which rents – our inverse firm-level measure of competition – are low experience higher productivity growth; however, this direct effect of rents is insignificant. But when

---

[11] To check for robustness, we re-estimated all regressions in Table 6.4, including these additional ownership characteristics. We still could not find any consistent relation between these measures and productivity growth. At the same time, none of our main findings in Table 6.4 is qualitatively altered.

we interact rents with our measure of tight owner control (*CONTROL*), as suggested by Nickell et al. (1997), we find that the interaction term is significantly negative. At the same time, the sign of ownership concentration is significantly positive. Taken together, this means that tight control by an ultimate owner has a positive impact on productivity growth, and that this effect is enhanced when competition on product markets is fierce. Hence, when taking into account competition we find strong support for **Hypothesis 6.1**. The evidence also supports **Hypothesis 6.7**, but only for firms under tight control.

Note that our industry-level measure of competition is not significantly associated with productivity growth. The business cycle proxy is also insignificant. These insignificant coefficients might be due to the fact that time and industry dummies absorb most of the variation in these industry-level variables. Also, we cannot assign industry-level competition variables to firms perfectly since we only have industry codes for the firms' primary products.

In Model (6) we interact rents with financial pressure (*BANK*), as also suggested by Nickell et al. (1997). We find that the positive impact of bank debt on productivity growth remains, but the interaction term is insignificant. This suggests that bank influence is not enhanced by fierce product market competition. Instead, in Model (7) we interact bank debt with our indicator of financial distress, as suggested by Model (3) of Table 6.3. As in Model (3), we find a significantly positive interaction term. This indicates that banks are in a position to influence productivity growth particularly when firm performance is poor; again this strongly supports **Hypothesis 6.5**. Note that the positive impact of shareholder control and its negative interaction with competition remains.

All versions of our GMM model are generally supported by the standard battery of specification tests. The Sargan tests do not reject the hypothesis of instrument validity. Also, the tests for second-order serial correlation of the residuals do not reject the null of zero correlation. Wald tests cannot reject the hypothesis of constant returns to scale. Finally, in all specifications we report, the slope coefficients and the sets of time and industry dummy variables are jointly significant according to our Wald tests (not reported). Finally, note that firm size, which is included in all models as a control, does not have a significant impact on productivity growth. The dummy for listed firms is significantly positive in some of the specifications.

6.5.2 Sensitivity of Results

To check the sensitivity of our main findings we conduct a range of robustness tests. One concern is the selection of variables measuring corporate governance and market discipline. Table 6.5 examines whether two alternative measures of ownership concentration, the largest block (*BLOCK*) and the Herfindahl index (*HERF*), have an additional impact on productivity growth besides our preferred measure (*CONTROL*). In contrast to

Table 6.3. Effects of corporate governance on productivity growth

	Dependent variable: output growth (Δy_{it})			
Indep. variables	Model (1)	Model (2)	Model (3)	Model (4)
Lagged output growth (Δy_{t-1})	0.027	0.028	0.002	0.001
	(0.159)	(0.159)	(0.133)	(0.132)
Labor growth (Δl_t)	0.803***	0.806***	0.801***	0.795***
	(0.165)	(0.165)	(0.159)	(0.161)
Capital growth (Δk_t)	-0.100	-0.114	-0.156	-0.132
	(0.228)	(0.223)	(0.202)	(0.213)
Business cycle ($CYCLE_t$)	0.012	0.012	0.010	0.010
	(0.019)	(0.019)	(0.019)	(0.019)
Owner conc. ($CONTROL_{t-1}$)	-0.014	-0.002	0.014	0.017
	(0.036)	(0.035)	(0.035)	(0.036)
Owner ($TYPE_{t-1}$ = private)	0.024	0.014	0.017	0.016
	(0.042)	(0.040)	(0.039)	(0.039)
Owner ($TYPE_{t-1}$ = fin.)	-0.114	-0.111	-0.113	-0.107
	(0.090)	(0.091)	(0.088)	(0.087)
Owner ($TYPE_{t-1}$ = gov.)	0.141	0.141	0.110	0.107
	(0.199)	(0.199)	(0.198)	(0.200)
Cross ownership ($CROSS_{t-1}$)	-0.060	-0.059	-0.052	-0.052
	(0.065)	(0.065)	(0.064)	(0.064)
Bank debt ($BANK_{t-1}$)		0.105**	0.007	-0.003
		(0.053)	(0.049)	(0.047)
Financial distress ($LOSS_{t-1}$)			-0.898	-0.877
			(0.954)	(0.959)
$BANK_{t-1}$ * $LOSS_{t-1}$			8.237**	8.199**
			(3.855)	(3.865)
Board ($BOARD_{t-1}$)				0.001
				(0.048)
Small board ($SMALL_{t-1}$)				0.026
				(0.031)
Total assets ($ASSET_{t-1}$)	0.010	0.011	0.010	0.008
	(0.013)	(0.013)	(0.011)	(0.012)
Listed ($LISTED_t$)	0.029	0.018	0.030	0.022
	(0.027)	(0.028)	(0.025)	(0.026)
Number of obs.	3,647	3,647	3,647	3,647
Instrument validity	p=0.497	p=0.456	p=0.315	p=0.286
AR(1) of residuals	p=0.027	p=0.027	p=0.015	p=0.015
AR(2) of residuals	p=0.418	p=0.414	p=0.430	p=0.429
Const. ret. to scale	p=0.301	p=0.279	p=0.223	p=0.261

Notes: GMM regression results relating measures of corporate governance to productivity growth. Estimates are obtained using the Arellano and Bond (1991) method. All regressions include time and two-digit industry dummies. Instruments are y_{it-j} for $j \geq 2$ and the second lags of $CONTROL$, $DEBT$, $CR6$, and $ASSET$. Asymptotic standard errors (reported in parentheses) are robust to general cross-section and time-series heteroskedasticity. *, **, *** indicates significance at the 0.10, 0.05, and 0.01 levels, respectively. For definitions, see Appendix.

Table 6.4. Effects of corporate governance and market discipline on productivity growth

	Dependent variable: output growth (Δy_{it})					
	Model (5)		Model (6)		Model (7)	
Indep. variables		Interaction $RENT_{t-1}$		Interaction $RENT_{t-1}$		Interaction $RENT_{t-1}$
Δy_{t-1}	-0.019		-0.025		-0.025	
	(0.133)		(0.130)		(0.122)	
Δl_t	0.825***		0.833***		0.833***	
	(0.167)		(0.166)		(0.161)	
Δk_t	0.438		0.467		0.446*	
	(0.329)		(0.328)		(0.248)	
$CYCLE_t$	0.011		0.012		0.012	
	(0.019)		(0.019)		(0.019)	
$CR6_{t-1}$	0.083		0.104		0.125	
	(0.093)		(0.097)		(0.094)	
$RENT_{t-1}$	-0.127		0.168		0.130	
	(0.258)		(0.246)		(0.223)	
$CONTROL_{t-1}$	0.231**	-0.684**	0.255**	-0.757**	0.367***	-1.072***
	(0.114)	(0.319)	(0.109)	(0.300)	(0.118)	(0.335)
$BANK_{t-1}$	0.189***		0.484*	-1.019	0.082*	
	(0.072)		(0.277)	(0.783)	(0.047)	
$LOSS_{t-1}$					-1.924*	
					(1.001)	
$BANK_{t-1}$ * $LOSS_{t-1}$					8.776**	
					(3.726)	
$ASSET_{t-1}$	0.020		0.022		0.019*	
	(0.015)		(0.015)		(0.011)	
$LISTED_t$	0.054**		0.060**		0.063**	
	(0.026)		(0.027)		(0.028)	
Number of obs.	3,647		3,647		3,647	
Instrument validity	p=0.206		p=0.153		p=0.377	
AR(1) of residuals	p=0.029		p=0.028		p=0.021	
AR(2) of residuals	p=0.524		p=0.486		p=0.513	
Const. ret. to scale	p=0.464		p=0.392		p=0.356	

Notes: GMM regression results relating measures of corporate governance and market discipline to productivity growth. Estimates are obtained using the Arellano and Bond (1991) method. All regressions include time and two-digit industry dummies. Instruments are y_{it-j} for $j \geq 2$ and the second lags of $CONTROL$, $DEBT$, $CR6$, and $ASSET$. Asymptotic standard errors (reported in parentheses) are robust to general cross-section and time-series heteroskedasticity. *, **, *** indicates significance at the 0.10, 0.05, and 0.01 levels, respectively. For definitions, see Appendix.

CONTROL, which measures concentration at the ultimate level of ownership, these alternative measures refer to the direct level of ownership. Taking Model (5) from Table 6.4 as the reference, we cannot find evidence for any additional impact of *BLOCK* or *HERF*. The other coefficients do not change qualitatively.

Next, we test the sensitivity of our finding that in Germany the impact of financial pressure is not enhanced or reduced when competition is intense, in particular because Nickell et al. (1997) find that they are substitutes. Table 6.6 examines whether two alternative measures of financial pressure, the debt ratio (*DEBT*) and interest coverage (*COVERAGE*), have an additional impact on productivity growth besides our preferred measure (*BANK*). Taking Model (6) from Table 6.4 as the reference, we find that both alternative measures are not significantly related to productivity growth, and all other results remain qualitatively unaffected.

In Table 6.7 we use two alternative measures of firm-level competition to address potential endogeneity issues. *RENTA* is the average of the firm's rents over the past two years. This time aggregation should smooth short-run firm-specific shocks that affect output directly and hence affect rents. *RENTI* is the year-specific average of our firm-specific rents measure across the respective three-digit industry. This cross-sectional aggregation also wipes out firm-specific shocks, and therefore avoids potential endogeneity problems associated with the rents variable. Taking Model (7) from Table 6.4 as the reference, we find that the interaction of rents and ownership concentration remains significantly negative. In addition, the positive impact of shareholder control as well as the positive interaction of bank debt and financial distress remain. However, using the time-adjusted as well as the industry-adjusted measure of rents in Models (7a) and (7b), the direct impact of bank debt turns insignificant. Overall, this robustness check gives us some confidence that our general approach – controlling for endogeneity problems using an instrumental variables GMM method – is appropriate.

To check whether our finding regarding financial pressure is robust against the definition of creditor influence, we examine two alternative measures, the debt ratio (*DEBT*) and leverage (*LEVERAGE*). Table 6.8 shows the results. Again using Model (7) from Table 6.4 as the reference, we find that these measures do not have any additional explanatory power for productivity growth, and our main findings are unchanged. Only when using leverage as alternative measure, the direct impact of bank debt becomes insignificant.

Since the measure of industry-level competition (*CR*6) is insignificant across all specifications, we consider two alternative measures described in Chapter 6.2.2. Using the Herfindahl index of producer concentration (*HHI*) instead, its coefficient is also insignificant and the other coefficients remain similar. Using the import ratio as a measure of foreign competition in addition to *CR*6 or *HHI*, its coefficient remains insignificant as well, and the other coefficients hardly change. This lack of explanatory power in industry-level measures of competition is likely due to measurement problems, which are hard to overcome with currently available data, as mentioned above.

All of our results are robust against alternative definitions of the capital stock. We experimented with capital stock measures constructed using the method applied by Nickell (1996) and Nickell et al. (1997). They also apply a perpetual inventory method, but they do not assume a constant rate of depreciation. We experimented with annual depreciation rates of 4% and 12%, but our estimation results turned out to be robust.

Finally, we experimented with alternative sets of instrumental variables. Our main results regarding the impact of corporate governance and market discipline are robust against variations of the lag length chosen for the instruments. They are also robust against using additional instruments, particularly the second lags of all time-varying measures of ownership structure and competition. In summary, we are confident that our main findings as presented in Chapter 6.5.1 are generally not sensitive to alternative specifications of explanatory variables or alternative sets of instruments.

6.6 Summary and Lessons

This chapter analyzes the impact of five corporate governance mechanisms (ownership concentration, ownership complexity, type of owner, financial pressure, and board size) and market discipline (product market competition) on productivity growth. We use a panel of 841 German manufacturing firms through the years 1986–1996.

We find that firms under concentrated ownership tend to show higher productivity growth, and this effect is larger for firms earning lower rents. Since we use rent as an inverse measure of the intensity of product market competition, this means that firms in more competitive markets tend to experience higher productivity growth, but only when owner control is tight. Our finding regarding the beneficial impact of competition is in line with evidence from the UK (Nickell et al., 1997), Italy (Bottasso and Sembenelli, 2001), Germany (Januszewski et al., 2002), and other major Western economies (Caves, 1992; Porter, 1992). Our finding that tight owner control has a disciplinary effect is consistent with evidence from Japan (Kaplan and Minton, 1994), the UK (Nickell et al., 1997), and Germany (Januszewski et al., 2002). We find that owner control and intense product market competition are complements; this stands in sharp contrast to Nickell et al. who find that they are substitutes.

Furthermore, also financial pressure from creditors has a positive impact on productivity growth. We find weak evidence that productivity grows faster for firms showing a large fraction of bank debt, and strong evidence that productivity grows faster when bank debt is high and at the same time performance is poor. Hence, creditors seem to be in a position to influence management decisions, which in turn affect productivity growth. And the creditors' position appears to be particularly strong for firms in financial distress. This

Table 6.5. Robustness tests: different measures of ownership structure

	Dependent variable: output growth (Δy_{it})					
	Model (5)		Model (5a)		Model (5b)	
Indep. variables		Interaction $RENT_{t-1}$		Interaction $RENT_{t-1}$		Interaction $RENT_{t-1}$
Δy_{t-1}	-0.019		-0.023		-0.021	
	(0.133)		(0.129)		(0.131)	
Δl_t	0.825***		0.833***		0.835***	
	(0.167)		(0.166)		(0.166)	
Δk_t	0.438		0.506		0.518	
	(0.329)		(0.344)		(0.346)	
$CYCLE_t$	0.011		0.011		0.011	
	(0.019)		(0.019)		(0.019)	
$CR6_{t-1}$	0.083		0.087		0.090	
	(0.093)		(0.095)		(0.096)	
$RENT_{t-1}$	-0.127		-0.664		-0.479	
	(0.258)		(0.597)		(0.445)	
$CONTROL_{t-1}$	0.231**	-0.684**	0.505**	-1.518**	0.419**	-1.258**
	(0.114)	(0.319)	(0.250)	(0.719)	(0.178)	(0.507)
$BLOCK_{t-1}$			-0.520	1.576		
			(0.456)	(1.332)		
$HERF_{t-1}$					-0.382	1.142
					(0.330)	(0.943)
$BANK_{t-1}$	0.189***		0.154***		0.149**	
	(0.072)		(0.058)		(0.059)	
$ASSET_{t-1}$	0.020		0.019		0.020	
	(0.015)		(0.014)		(0.014)	
$LISTED_t$	0.054**		0.063**		0.063**	
	(0.026)		(0.030)		(0.031)	
Number of obs.	3,647		3,647		3,647	
Instrument validity	p=0.206		p=0.273		p=0.262	
AR(1) of residuals	p=0.029		p=0.030		p=0.030	
AR(2) of residuals	p=0.524		p=0.493		p=0.485	
Const. ret. to scale	p=0.464		p=0.352		p=0.335	

Notes: GMM regression results relating measures of corporate governance and market discipline to productivity growth. Estimates are obtained using the Arellano and Bond (1991) method. All regressions include time and two-digit industry dummies. Instruments are y_{it-j} for $j \geq 2$ and the second lags of $CONTROL$, $DEBT$, $CR6$, and $ASSET$. Asymptotic standard errors (reported in parentheses) are robust to general cross-section and time-series heteroskedasticity. *, **, *** indicates significance at the 0.10, 0.05, and 0.01 levels, respectively. For definitions, see Appendix.

Table 6.6. Robustness tests: different measures of capital structure interacted with competition

	Dependent variable: output growth (Δy_{it})					
	Model (6)		Model (6a)		Model (6b)	
Indep. variables		Interaction $RENT_{t-1}$		Interaction $RENT_{t-1}$		Interaction $RENT_{t-1}$
Δy_{t-1}	-0.025		-0.029		0.009	
	(0.130)		(0.126)		(0.150)	
Δl_t	0.833***		0.793***		0.838***	
	(0.166)		(0.153)		(0.168)	
Δk_t	0.467		0.541*		0.543	
	(0.328)		(0.307)		(0.336)	
$CYCLE_t$	0.012		0.014		0.012	
	(0.019)		(0.019)		(0.019)	
$CR6_{t-1}$	0.104		0.135		0.111	
	(0.097)		(0.104)		(0.100)	
$RENT_{t-1}$	0.168		0.731		-0.006	
	(0.246)		(0.540)		(0.352)	
$CONTROL_{t-1}$	0.255**	-0.757**	0.233**	-0.636**	0.290**	-0.837**
	(0.109)	(0.300)	(0.102)	(0.284)	(0.121)	(0.331)
$BANK_{t-1}$	0.484*	-1.019	0.486*	-0.682	0.464*	-0.773
	(0.277)	(0.783)	(0.289)	(0.798)	(0.279)	(0.803)
$DEBT_{t-1}$			0.177	-1.605		
			(0.486)	(1.415)		
$COVERAGE_{t-1}$					0.000	0.000
					(0.001)	(0.002)
$ASSET_{t-1}$	0.022		0.016		0.022	
	(0.015)		(0.013)		(0.016)	
$LISTED_t$	0.060**		0.053*		0.076**	
	(0.027)		(0.028)		(0.034)	
Number of obs.	3,647		3,647		3,628	
Instrument validity	p=0.153		p=0.161		p=0.285	
AR(1) of residuals	p=0.028		p=0.030		p=0.032	
AR(2) of residuals	p=0.486		p=0.512		p=0.193	
Const. ret. to scale	p=0.392		p=0.284		p=0.324	

Notes: GMM regression results relating measures of corporate governance and market discipline to productivity growth. Estimates are obtained using the Arellano and Bond (1991) method. All regressions include time and two-digit industry dummies. Instruments are y_{it-j} for $j \geq 2$ and the second lags of $CONTROL$, $DEBT$, $CR6$, and $ASSET$. Asymptotic standard errors (reported in parentheses) are robust to general cross-section and time-series heteroskedasticity. *, **, *** indicates significance at the 0.10, 0.05, and 0.01 levels, respectively. For definitions, see Appendix.

Table 6.7. Robustness tests: different measures of firm-level competition

	Dependent variable: output growth (Δy_{it})					
	Model (7)		Model (7a)		Model (7b)	
Indep. variables		Interaction $CONTR._{t-1}$		Interaction $CONTR._{t-1}$		Interaction $CONTR._{t-1}$
Δy_{t-1}	-0.025		-0.048		-0.004	
	(0.122)		(0.124)		(0.131)	
Δl_t	0.833***		0.828***		0.816***	
	(0.161)		(0.159)		(0.160)	
Δk_t	0.446*		0.296		-0.099	
	(0.248)		(0.216)		(0.195)	
$CYCLE_t$	0.012		0.011		0.009	
	(0.019)		(0.019)		(0.019)	
$CR6_{t-1}$	0.125		0.110		0.096	
	(0.094)		(0.091)		(0.088)	
$RENT_{t-1}$	0.130	-1.072***				
	(0.223)	(0.335)				
$RENTA_{t-1}$			0.289	-1.011***		
			(0.255)	(0.337)		
$RENTI_{t-1}$					-0.184	-0.608**
					(0.297)	(0.295)
$CONTROL_{t-1}$	0.367***		0.341***		0.203*	
	(0.118)		(0.116)		(0.105)	
$BANK_{t-1}$	0.082*		0.070		0.053	
	(0.047)		(0.048)		(0.048)	
$LOSS_{t-1}$	-1.924*		-1.760*		-1.041	
	(1.001)		(0.958)		(0.963)	
$BANK_{t-1}$	8.776**		8.831**		8.373**	
* $LOSS_{t-1}$	(3.726)		(3.751)		(3.844)	
$ASSET_{t-1}$	0.019*		0.017		0.010	
	(0.011)		(0.011)		(0.010)	
$LISTED_t$	0.063**		0.054**		0.043	
	(0.028)		(0.026)		(0.027)	
Number of obs.	3,647		3,647		3,647	
Instrument validity	p=0.377		p=0.265		p=0.576	
AR(1) of residuals	p=0.021		p=0.018		p=0.015	
AR(2) of residuals	p=0.513		p=0.432		p=0.435	
Const. ret. to scale	p=0.356		p=0.579		p=0.312	

Notes: GMM regression results relating measures of corporate governance and market discipline to productivity growth. Estimates are obtained using the Arellano and Bond (1991) method. All regressions include time and two-digit industry dummies. Instruments are y_{it-j} for $j \geq 2$ and the second lags of $CONTROL$, $DEBT$, $CR6$, and $ASSET$. Asymptotic standard errors (reported in parentheses) are robust to general cross-section and time-series heteroskedasticity. *, **, *** indicates significance at the 0.10, 0.05, and 0.01 levels, respectively. For definitions, see Appendix.

Table 6.8. Robustness tests: different measures of capital structure interacted with financial distress

	Dependent variable: output growth (Δy_{it})					
	Model (7)		Model (7c)		Model (7d)	
Indep. variables		Interaction $LOSS_{t-1}$		Interaction $LOSS_{t-1}$		Interaction $LOSS_{t-1}$
Δy_{t-1}	-0.025		-0.017		-0.016	
	(0.122)		(0.123)		(0.118)	
Δl_t	0.833***		0.852***		0.845***	
	(0.161)		(0.149)		(0.147)	
Δk_t	0.446*		0.512**		0.502**	
	(0.248)		(0.244)		(0.234)	
$CYCLE_t$	0.012		0.012		0.012	
	(0.019)		(0.019)		(0.018)	
$CR6_{t-1}$	0.125		0.130		0.138	
	(0.094)		(0.095)		(0.092)	
$RENT_{t-1}$	0.130		0.068		0.097	
	(0.223)		(0.231)		(0.237)	
$CONTROL_{t-1}$	0.367***		0.370***		0.372***	
	(0.118)		(0.122)		(0.122)	
$RENT_{t-1}$	-1.072***		-1.049***		-1.074***	
$* CONTROL_{t-1}$	(0.335)		(0.346)		(0.350)	
$LOSS_{t-1}$	-1.924*		-1.119		-1.732	
	(1.001)		(1.969)		(1.117)	
$BANK_{t-1}$	0.082*	8.776**	0.161**	9.488**	0.117	9.365**
	(0.047)	(3.726)	(0.081)	(4.172)	(0.084)	(3.929)
$DEBT_{t-1}$			-0.215	-1.780		
			(0.144)	(4.283)		
$LEVERAGE_{t-1}$					-0.021	-0.108
					(0.041)	(0.447)
$ASSET_{t-1}$	0.019*		0.020*		0.020*	
	(0.011)		(0.010)		(0.011)	
$LISTED_t$	0.063**		0.062**		0.061**	
	(0.028)		(0.028)		(0.027)	
Number of obs.	3,647		3,647		3,647	
Instrument validity	p=0.377		p=0.254		p=0.269	
AR(1) of residuals	p=0.021		p=0.024		p=0.022	
AR(2) of residuals	p=0.513		p=0.497		p=0.500	
Const. ret. to scale	p=0.356		p=0.216		p=0.230	

Notes: GMM regression results relating measures of corporate governance and market discipline to productivity growth. Estimates are obtained using the Arellano and Bond (1991) method. All regressions include time and two-digit industry dummies. Instruments are y_{it-j} for $j \geq 2$ and the second lags of $CONTROL$, $DEBT$, $CR6$, and $ASSET$. Asymptotic standard errors (reported in parentheses) are robust to general cross-section and time-series heteroskedasticity. *, **, *** indicates significance at the 0.10, 0.05, and 0.01 levels, respectively. For definitions, see Appendix.

disciplinary effect of financial pressure is consistent with evidence from Germany on the early 1970s (Cable, 1985), and with recent evidence from the US (Zingales, 1998), the UK (Nickell and Nicolitsas, 1999), and Belgium (Renneboog, 2000).

We cannot confirm that the type of the ultimate owner has a particular impact on productivity growth. Likewise, we do not find evidence that complex ownership structures (e.g., cross ownership or pyramid structures) or large board size have an adverse impact on performance. One reason for the insignificant relation of board size and performance could be that the size of German supervisory boards is tightly regulated by law. Hence, board size is likely to be determined by other factors such as firm size and industry, not necessarily by considerations regarding optimal governance structure. In summary, our results suggest that corporate governance (ownership and capital structure of a firm) as well as market discipline (product market competition) are important governance devices. The combination of these mechanisms forms the basis for higher productivity growth.

Our findings have implications for future empirical research. First, we find a positive impact of ownership concentration on productivity growth, but only when we consider ownership at the ultimate level, not at the direct level. This suggests that *ultimate* ownership matters, not *direct* ownership. Hence, studies relying on measures of direct ownership, which are typically more easily to obtain, might come to misleading results. Second, we find that ownership concentration does not affect productivity growth when not taking into account product market competition. Only when additionally using competition measures and their interaction with measures of corporate governance, we find a significant impact. This is a good example of a missing variables problem (see Chapter 2.3). Hence, studies investigating only one or a few of all mechanisms, which potentially affect productivity growth, might come to misleading results as well.

7 Concluding Remarks

This study makes two contributions. First, we assemble a unique database – the German Corporations Database (GCD) – that provides a solid basis for corporate governance analysis in Germany (Chapter 3). Compared with previously available data sets, GCD is less likely to suffer from selectivity bias because it includes listed and non-listed corporations, private as well as public. In addition, GCD allows to avoid common methodological drawbacks of previous studies such as endogeneity or missing variables because it is a large unbalanced panel and because it contains a much richer set of information on all relevant corporate governance mechanisms.

Second, guided by methodological lessons from previous empirical work (Chapter 2) this study explores three specific topics of corporate governance that have not been covered sufficiently before and are crucial to our understanding of corporate governance: the frequency, causes, and consequences of control transfers (Chapter 4), the determinants of acquisition and failure (Chapter 5), and the role of corporate governance and market discipline for productivity growth (Chapter 6). Essentially, these studies are a direct application of GCD. The main results are summarized in Chapter 1; detailed results are provided at the end of each of the Chapters 4–6. In this final chapter we derive some tentative conclusions from the empirical results presented in this study. In particular, we discuss implications for economic policy, implications for the design of empirical studies of corporate governance, and requirements for data that would allow to examine other important issues in corporate governance, but are currently not available in Germany.

Implications for Economic Policy

The findings of this study have implications for economic policy. They can be described as follows:

For Germany it might be necessary to extend the new Law on Securities Purchases and Takeovers[1] *to non-listed (public) corporations.* Chapter 4 shows that the frequency of control transfers in corporate Germany is greater than often assumed. It is comparable to those observed for other countries.

[1] Wertpapiererwerbs- und Übernahmegesetz.

Interestingly, the rate of control transfers is also similar for listed and non-listed German corporations. However, the new Law on Securities Purchases and Takeovers, coming into effect in the year 2002, covers only listed firms. This takeover code intends to establish a framework for fair and transparent transactions of large share blocks, to ensure an equal level of information to be provided to all the target's shareholders and workers, and to hinder price discrimination against target's minority shareholders. Therefore, this law is an important step forward. But since non-listed (public) corporations have minority shareholders as well (Chapter 4.3.1), it is not obvious why these firms are not covered by this law and do not receive similar minority shareholder protection.[2]

For other European countries it might be recommendable to reduce the transaction costs associated with block trades, similar to the repeal of the corporate capital gains tax in Germany. A key finding from Chapter 5 is that poorly performing firms are more likely to be acquired. This result is consistent with the notion that acquisitions can play an important governance role. At the same time, we find that firms with complex ownership structures, reflected for example in cross ownership, are less likely to experience an acquisition. This indicates that ownership complexity acts as a takeover deterrent. In most European countries capital gains from sales of corporate assets are subject to the regular corporate tax. Lang et al. (2001) argue that this tax increases the transaction costs associated with block trades and therefore acts as a barrier to efficient allocation of ownership and investment. In Germany, from January 2002 on these capital gains will be tax-free. This change in the tax system could, at least in the next few years, induce a significant reallocation of corporate assets. For example, financial conglomerates, which are still heavily involved in cross ownership, can capitalize hidden reserves and strategically refocus their portfolio. These arguments are confirmed by a recent survey among 277 financial analysts: An overwhelming majority of 90% of these experts expect an increase in acquisitions and divestitures activity from the year 2002 on, and about 87% expect that banks as well as insurers will gain the most from this measure (Köke, 2001e). In a macroeconomic perspective, reducing the transaction costs associated with block trades can support structural change, and thus be recommendable for other continental European countries where corporate ownership is often complex as well; see Becht et al. (2001) for Belgium and Bloch and Kremp (2001) for France.

Competition in product markets should be fostered. An important finding from Chapter 6 is that firms operating in markets with intense competition tend to experience higher productivity growth. Since product market competition generally is less intense in continental Europe than in the US

[2] In contrast to the owners of a public corporation (*AG*), owners of a private corporation (*GmbH*) have a legally secured right to command information on all matters concerning the corporation (§51a GmbHG). In this sense, an abuse of minority rights is less likely for a private corporation.

(Börsch-Supan, 1999), there is still room for policy action. Most importantly, remaining obstacles to an integrated Internal Market should be removed.

Economic policy should take a neutral position towards concentrated versus dispersed ownership. The results from Chapter 6 also show that this beneficial impact of competition only holds for firms under concentrated ownership. Hence, tight shareholder control appears to be a precondition for this competition effect to materialize in higher growth rates of productivity. Moreover, results from Chapter 5 show that firms under concentrated ownership are less likely to fail than firms under dispersed ownership. These findings are consistent with Shleifer and Vishny (1986) who predict that the incentive to monitor management is positively related to shareholder concentration. One might conclude that economic policy should encourage concentrated ownership. However, we also find that some degree of ownership dispersion makes changes in ownership more likely. As mentioned above, such ownership changes can be an essential governance device. Other advantages of dispersed ownership are access to a larger pool of investors as well as higher liquidity of the firm's stock; the latter typically is an important selection criterion for institutional investors. Taken together, there are advantages to concentrated as well as to dispersed ownership, and the recommendation for policy can only be to take a neutral position. Unilateral promotion of an Anglo-Saxon type (typically dispersed) ownership structure can be wrong, in particular because some characteristics of the German system of corporate finance are still not well understood. For example, large conglomerates combine tight owner control with access to an internal capital market, which can play a key role for financing investment (Hellwig, 2001).

Economic policy should react to foreseeable changes in corporate ownership by ensuring a fair treatment of minority shareholders. Finally, the results from Chapter 6 suggest that also creditors enhance productivity growth, in particular for firms in financial distress. While we do not explicitly test for the impact of 'housebank' relations, our results suggest that lending relationships in Germany cannot simply be dismissed as too inflexible and outdated, as often argued. But we also find that this beneficial impact of creditors depends on a strong creditor position, measured as a large fraction of bank debt. This implies that reduced bank lending, for example as a consequence from increased securitization of loans, could negatively affect the banks' incentives or ability to monitor. One way to address a potential decline in monitoring by creditors could be to strengthen other parties involved in corporate governance. In the US and the UK we observe an increasingly active participation of small shareholders, often called 'shareholder activism'. Mostly these investors are financial institutions such as pension funds, which hold blocks well below 5%. But the largest of them appear to be able to influence particular corporate decisions, for example through private negotiations (Smith, 1996; Carleton et al., 1998). Although the evidence regarding the impact of institutional investors on performance is mixed,[3] the general trend towards more institutional investment is clear (Blommestein, 1998). For Germany, the transition from the current pay-as-you-go pension system to a partially funded system is likely to spur this development (Börsch-Supan and Winter, 1999). Hence, to strengthen corporate governance the bottom line for policy is to ensure a fair treatment of minority shareholders.

Implications for Research Design

The findings of this study have implications for the design of future empirical studies on corporate governance. They can be summarized as follows:

Panel data, particularly on ownership structures, are essential to avoid problems of structural reverse causality or spurious correlation. The analysis of the market for large share blocks (Chapter 4) shows that ownership structures in Germany exhibit significant variation over time. This implies that using cross-section data on ownership is not sufficient to explain variation in performance because any unobserved variation in ownership will be included in the error term. But correlation of the error term with (observed) cross-section data on ownership will cause coefficients to be biased and inconsistent. Similarly, explaining firm performance without data on ownership, but instead applying fixed-effect models to account for unobserved firm heterogeneity will also yield biased and inconsistent coefficients because unobserved (ownership) variables are *not* fixed over time.

Data on listed as well as non-listed firms are essential to avoid selection bias. The results from Chapter 4 also show that the control transfer process works differently in listed and non-listed firms. For example, complex ownership structures limit control changes only in non-listed firms. This indicates that empirical studies focusing on listed firms tend to underestimate the impact of ownership complexity on control transfers.

Analyses that model sample attrition should examine acquisition as well as failure simultaneously. The results from Chapter 5 point to a second potential source of selection bias. We find that acquisition and failure of sample firms are determined by common factors. Both events are important sources of sample attrition. Hence, examining one source but disregarding the other is likely to bias estimation results. Modelling sample attrition appropriately requires accurate information on the reason for sample exit.

To avoid problems of missing variables, it is important to analyze simultaneously the impact of all relevant governance mechanisms (including product market competition) and their interaction. A key result of Chapter 6 is that firms under concentrated ownership tend to show higher productivity growth,

[3] See Black (1998) and Karpoff (1998) for surveys. See del Guercio and Hawkins (1999) and Faccio and Lasfer (2000) for more recent evidence on the US and the UK, respectively.

and this effect is larger for firms operating in more competitive markets. However, we find no evidence of a beneficial impact of ownership concentration as long as not taking into account product market competition. This is a good example of a missing variables problem.

To reduce problems of measurement error, the crucial task is to measure all variables correctly. While this advise seems obvious, it is often not obvious which variable is incorrectly measured. For example, studies on corporate governance mostly measure ownership at the *direct* level. But theoretical considerations in Chapter 2 suggest that for Germany ownership should be measured at the *ultimate* level. Results from Chapter 6 confirm that ultimate ownership matters for productivity growth, not direct ownership. Since direct ownership is typically not perfectly correlated with ultimate ownership, it is incorrectly measured. A major obstacle for research, however, is that such data on ultimate firm ownership are not readily available. As explained below, a lack of appropriate data also limits future research on other important aspects of corporate governance.

Need for High-Quality Data

Finally, the empirical analyses of this study reveal some limitations of the data currently available for Germany. These limitations are serious because they constrain studies on new and essential issues in corporate governance.

There is a need for a firm panel based on plant-level data, similar to the Longitudinal Research Database in the US. The most difficult and time-consuming part of assembling GCD was to collect information on the full ownership structure of sample firms and to track them over time. Understanding firm dynamics is important because the reallocation of corporate assets plays a key role for economic change. While this study is the first to examine dynamics in ultimate firm ownership for Germany, it is only a first step. For example, currently available data do not allow to consistently track firms at the plant-level over time. This would be important because changes in ownership occur more frequently for smaller firms (Chapters 4 and 5) and because all subsidiaries of a conglomerate could be assigned to their respective industry (which would reduce measurement error considerably). In the US, such data are available in the Longitudinal Research Database (LRD), maintained by the Center for Economic Studies at the Bureau of Census. A recent study by Maksimovic and Phillips (2001) exploits these data. They find that conglomerates tend to sell peripheral plants with low productivity, and that productivity improves after reallocating these assets to new owners. In contrast, single-plant firms are sold when they are more productive, and productivity does not increase after the sale. For Germany, such analysis is currently impossible; nevertheless, it is important because firm dynamics also affect employment and the efficiency in the allocation of resources. And such analysis will become even more important when the repeal of the corporate capital gains tax, effective from the year 2002 on, increases the number of acquisitions and divestitures, as discussed above.

There is a need for panel data on ownership and voting rights of small investors (such as pension funds). A second constraint to assembling GCD was that German firms were required to disclose the distribution of ownership rights, but not the distribution of voting rights during most of the sample years. Although we are confident that in the vast majority of sample firms voting rights coincide with ownership rights, as explained in Chapter 4.2.2, using voting rights data could be interesting in particular for the largest firms, which typically show dispersed ownership. Here, proxy voting of banks might be significant. For Germany, information on voting rights representation at the general meeting of shareholders is accessible only at local courts. Edwards and Nibler (2000) make the effort to collect these data for 156 large firms in the year 1992. Unfortunately, such cross-section data are not sufficient to examine the dynamics in voting behavior. This is not a minor issue. In recent years, institutional investors, domestic as well as from abroad, are taking stock in German corporations (Steiger, 2000). As mentioned above, this growing class of investors could effectively monitor management by acting in coalitions or by putting firms under public pressure. For Germany, there are no systematic data on institutional ownership or voting rights because the individual stakes are typically below the threshold of 5% that triggers compulsory disclosure (Law for Transparency and Control). Similarly, there are no consistent data on shareholder proposals as they are available in the US (del Guercio and Hawkins, 1999). But understanding the contribution of institutional investors to improving corporate governance will become even more important in light of the changing system of social security.

Appendix

For better handling, the German Corporations Database (GCD) is split into several smaller data sets. Each of these data sets covers a specific topic of empirical research on corporate governance. These topics are: ownership structure, capital structure, board structure, and structure of the firms' product markets. Additional data sets contain information on performance, market exit behavior, other firm-specific characteristics (e.g. firm size and firm age), and macroeconomic indicators (e.g. interest rates and prices for inputs and outputs). The structure of GCD is depicted in Figure 3.1 of Chapter 3.2.

In the following, we describe the content of each of these data sets and provide definitions of all variables contained. The variable names used below (`variable`) are identical with those used in GCD. Firm years are exactly identified with the two variables `nummer`, the firm identifier, and `year`, the year for a particular observation. Macroeconomic data (contained in the file `macro.dta`) are to be merged using `year`. As far as ratios are used, these ratios have been truncated at the 1- and 99-percentile to avoid bias resulting from potential outliers. A dummy `Xt` indicates for each firm year whether the variable `X` has been truncated in that particular firm year or not. For example, if `borrowt` is equal to one, this means that for the particular observation the borrowing ratio (`borrow`) is truncated.

Measuring Performance

To measure firm performance we use a range of variables because it is not clear from a theoretical point of view how performance ought to be measured. The performance measures in GCD are based either on accounting or capital market data. Table A.1 summarizes those measures.

Our key measure of operating surplus is earnings before interest, taxes, and depreciation (`ebitda`). If measured using the standard accounting definition, this quantity contains a number of balance-sheet items that can potentially distort the economic content of this variable, resulting in measures of EBITDA that are downward-biased measures of operating surplus. This problem is particularly severe in Germany where firms are entitled to retain a large fraction of earnings to build up reserves. Therefore we prefer an economic definition that measures operating surplus as sales less expenses for

Table A.1. Variables measuring performance

Variable	Definition
EBITDA (`ebitda`)	Sales less costs for labor and materials (economic definition)
EBITDA2 (`ebitda2`)	Profit on ordinary and extraordinary activities plus interest and depreciation (accounting definition)
Return on assets (ROA) (`roaat`)	EBITDA/total assets
Change in ROA (`droaat`)	$\Delta ROA_t = ROA_t - ROA_{t-1}$
Return on equity (ROE) (`roeat`)	EBITDA/total equity
Change in ROE (`droeat`)	$\Delta ROE_t = ROE_t - ROE_{t-1}$
Return on sales (ROS) (`rosat`)	EBITDA/total sales
Cash flow on equity (`cfeqt`)	(EBITDA + change in working capital)/total equity
Cash flow on assets (`cfast`)	(EBITDA + change in working capital)/total assets
Market-to-book ratio (`marat`)	Market value of equity/book value of equity
Stock market return (`yearrent`)	Continuous yearly return $R_t^c = \sum_{w=1}^{n} \frac{R_w^c}{n} * 52$, where continuous weekly return $R_w^c = ln(\frac{K_w^p}{K_{w-1}^p})$ and K_w^p price on Wednesday of week w. K_w^p is corrected for changes in capital and stock's face value, stock splits, and dividends.
Operating loss (1 year) (`lossc`)	$lossc_t = 1$ if EBITDA is negative in t, zero otherwise
Operating loss (2 years) (`loss`)	$loss_t = 1$ if EBITDA is negative in t and $t-1$, zero otherwise
Growth rate of sales (`rsales`)	$rsales = \frac{sales_t - sales_{t-1}}{sales_{t-1}}$
Total factor productivity (`resid`)	Residual from OLS estimation of Cobb-Douglas production function, $y = \alpha + \beta_K k + \beta_L l$, where y=ln(value added), k=ln(replacement costs of tangible assets), and l=ln(total number of employees). Value added and capital stock are deflated using appropriate price indices. Time and two-digit industry dummies are included.
Labor productivity (`lprodv lprods`)	Value added/labor; total sales/labor
Capital productivity (`cprodv cprods`)	Value added/capital; total sales/capital

labor and materials; see also Lehmann and Weigand (2000). Nevertheless, the database contains the accounting version of EBITDA as well (Table A.1).

Note that GCD not only contains the absolute value of each performance measure but also two types of relative measures. First, most variables are adjusted for median industry performance to correct for industry differentials in the level of performance. These variables are denoted similarly. For example, `roaat` denotes return on assets in year *t*, measured in absolute value, and `roait` denotes industry-adjusted return on assets in year *t*, calculated as `roaat` less the median value of return on assets in the respective two-digit industry. Second, most variables are adjusted for median performance in the same accounting year to correct for cyclical movements in the level of performance. Analogously, `roart` denotes year-adjusted return on assets in year *t*, calculated as `roaat` less the median value of return on assets in that year. For annual stock market return this adjustment is slightly different. Here, `yearrent` denotes the absolute value of return, while `rmkat` denotes a market-adjusted return using `dafox`, the market index provided by the University of Karlsruhe (see Chapter 3.1). Industry-adjusted return is denoted as `ricap`, calculated as `yearrent` less the median return in the respective two-digit industry.

The data set labeled `perform.dta` contains the following measures of performance, which can be merged to the other subsamples using `nummer` and `year`:

```
ebitda ebitda2
roaat roart roait roaatt roartt roaitt
droaat droart droait droaatt droartt droaitt
roeat roert roeit roeatt roertt roeitt
droeat droert droeit droeatt droertt droeitt
rosat rosrt rosit rosatt rosrtt rositt
cfeqt cfeqrt cfeqit cfeqtt cfeqrtt cfeqitt
cfast cfasrt cfasit cfastt cfasrtt cfasitt
marat marrt marit maratt marrtt maritt
yearrent yearret rmkat ricap dafox
lossc loss rsales rsalest resid
lprods lprodst lprodv lprodvt
cprods cprodst cprodv cprodvt
```

Measuring Ownership Structure

To measure firms' ownership structure, GCD uses the concept of ultimate ownership. This concept is described in detail in Chapter 4.2.2. It allows to classify firms according to the type of their ultimate owner. Table A.2 summarizes the variables that describe the firms' ownership structure, and Table A.3 defines the shareholder categories used in GCD.

The data set labeled `owner.dta` contains the following measures of ownership structure, which can be merged to the other subsamples using `nummer` and `year`:

```
block block3 blockall
c1ndla1 c1ndla2 c1ndla3 c1ndla4 c1ndla5 c1ndla6 c1ndla7
c2ndla1 c2ndla2 c2ndla3 c2ndla4 c2ndla5 c2ndla6 c2ndla7
c3ndla1 c3ndla2 c3ndla3 c3ndla4 c3ndla5 c3ndla6 c3ndla7
c4ndla1 c4ndla2 c4ndla3 c4ndla4 c4ndla5 c4ndla6 c4ndla7
c5ndla1 c5ndla2 c5ndla3 c5ndla4 c5ndla5 c5ndla6 c5ndla7
c6ndla1 c6ndla2 c6ndla3 c6ndla4 c6ndla5 c6ndla6 c6ndla7
c7ndla1 c7ndla2 c7ndla3 c7ndla4 c7ndla5 c7ndla6 c7ndla7
c9ndla1 c9ndla2 c9ndla3 c9ndla4 c9ndla5 c9ndla6 c9ndla7
c10ndla1 c10ndla2 c10ndla3 c10ndla4 c10ndla5 c10ndla6 c10ndla7
c11ndla1 c11ndla2 c11ndla3 c11ndla4 c11ndla5 c11ndla6 c11ndla7
c12ndla1 c12ndla2 c12ndla3 c12ndla4 c12ndla5 c12ndla6 c12ndla7
c13ndla1 c13ndla2 c13ndla3 c13ndla4 c13ndla5 c13ndla6 c13ndla7
c14ndla1 c14ndla2 c14ndla3 c14ndla4 c14ndla5 c14ndla6 c14ndla7
c1ndsum c2ndsum c3ndsum c4ndsum c5ndsum c6ndsum c7ndsum c9ndsum
c10ndsum c11ndsum c12ndsum c13ndsum c14ndsum c61ndsum
ckat11 ckat12 ckat13 ckat14 ckat61
herf cubbin95 cubbin99 control ctyp kontrole cross pyramid cname
```

A major advantage of the panel structure for ownership data contained in GCD is that changes in ownership can be calculated. Table A.4 describes the variables that are used to measure these changes.

The data set labeled `downer.dta` contains the following measures of changes in ownership, which can be merged to the other subsamples using `nummer` and `year`:

```
inew1nd inew2nd inew3nd inew4nd inew5nd inew7nd
inew11nd inew12nd inew13nd inew61nd
iold1nd iold2nd iold3nd iold4nd iold5nd iold7nd
iold11nd iold12nd iold13nd iold61nd
dold1nd dold2nd dold3nd dold4nd dold5nd dold7nd
dold11nd dold12nd dold13nd dold61nd
inewnd ioldnd doldnd dcontrol newtyp oldtyp
```

Measuring Capital Structure

Table A.5 summarizes the variables that describe the firms' capital structure and liquidity status.

Table A.2. Variables measuring ownership structure

Variable	Definition
Largest block (`block`)	Size of largest share block at direct level
Three largest blocks (`block3`)	Sum of three largest share blocks at direct level
All large blocks (`blockall`)	Sum of all large share blocks at direct level
X'th largest block in Y (`cXndlaY`)	Size of X'th largest share block in (ultimate) shareholder category Y
Sum of all large blocks in Y (`cYndsum`)	Sum of all large blocks in (ultimate) shareholder category Y
Type of ultimate owner (`ckatY`)	Dummy indicating whether ultimate owner is of category Y
Herfindahl index (`herf`)	$herf = \sum_{j=1}^{n} P_j^2$, where P_j size of individual block
Cubbin and Leech index (`cubbinX`)	$cubbinX = 1$ if probability exceeds X percent that largest shareholder wins a vote, zero otherwise: $\alpha = \Phi(\frac{block}{\sqrt{herf-block^2}})$, where X is 95% or 99%
Control (`control`)	$control = 1$ if firm has ultimately controlling shrh. based on concept of control, zero otherwise
Ultimate owner (type) (`ctyp`)	Type of ultimate shrh. that sells control block
Level of control (`kontrole`)	Level of the end of a control chain in pyramids. For $kontrole = 1$, control resides with direct shrh.
Cross ownership (`cross`)	$cross = 1$ if ultimate owner is part of the web of firms identified by Wenger and Kaserer (1998) and if ultimate owner indirectly owns share block in itself, zero otherwise
Pyramid (`pyramid`)	$pyramid = 1$ if level of control is larger than two, zero otherwise
Ultimate owner (name) (`cname`)	Name of ultimate owner

Table A.3. Shareholder categories

Category	Definition
1	Holding companies (Vermögensverwaltungsges., Beteiligungsges.)
2	Banks
3	Insurance companies
4	Investment funds
5	Industrial and commercial companies
6	Individuals and families not related to a director including privately held companies in the legal form of KG and OHG
7	Government authorities
9	Executive directors (members of management board)
10	Non-executive directors (members of supervisory board)
11	All individuals (sum of 6, 9, and 10)
12	All financial firms (sum of 2, 3, and 4)
13	All non-financial firms (sum of 1 and 5)
14	All directors, i.e. insiders (sum of 9 and 10)
61	Dispersed shares and shares not attributable to any category

Notes: A distiction between executive directors, non-executive directors, and other individuals not owning shares is possible only for the years 1986–1994.

The data set labeled `capital.dta` contains the following measures of capital structure, which can be merged to the other subsamples using **`nummer`** and **`year`**:

```
borrow borrowt debt coverage covert leverage levert
nowork work workt curr currt quick quickt
```

Measuring Board Structure

To describe the firms' board structure, GCD contains information on the management board (*Vorstand*) as well as the supervisory board (*Aufsichtsrat*), which in Germany are legally separate entities. This information refers to the size and composition of both boards, and also to changes in board structure. Table A.6 summarizes the respective variables.

Note that in Germany the number of directors on the supervisory board is regulated by law, with a minimum of three and a maximum of 21 members; see Hopt (1997) for details. Determining the minimum number of directors is a complex process because different laws are to be applied, depending on firm size and industry (Stock Corporation Law; Iron and Steel Codetermination

Table A.4. Variables measuring changes in ownership structure

Variable	Definition
Increase by new shareholder (**inewYnd**)	Sum of blocks purchased by new (ultimate) shareholders in category Y
Increase by old shareholder (**ioldYnd**)	Sum of blocks purchased by old (ultimate) shareholders in category Y
Decrease by old shareholder (**ioldYnd**)	Sum of blocks sold by old (ultimate) shareholders in category Y
Total increase by new shareholder (**inewnd**)	Sum of blocks purchased by new (ultimate) shareholders across all shareh. categories
Total increase by old shareholder (**ioldnd**)	Sum of blocks purchased by old (ultimate) shareholders across all shareh. categories
Total decrease by old shareholder (**ioldnd**)	Sum of blocks sold by old (ultimate) shareholders across all shareh. categories
Change in control (**dcontrol**)	$dcontrol = 1$ if ultimate shareholder changes, zero otherwise
Buying ultimate owner (**newtyp**)	Type of ultimate shareholder that buys control block
Selling ultimate owner (**oldtyp**)	Type of ultimate shareholder that sells control block

Table A.5. Variables measuring capital structure

Variable	Definition
Borrowing ratio (**borrow**)	Interest payments/EBITDA
Debt-to-assets ratio (**debt**)	Total debt to total assets
Interest coverage (**coverage**)	EBITDA/interest payments
Leverage (**leverage**)	Total debt/total equity
Negative working capital (**nowork**)	$nowork = 1$ if current assets smaller than current liabilities, zero otherwise
Working capital ratio (**work**)	(Current assets less current liabilities)/total assets
Current ratio (**curr**)	Current assets/short-term liabilities
Quick ratio (**quick**)	(Current assets less inventories)/short-term liabilities

Law, 1951; Amendment to Codetermination Law, 1967; Law on Codetermination, 1976).[1] In addition, a firm belonging to a group company (*Konzern*) can be subject to codetermination laws and therefore must comply with different requirements regarding board size, even when firm size is smaller than the thresholds specified in codetermination laws. However, a group company cannot be identified from our data; groups can only be identified by consulting individual corporate charters, which have not been available to us when constructing GCD. Therefore, the dummy indicating whether a supervisory board is larger than the legally prescribed size (`small`) might contain some classification error, particularly for subsidiaries of conglomerates.

Table A.6. Variables measuring board structure

Variable	Definition
Supervisory board (`board`)	$board = 1$ if supervisory board exists, zero otherwise
Size of supervisory board (`bsize`)	Number of non-executive directors N_t
Small supervisory board (`small`)	$small = 1$ if number of directors on supervisory board is equal to legal minimum, zero otherwise
Size of management board (`execdir`)	Number of executive directors E_t
Union representation (`dstaker`)	Fraction of union representatives on supervisory board
Turnover of CEO (`turceo`)	$turceo_t = 1$ if chairman of managerial board changes from year $t-1$ to t, zero otherwise
Turnover of Chairman (`turchair`)	$turchair_t = 1$ if chairman of supervisory board changes from year $t-1$ to t, zero otherwise
Turnover of executive directors (`rexec`)	$\frac{J_t+L_t}{E_t+E_{t-1}}$, where J_t (L_t) number of joining (leaving) exec. directors and E_t number of exec. directors
Turnover of non-executive directors (`rdir`)	$\frac{J_t+L_t}{N_t+N_{t-1}}$, where J_t (L_t) number of joining (leaving) non-exec. dirs. and N_t number of non-exec. dirs.

The data set labeled `board.dta` contains the following measures of board structure, which can be merged to the other subsamples using `nummer` and `year`:

```
board bsize small execdir dstaker
turceo turchair rexec rdir
```

[1] *Aktiengesetz; Montan-Mitbestimmungsgesetz, 1951; Mitbestimmungs-Ergänzungsgesetz, 1967; Mitbestimmungsgesetz, 1976.*

Measuring Corporate Restructuring

To examine the impact of changes in corporate governance or changes in the firms' environment, measures on corporate restructuring can be useful. Table A.7 summarizes the respective measures contained in GCD, in particular sales of assets, employee layoffs, and cost cutting.

Table A.7. Variables measuring corporate restructuring

Variable	Definition
Sales of assets (`ssac smas sgru sfin sbet swpd`)	$s_{jt} = \frac{S_{jt}}{T_{jt}}$, where S_{jt} sales of asset class j in year t and T_{jt} stock of asset class j at the beginning of year t. The following asset classes are included: total fixed assets (`ssac`), machinery (`smas`), real estate and housing (`sgru`), total financial assets (`sfin`), equity holdings (`sbet`), and other securities (`swpd`)
Growth rate of employment (`rlabor`)	$n_t = \frac{N_t - N_{t-1}}{N_{t-1}}$, where N_t total number of employees
Growth rate of labor costs (`dperso`)	$c_t = \frac{C_t - C_{t-1}}{C_{t-1}}$,where C_t total labor expenditures

The data set labeled `restruct.dta` contains the following measures of restructuring, which can be merged to the other subsamples using `nummer` and `year`:

```
ssac smas sgru sfin sbet swpd
rlabor dperso
```

Measuring Product Market Competition

The intensity of product market competition is measured both at the industry and at the firm level. Table A.8 summarizes the respective variables.

At the industry level, competition is measured using measures of domestic producer concentration (`cr6`, `hhi`) and a measure of competition from abroad (`import`). At the firm level, the intensity of competition is measured using the firm's rent from production, which can be interpreted as an ex post measure of market power. The motivation for using this measure is that firms operating in less competitive markets should be able to sell their products well above marginal cost, and therefore earn higher rents after covering their expenses (on capital, labor, and materials). The abstract definition of production rents, R_t, is as follows:

Table A.8. Variables measuring product market competition

Variable	Definition
Industry concentration I (`cr6`)	Market share of six largest suppliers in four-digit industry
Industry concentration II (`hhi`)	Herfindahl index of all suppliers in four-digit industry
Import penetration (`import`)	Value of imports divided by sum of domestic production and imports in two-digit industry
Firm-specific rent (`rentXY`)	Ex post rents from production, where X and Y denote alternative definitions (see below)

$$R_t = \frac{S_t - r_t^K p_t^K K_t}{Q_t} \,. \tag{A.1}$$

The denominator, Q_t, is real output measured as real value added, $\frac{Y_t}{p_t^Y} - \frac{M_t}{p_t^M}$, or real total sales, $\frac{Y_t}{p_t^Y}$. The numerator is a measure of the firm's real operating surplus measured as EBITDA, S_t, less real cost of capital, $\frac{r_t^K K_t}{p_t^K}$. In this notation, Y_t is nominal output, L_t, K_t, and M_t are nominal labor, capital, and materials inputs, while p_t^Y, p_t^L, p_t^K, and p_t^M are the corresponding prices. Finally, r_t^K is the user cost of capital, defined as $r_t^K = \delta + r_t$, where δ is the depreciation rate and r_t is the risk-free market interest rate. Taking either real value added or real sales as denominator in equation (A.1), rent is denoted as `rentv` or `rents`, respectively.

To address potential endogeneity issues, we calculate the average of the firm's rents over the past two years. This time aggregation should smooth short-run firm-specific shocks that affect output directly and hence affect rents. Rent is denoted as `rentva` or `rentsa`, respectively. In addition, we calculate the year-specific average of firm-specific rents across the respective two- or three-digit industry. This cross-sectional aggregation also wipes out firm-specific shocks, and therefore avoids potential endogeneity problems associated with the rent variable. Using real value added as the denominator, rent is denoted as `rentvx2` or `rentvx3`, respectively. Using real sales as the denominator, rent is denoted as `rentsx2` or `rentsx3`, respectively.

The data set labeled `comp.dta` contains the following measures of competition, which can be merged to the other subsamples using `nummer` and `year`:

```
cr6 hhi import
rentv rentva rentvx2 rentvx3
rents rentsa rentsx2 rentsx3
```

Measuring Reason for Non-Reporting

GCD contains information on the reason for why time series of balance sheet data end before the end of the panel. As described in Chapter 3.1, we identify the reason for non-reporting by searching the Mannheim Company Database (MUP), by interviewing people from Hoppenstedt, and by conducting telephone interviews with the firm in consideration or with its last owner. In total, interrupted time series of balance sheet data occur for 1,816 firms out of the 2,959 firms contained in GCD. For all cases, information on the reason for non-reporting is collected.

However, the obtained data have two problems: First, the information turned out to be unreliable when at the same time detailed information on ownership structure was lacking for a particular firm. Specifically, the survey respondents often reported a change in ownership when in fact the *ultimate* owner did not change, but only the *direct* owner. This difference is important because, as argued in Chapter 4.2.2, the concept of ultimate ownership should be applied when assembling ownership information. Hence, detailed information on ownership for the years before balance sheet data end is essential. Second, for a large fraction of non-listed firms there is no balance sheet information for the year 1997 because the BSD release was still incomplete at the time of purchase by ZEW. This could introduce a bias when the balance sheet data are missing not randomly. To obtain reliable data on the reason for non-reporting, we focus on firms that (1) have ownership information and (2) have ending time series for any year before 1996.

This resulting subsample consists of 1,535 firms (9,000 firm years) for the years 1986–1996. By definition, a sample exit can occur only before 1996.[2] Table A.9 shows the variable used to describe the reason for non-reporting.

Table A.9. Variable measuring reason for non-reporting

Reason for non-reporting (`reason`)	Reason for time series of balance sheet data ending before 1996 (0 ongoing without major change in ownership; 1 non-voluntary liquidation or bankruptcy; 2 takeover; 3 voluntary liquidation

The data set labeled `exit.dta` contains this measure of non-reporting, which can be merged to the other subsamples using `nummer` and `year`:

`reason`

[2] For the incidence of sample exit and the respective reason, see Chapter 5.2.

Measuring Other Firm-Specific Variables

Finally, GCD contains general information on each sample firm as well as some important balance sheet items. Table A.10 summarizes the respective measures.

In total, GCD contains six different measures of capital stock. This allows the researcher to test whether empirical results are sensitive against particular assumptions underlying the construction of the capital stock measures. All measures of capital stock are defined as replacement costs of tangible assets, and all measures use a perpetual inventory method.

In general, the firm's capital stock, K_t, is defined as replacement costs of tangible assets including machines, buildings, and land, deflated using a combined input price index for capital goods and land, weighted by their empirical distribution (Statistisches Bundesamt, Fachserie 17, Reihe 2, and Fachserie 17, Reihe 4, 1998). Replacement costs of capital are calculated using the method of Bond et al. (1999). They adjust the historical cost values for inflation and then apply a perpetual inventory method with a constant annual depreciation rate of $\delta = 0.08$. Specifically,

$$p_t^K K_t = (1-\delta) p_{t-1}^K K_{t-1} \frac{p_t^K}{p_{t-1}^K} + p_t^K I_t \,, \tag{A.2}$$

where K_t is the capital stock, p_t^K is the price index for capital goods, I_t is real investment, and δ the depreciation rate. The starting value is the net book value of tangible assets, adjusted for inflation in previous years.

The measures of capital stock contained in GCD are constructed using alternative rates of depreciation (4%, 8%, and 12%) and using two alternative methods to determine the age of the capital stock; capital stock's age is required to construct the starting values for the perpetual inventory method. Specifically, the first method to determine capital stock's age is

$$age_1 = \sum_{i=1}^{n} \frac{C_t}{D_t} \,, \tag{A.3}$$

where C_t is cumulated depreciation on tangible assets in year t, and D_t is depreciation on tangible assets in year t. Both items are taken from firms' fixed-assets movement schedule. The second method is

$$age_2 = \sum_{i=1}^{n} \frac{B_t}{D_t} \,, \tag{A.4}$$

where B_t is book value of tangible assets in year t, and D_t is depreciation on tangible assets in year t. Both methods follow Wadhwani and Wall (1986).

In addition to the firm identifier `nummer`, GCD contains a stock identification number (`wpn`) used by the German Stock Exchange, an identification number (`kis`) used by Hoppenstedt to construct ownership hierarchies within the Group Structure Database, an identification number (`crefo`) used by the Mannheim Company Database, as well as a firm year identifier (`idneu`) used in Hoppenstedt's Balance Sheet Database. These codes can be useful when adding further observations to GCD.

Table A.10. Variables measuring other firm-specific characteristics

Name (`name`)	Name of firm
City (`city`)	City in which firm is registered
Listing (`listed`)	*listed* = 1 if firm is listed on stock exchange, zero otherwise
Legal form (`gmbh`)	*gmbh* = 1 if firm operates in legal form of GmbH, zero otherwise
Industry (`nace2 nace3 nace5`)	Primary X-digit industry in which firm operates
Diversification (`divers`)	Number of five-digit industries (NACE) in which firm operates
Firm age (`found`)	Year of (first) foundation
Firm size (`asset sales`)	Firm size measured by total assets or total sales
Factor inputs (`labor mater capXY`)	Factor inputs for production: labor, materials, and capital (at replacement value), where X denotes the method to determine the capital stock's age and Y denotes the rate of depreciation
Other items (`equity debt value`)	Total debt, total equity, value added (which is defined as total sales less expenses for materials)

The data set labeled `other.dta` contains the following additional firm-specific measures, which can be merged to the other subsamples using `nummer` and `year`:

```
name city listed gmbh
nace2 nace3 nace5 divers found
asset sales labor mater
cap104 cap108 cap112 cap204 cap208 cap212
equity debt value
wpn kis crefo idneu
```

Measuring Macroeconomic Variables

Finally, GCD contains a range of macro-economic and industry-specific variables, part of which are needed to construct measures discussed above (e.g. replacement costs of capital stock or firm-level measures of competition). Table A.11 summarizes the respective variables.

The data set labeled `macro.dta` contains the following macroeconomic or industry-specific measures, which can be merged to the other subsamples using `nummer` and `year`:

```
poutput pkapital pwaren cycle
urendite inflatio realzins steuereg
```

Table A.11. Variables measuring macroeconomic conditions

Output price (`poutput`)	Output price index measured at two-digit industry level (SYPRO code)
Input price (capital) (`pkapital`)	Combined input price index for machinery, buildings, and real estate measured at two-digit industry level (SYPRO code)
Input price (material) (`pwaren`)	Input price index for materials measured at two-digit industry level (SYPRO code)
Risk-free interest rate (`urendite`)	Rate of return on ten-year government bonds
Capacity utilization (`cycle`)	Capacity utilization ratios at two-digit industry level
Inflation rate (`inflatio`)	Growth rate in price index for four-person household
Real interest rate (`realzins`)	Risk-free interest rate less inflation rate
Taxes (`steuereg`)	Tax rate on retained earnings

Bibliography

Adams, M. (1994), Die Usurpation von Aktionärsbefugnissen mittels Ringverflechtung in der „Deutschland AG“, *Die Aktiengesellschaft* 4, 148-158.

Agnblad, J., E. Berglöf, P. Högfeldt, and H. Svancar (2001), Ownership and Control in Sweden: Strong Owners, Weak Minorities, and Social Control, in: F. Barca and M. Becht (Eds.), *The Control of Corporate Europe*, Oxford, 228-258.

Agrawal, A. and C.R. Knoeber (1996), Firm Performance and Mechanisms to Control Agency Problems Between Managers and Shareholders, *Journal of Financial and Quantitative Analysis* 31 (3), 377-397.

Allen, F. and D. Gale (2000), Corporate Governance and Competition, in: X. Vives (Ed.), *Corporate Governance: Theoretical and Empirical Perspectives*, Cambridge.

Allen, C., M. Gasiorek, and A. Smith (1998), The Competition Effects of the Single Market in Europe, *Economic Policy* 13 (2), 439-486.

Almus, M. (2000), *The Shadow of Death: An Empirical Analysis of the Pre-Exit Performance of Young German Firms*, ZEW Discussion Paper 00-44, Centre for European Economic Research, Mannheim.

Altman, E. (1968), Financial Ratios, Discriminant Analysis, and the Prediction of Corporate Bankruptcy, *Journal of Finance* 23, 589-609.

Anderson, T.W. and C. Hsiao (1981), Estimation of Dynamic Models with Error Components, *Journal of the American Statistical Association* 76 (375), 598-606.

Anderson, T.W. and H. Rubin (1949), Estimation of the Parameters of a Single Equation in a Complete System of Stochastic Equations, *Annals of Mathematical Science* 20 (1), 46-63.

Andrade, G., M. Mitchell, and E. Stafford (2001), New Evidence and Perspectives on Mergers, *Journal of Economic Perspectives* 15 (2), 103-120.

Arellano, M. and S. Bond (1991), Some Tests of Specification for Panel Data: Monte Carlo Evidence and an Application to Employment Equations, *Review of Economic Studies* 58, 277-297.

Astebro, T. and J. Winter (2001), *More Than a Dummy: The Probability of Survival, Failure, and Acquisition of Firms in Financial Distress*, Working Paper, University of Waterloo and University of Mannheim.

Baily, M.N. and H. Gersbach (1995), Efficiency in Manufacturing and the Need for Global Competition, *Brookings Papers on Economic Activity (Microeconomics)*, 307-347.

Barber, B.M., D. Palmer, and J. Wallace (1995), Determinants of Conglomerate and Predatory Acquisitions: Evidence from the 1960s, *Journal of Corporate Finance* 1, 283-318.

Barcley, M.J. and C.G. Holderness (1991), Negotiated Block Trades and Corporate Control, *Journal of Finance* 46, 861-878.

Bartelsman, E.J. and M. Doms (2000), Understanding Productivity: Lessons from Longitudinal Micro Data, *Journal of Economic Literature* 38, 569-594.

Bebchuk, L.A. (1994), Efficient and Inefficient Sales of Corporate Control, *Quarterly Journal of Economics* 109, 957-993.

Bebchuk, L.A., R. Kraakman, and G. Triantis (2000), Stock Pyramids, Cross Ownership, and Dual Class Equity, in: R.K. Morck (Ed.), *Concentrated Corporate Ownership*, Chicago, 295-315.

Becht, M. and E. Böhmer (2001), Ownership and Voting Power in Germany, in: F. Barca and M. Becht (Eds.), *The Control of Corporate Europe*, Oxford, 128-153.

Becht, M. and E. Böhmer (2002), Voting Control in German Corporations, *International Review of Law and Economics*, forthcoming.

Becht, M. and A. Röell (1999), Blockholdings in Europe: An International Comparison, *European Economic Review* 43, 1049-1056.

Becht, M., A. Chapelle, and L. Renneboog (2001), Shareholding Cascades: The Separation of Ownership and Control in Belgium, in: F. Barca and M. Becht (Eds.), *The Control of Corporate Europe*, Oxford, 71-105.

Berle, A.A. and G.C. Means (1932), *The Modern Corporation and Private Property*, New York.

Bethel, J.E., J.P. Liebeskind, and T. Opler (1998), Block Share Purchases and Corporate Performance, *Journal of Finance* 53 (2), 605-634.

Bianchi, M., M. Bianco, and L. Enriques (2001), Pyramidal Groups and the Separation Between Ownership and Control in Italy, in: F. Barca and M. Becht (Eds.), *The Control of Corporate Europe*, Oxford, 154-187.

Black, B.S. (1998), Shareholder Activism and Corporate Governance in the United States, in: P. Newman (Ed.), *The New Palgrave Dictionary of Economics and Law*, London.

Bloch, L. and E. Kremp (2001), Ownership and Voting Power in France, in: F. Barca and M. Becht (Eds.), *The Control of Corporate Europe*, Oxford, 106-127.

Blommestein, H.J. (1998), The New Financial Landscape and Its Impact on Corporate Governance, in: M. Balling, E. Hennessy, and R. O'Brien (Eds.), *Corporate Governance, Financial Markets, and Global Convergence*, Dordrecht, 41-70.

Blundell, R. and S. Bond (1998), Initial Conditions and Moment Restrictions in Dynamic Panel Data Models, *Journal of Econometrics* 87, 115-143.

Bond, S., D. Harhoff, and J. van Reenen (1999), *Investment, R&D, and Financial Constraints in Britain and Germany*, Working Paper, Institute for Fiscal Studies, London.

Börsch-Supan, A. (1999), Capital Productivity and the Nature of Competition, *Brookings Papers on Economic Activity (Microeconomics)*, 205-244.

Börsch-Supan, A. and J. Köke (2002), An Applied Econometricians' View of Empirical Corporate Governance Studies, *German Economic Review*, forthcoming.

Börsch-Supan, A. and J. Winter (1999), *Pension Reform, Savings Behavior, and Corporate Governance*, SFB Working Paper No. 48, University of Mannheim.

Bottasso, A. and A. Sembenelli (2001), Market Power, Productivity, and the EU Single Market Program: Evidence from a Panel of Italian Firms, *European Economic Review* 45, 167-186.

Boycko, M., A. Shleifer, and R.W. Vishny (1995), *Privatizing Russia*, Cambridge.

Brickley, J.A., R.C. Lease, and C.W. Smith, Jr. (1988), Ownership Structure and Voting on Anti-Takeover Amendments, *Journal of Financial Economics* 20, 267-291.

Burkart, M., D. Gromb, and F. Panunzi (2000), Agency Conflicts in Public and Negotiated Transfers of Corporate Control, *Journal of Finance* 55 (2), 647-677.

Cable, J. (1985), Capital Market Information and Industrial Performance: The Role of West German Banks, *Economic Journal* 95, 118-132.

Campa, J.M. and S. Kedia (2000), *Explaining the Diversification Discount*, Working Paper, New York University and Harvard University.

Carleton, W.T., J.M. Nelson, and M.S. Weisbach (1998), The Influence of Institutions on Corporate Governance Through Private Negotiations: Evidence from TIAA-CREF, *Journal of Finance* 53 (4), 1335-1362.

Caves, R.E. (1992), *Industrial Efficiency in Six Nations*, Cambridge.

Chirinko, R.S. and J.A. Elston (1996), Banking Relationships in Germany: Empirical Results and Policy Implications, *Bank Relationships*, 239-255.

Cho, M. (1998), Ownership Structure, Investment, and the Corporate Value: An Empirical Analysis, *Journal of Financial Economics* 47, 103-121.

Conyon, M.J. and J. Schwalbach (1997a), *European Differences in Executive Pay and Corporate Governance*, Working Paper, University of Warwick and Humboldt University Berlin.

Conyon, M.J. and J. Schwalbach (1997b), *Pay for Performance and Board Effectiveness in Britain and Germany*, Working Paper, University of Warwick and Humboldt University Berlin.

Corts, K.S. (1998), Conduct Parameters and the Measurement of Market Power, *Journal of Econometrics* 88, 227-250.

Crespi-Cladera, R. and M. Garcia-Cestona (2001), Ownership and Control of Spanish Listed Firms, in: F. Barca and M. Becht (Eds.), *The Control of Corporate Europe*, Oxford, 207-227.

Cubbin, J. and D. Leech (1983), The Effect of Shareholder Dispersion on the Degree of Control in British Companies: Theory and Measurement, *Economic Journal* 93, 351-369.

De Jong, A., R. Kabir, T. Marra, and A. Röell (2001), Ownership and Control in the Netherlands, in: F. Barca and M. Becht (Eds.), *The Control of Corporate Europe*, Oxford, 188-206.

Del Guercio, D. and J. Hawkins (1999), The Motivation and Impact of Pension Fund Activism, *Journal of Financial Economics* 52, 293-340.

Demsetz, H. and K. Lehn (1985), The Structure of Corporate Ownership: Causes and Consequences, *Journal of Political Economy* 93 (6), 1155-1177.

Denis, D.J. and T.A. Kruse (2000), Managerial Discipline and Corporate Restructuring Following Performance Declines, *Journal of Financial Economics* 55, 391-424.

Denis, D.J. and A. Sarin (1999), Ownership and Board Structures in Publicly Traded Corporations, *Journal of Financial Economics* 52, 187-223.

Doms, M., T. Dunne, and M.J. Roberts (1995), The Role of Technology Use in the Survival and Growth of Manufacturing Plants, *International Journal of Industrial Organization* 13 (4), 523-542.

Eckbo, B.E., V. Maksimovic, and J. Williams (1990), Conditional Estimation of Cross-Sectional Models in Event Studies, *Review of Financial Studies* 3 (3), 343-365.

Edwards, J. and K. Fischer (1994), *Banks, Finance, and Investment in Germany*, Cambridge.

Edwards, J. and M. Nibler (2000), Corporate Governance: Banks Versus Ownership Concentration in Germany, *Economic Policy* 15 (2), 237-267.

Faccio, M. and A.M. Lasfer (2000), Do Occupational Pension Funds Monitor Companies in Which They Hold Large Stakes?, *Journal of Corporate Finance* 6, 71-110.

Fama, E.F. and M.C. Jensen (1983), Separation of Ownership and Control, *Journal of Law and Economics* 26, 301-325.

Franks, J. and C. Mayer (1990), Capital Markets and Corporate Control: A Study of France, Germany, and the UK, *Economic Policy* 10 (1), 189-231.

Franks, J. and C. Mayer (1994), *The Ownership and Control of German Corporations*, Working Paper, London Business School and University of Oxford.

Franks, J. and C. Mayer (1995), Ownership and Control, in: H. Siebert (Ed.), *Trends in Business Organization*, Tübingen, 171-200.

Franks, J. and C. Mayer (1998), Bank Control, Takeovers, and Corporate Governance in Germany, *Journal of Banking and Finance* 22, 1385-1403.

Franks, J. and C. Mayer (2001), Ownership and Control of German Corporations, *Review of Financial Studies* 14, 943-977.

Franks, J., C. Mayer, and L. Renneboog (2001), Who Disciplines the Management of Poorly Performing Companies?, *Journal of Financial Intermediation* 10, 209-248.

Garvey, G.T. and G. Hanka (1999), Capital Structure and Corporate Control: The Effect of Anti-Takeover Statutes on Firm Leverage, *Journal of Finance* 54 (2), 519-546.

Gerke, W. and M. Steiger (2001), Einfluss der Kapitalmärkte auf die Corporate-Governance-Strukturen in Europa, in: D. Hummel (Ed.), *Handbuch Europäischer Kapitalmarkt*, Wiesbaden, 207-223.

Geroski, P.A. (1998), An Applied Econometrican's View of Large Company Performance, *Review of Industrial Organization* 13 (3), 271-294.

Goergen, M. and L. Renneboog (2001), Strong Owners and Passive Institutional Investors in the United Kingdom, in: F. Barca and M. Becht (Eds.), *The Control of Corporate Europe*, Oxford, 259-284.

Göppl, H. (1996), *Risk Book: German Stocks 1976-1995; Risk, Return and Liquidity*, Frankfurt.

Gordon, A.L. and J. Pound (1993), Information, Ownership Structure, and Shareholder Voting: Evidence from Shareholder-Sponsored Corporate Governance Proposals, *Journal of Finance* 48 (2), 697-718.

Gorton, G. and F.A. Schmid (2000), Universal Banking and the Performance of German Firms, *Journal of Financial Economics* 58, 29-80.

Granger, C. (1969), Investigating Causal Relations by Econometric Models and Cross-Spectral Models, *Econometrica* 37, 424-438.

Green, A. and D. Mayes (1991), Technical Inefficiency in Manufacturing Industries, *Economic Journal* 101, 523.

Greene, W.H. (1997), *Econometric Analysis*, 3rd ed., Upper Saddle River/NJ.

Grossman, S.J. and O.D. Hart (1980), Takeover Bids, the Free-Rider Problem, and the Theory of the Corporation, *Bell Journal of Economics* 11, 42-64.

Gugler, K., S. Kalss, A. Stomper, and J. Zechner (2001), The Separation of Ownership and Control in Austria, in: F. Barca and M. Becht (Eds.), *The Control of Corporate Europe*, Oxford, 46-70.

Hanley, K. and W. Wilhelm (1995), Evidence on the Strategic Allocation of Initial Public Offerings, *Journal of Financial Economics* 37, 239-257.

Harhoff, D., K. Stahl, and M. Woywode (1998), Legal Form, Growth, and Exit of West German Firms: Empirical Results for Manufacturing, Construction, Trade, and Service Industries, *Journal of Industrial Economics* 46 (4), 453-488.

Hart, O.D. (1983), The Market Mechanism as an Incentive Scheme, *Bell Journal of Economics* 14 (3), 366.

Hausman, J.A. (1978), Specification Tests in Econometrics, *Econometrica* 46, 1251-1271.

Heckman, J. (1976), The Common Structure of Statistical Models of Truncation, Sample Selection, and Limited Dependent Variables and a Simple Estimator for Such Models, *The Annals of Economic and Social Measurement* 5, 475-492.

Heiss, F. and J. Köke (2001), *Dynamics in Ownership and Firm Survival: Evidence From Corporate Germany*, ZEW Discussion Paper No. 01-63, Centre for European Economic Research, Mannheim.

Hellwig, M. (1997), Unternehmensfinanzierung, Unternehmenskontrolle und Ressourcenallokation: Was leistet das Finanzsystem?, in: B. Gahlen, H. Hesse, and H.J. Ramser (Eds.), *Finanzmärkte*, Tübingen, 211-243.

Hellwig, M. (2001), Corporate Governance and the Financing of Investment for Structural Change, in: Deutsche Bundesbank (Ed.), *Investing Today for the World of Tomorrow: Studies on the Investment Process in Europe*, Berlin, 203-223.

Hermalin, B.E. (1992), The Effects of Competition on Executive Behavior, *Rand Journal of Economics* 23 (3), 350-365.

Hermalin, B.E. and M.S. Weisbach (2002), Boards of Directors as an Endogenously Determined Institution: A Survey of the Economic Literature, *Economic Policy Review*, forthcoming.

Himmelberg, C.P., G.R. Hubbard, and D. Palia (1999), Understanding the Determinants of Managerial Ownership and the Link Between Ownership and Performance, *Journal of Financial Economics* 53 (3), 353-384.

Holderness, C.G. (2002), A Survey of Blockholders and Corporate Control, *Economic Policy Review*, forthcoming.

Holderness, C.G. and D.P. Sheehan (1988), The Role of Majority Shareholders in Publicly Held Corporations: An Exploratory Analysis, *Journal of Financial Economics* 20, 317-346.

Holmström, B. and J. Tirole (1993), Market Liquidity and Performance Monitoring, *Journal of Political Economy* 101 (4), 679-709.

Hopt, K.J. (1997), The German Two-Tier Board (Aufsichtsrat): A German View on Corporate Governance, in: K.J. Hopt and E. Wymeersch (Eds.), *Comparative Corporate Governance: Essays and Materials*, Berlin, 3-20.

Januszewski, S.I., J. Köke, and J.K. Winter (2002), Product Market Competition, Corporate Governance, and Firm Performance: An Empirical Analysis for Germany, *Research in Economics*, forthcoming.

Jarrell, G.A., J. Brickley, and J. Netter (1988), The Market for Corporate Control: The Empirical Evidence Since 1980, *Journal of Economic Perspectives* 2, 49-68.

Jenkinson, T. and A. Ljungqvist (2001), Hostile Stakes and the Role of Banks in German Corporate Governance, *Journal of Corporate Finance*, 7 (4), 397-446.

Jensen, M.C. (1986), Agency Costs of Free Cash Flow, Corporate Finance, and Takeovers, *American Economic Review* 76, 323-329.

Jensen, M.C. (1988), Takeovers: Their Causes and Consequences, *Journal of Economic Perspectives* 2, 21-48.

Jensen, M.C. (1993), The Modern Industrial Revolution, Exit, and the Failure of Internal Control Systems, *Journal of Finance* 48 (3), 831-880.

Jensen, M.C. and W.H. Meckling (1976), Theory of the Firm: Managerial Behavior, Agency Costs, and Ownership Structure, *Journal of Financial Economics* 3, 305-360.

Jensen, M.C. and K.J. Murphy (1990), Performance Pay and Top-Management Incentives, *Journal of Political Economy* 98 (2), 225-264.

Jensen, M.C. and R. Ruback (1983), The Market for Corporate Control, *Journal of Financial Economics* 11, 5-50.

Kahan, M. (1993), Sales of Corporate Control, *Journal of Law, Economics, and Organization* 9, 368-379.

Kang, D.L (1998), *The Internal Control of Organizations: How Large-Block Ownership by Insiders Leads to Increase Firm Performance*, Working Paper, Harvard Business School.

Kaplan, S.N. (1994a), Top Executives, Turnover, and Firm Performance in Germany, *Journal of Law, Economics and Organization* 10 (1), 142-159.

Kaplan, S.N. (1994b), Top Executive Rewards and Firm Performance: A Comparison of Japan and the United States, *Journal of Political Economy* 102 (3), 510-546.

Kaplan, S.N. (1997), Corporate Governance and Corporate Performance: A Comparison of Germany, Japan, and the US, in: K.J. Hopt and E. Wymeersch (Eds.), *Comparative Corporate Governance: Essays and Materials*, Berlin, 195-210.

Kaplan, S.N. and B. Minton (1994), Appointments of Outsiders to Japanese Boards: Determinants and Implications for Managers, *Journal of Financial Economics* 36 (2), 225-258.

Karpoff, J.M. (1998), The Impact of Shareholder Activism on Target Companies: A Survey of Empirical Findings, Working Paper, University of Washington.

Klette, T.J. (1999), Market Power, Scale Economies, and Productivity: Estimates from a Panel of Establishment Data, *Journal of Industrial Economics* 47 (4), 451-476.

Köke, J. (2000), *Control Transfers in Corporate Germany: Their Frequency, Causes, and Consequences*, ZEW Discussion Paper No. 00-67, Centre for European Economic Research, Mannheim.

Köke, J. (2001a), *Corporate Governance, Market Discipline, and Productivity Growth*, ZEW Discussion Paper No. 01-55, Centre for European Economic Research, Mannheim.

Köke, J. (2001b), *Determinants of Acquisition and Failure: Stylized Facts and Lessons for Empirical Studies*, ZEW Discussion Paper No. 01-30, Centre for European Economic Research, Mannheim.

Köke, J. (2001c), New Evidence on Ownership Structures in Germany, *Kredit und Kapital* 34 (2), 257-292.

Köke, J. (2001d), *The German Corporations Database: A User Guide*, ZEW Documentation, Centre for European Economic Research, Mannheim.

Köke, J. (2001e), Unternehmensübernahmen in Deutschland, *ZEW Finanzmarktreport* 7, 3.

Kole, S. and K. Lehn (1997), Deregulation, the Evolution of Corporate Governance Structure, and Survival, *American Economic Review* 87, 421-425.

Kole, S. and K. Lehn (1999), Deregulation and the Adaptation of Governance Structure: The Case of the US Airline Industry, *Journal of Financial Economics* 52, 79-117.

Koopmans, T.C. and W.C. Hood (1953), The Estimation of Simultaneous Linear Economic Relationships, in: W.C. Hood and T.C. Koopmans (Eds.), *Studies in Econometric Method*, Cowles Commission Monograph 14, New York.

Lamont, O. (1997), Cash Flow and Investment: Evidence from Internal Capital Markets, *Journal of Finance* 52, 83-110.

Lang, M.H., E.L. Maydew, and D.A. Shackelford (2001), *Bringing Down the Other Berlin Wall: Germany's Repeal of the Corporate Capital Gains Tax*, Working Paper, University of North Carolina.

La Porta, R., F. Lopez-de-Silanes, and A. Shleifer (1999), Corporate Ownership Around the World, *Journal of Finance* 54 (2), 471-517.

Leech, D. and J. Leahy (1991), Ownership Structure, Control Type Classifications, and the Performance of Large British Companies, *Economic Journal* 101, 1418-1437.

Lehmann, E. and J. Weigand (2000), Does the Governed Corporation Perform Better? Governance Structures and Corporate Performance in Germany, *European Finance Review* 4, 157-195.

Leland, H. and D. Pyle (1977), Information Asymmetries, Financial Structure, and Financial Intermediation, *Journal of Finance* 42 (5), 371-387.

Maddala, G.S. (1983), *Limited Dependent Variables and Qualitative Variables in Econometrics*, Cambridge.

Maksimovic, V. and G. Phillips (2001), The Market for Corporate Assets: Who Engages in Mergers and Asset Sales and Are There Efficiency Gains? *Journal of Finance* 56 (6), 2019-2065.

Maug, E. (1997), Boards of Directors and Capital Structure: Alternative Forms of Corporate Restructuring, *Journal of Corporate Finance* 3, 113-139.

Mayer, C. (1988), New Issues in Corporate Finance, *European Economic Review* 32, 1167-1189.

Mayer, C. (1998), Financial Systems and Corporate Governance: A Review of the International Evidence, *Journal of Institutional and Theoretical Economics* 154, 144-176.

McConnell, J.J. and H. Servaes (1990), Additional Evidence on Equity Ownership and Corporate Value, *Journal of Financial Economics* 27, 595-612.

McWilliams, V.B. and N. Sen (1997), Board Monitoring and Anti-Takeover Amendments, *Journal of Financial and Quantitative Analysis* 32 (4), 491-505.

Mello, A.S. and J.E. Parsons (1998), Going Public and the Ownership Structure of the Firm, *Journal of Financial Economics* 49, 79-109.

Mitchell, M.L. and J.H. Mulherin (1996), The Impact of Industry Shocks on Takeover and Restructuring Activity, *Journal of Financial Economics* 41, 193-229.

Monopolkommission (1996), *Wettbewerbspolitik in Zeiten des Umbruchs: Hauptgutachten 1994/1995*, Baden-Baden.

Morck, R., A. Shleifer, and R.W. Vishny (1988), Management Ownership and Market Valuation, *Journal of Financial Economics* 20, 292-315.

Mulherin, J.H. and A.L. Boone (2000), Comparing Acquisitions and Divestitures, *Journal of Corporate Finance* 6, 117-139.

Murali, R. and J.B. Welch (1989), Agents, Owners, Control, and Performance, *Journal of Business Finance and Accounting* 16 (3), 385-398.

Murphy, K.J. (1998), Executive Compensation, in: O. Ashenfelter and D. Card (Eds.), *Handbook of Labor Economics*, Vol. 3., North Holland, 2485-2557.

Nickell, S. (1996), Competition and Corporate Performance, *Journal of Political Economy* 104 (4), 724-746.

Nickell, S. and D. Nicolitsas (1999), How Does Financial Pressure Affect Firms? *European Economic Review* 43, 1435-1456.

Nickell, S., D. Nicolitsas, and N. Dryden (1997), What Makes Firms Perform Well?, *European Economic Review* 41, 783-796.

OECD (1998), Shareholder Value and the Market in Corporate Control in OECD Countries, *Financial Market Trends* 69, 15-37.

Pagano, M. and A. Röell (1996), The Choice of Stock Ownership Structure: Agency Costs, Monitoring, and the Decision To Go Public, in: M. Pagano and A. Röell (Eds.), *The Decision to Go Public and the Stock Market*, Rom, 41-75.

Porter, M.E. (1992), *The Competitive Advantage of Nations*, London.

Pound, J. (1988), Proxy Contests and the Efficiency of Shareholder Oversight, *Journal of Financial Economics* 20, 237-265.

Powell, R.G. (1997), Modelling Takeover Likelihood, *Journal of Business Finance and Accounting* 24, 1009-1030.

Prabhala, N.R. (1997), Conditional Methods in Event Studies and an Equilibrium Justification for Standard Event-Study Procedures, *Review of Financial Studies* 10 (1), 1-38.

Prowse, S. (1994), *Corporate Governance in an International Perspective: A Survey of Corporate Governance Mechanisms Among Large Firms in the United States, the United Kingdom, Japan, and Germany*, Working Paper No. 41, Bank for International Settlements, Basel.

Renneboog, L. (2000), Ownership, Managerial Control, and the Governance of Companies Listed on the Brussels Stock Exchange, *Journal of Banking and Finance* 24 (12), 1959-1995.

Roe, M. (1993), Some Differences in Corporate Structure in Germany, Japan, and the United States, *The Yale Law Review* 102, 1927-2003.

Scharfstein, D. (1988), Product-Market Competition and Managerial Slack, *Rand Journal of Economics* 19 (1), 147.

Schwert, W.G., (2000), Hostility in Takeovers: In the Eyes of the Beholder? *Journal of Finance* 55 (6), 2599-2640.

Scott, J. (1981), The Probability of Bankruptcy: A Comparison of Empirical Predictions and Theoretical Models, *Journal of Banking and Finance* 5, 317-344.

Seger, F. (1997), *Banken, Erfolg und Finanzierung*, Wiesbaden.

Shleifer, A. and R.W. Vishny (1986), Large Shareholders and Corporate Control, *Journal of Political Economy* 94 (3), 461-488.

Shleifer, A. and R.W. Vishny (1988), Value Maximization and the Acquisition Process, *Journal of Economic Perspectives* 2 (1), 7-20.

Shleifer, A. and R.W. Vishny (1992), Liquidation Values and Debt Capacity: A Market Equilibrium Approach, *Journal of Finance* 47 (4), 1343-1366.

Shleifer, A. and R.W. Vishny (1997), A Survey of Corporate Governance, *Journal of Finance* 52 (2), 737-783.

Short, H. (1994), Ownership, Control, Financial Structure, and the Performance of Firms, *Journal of Economic Surveys* 8 (3), 203-247.

Shumway, T. (2001), Forecasting Bankruptcy More Accurately: A Simple Hazard Rate Model, *Journal of Business* 74, 101-124.

Smith, M.P. (1996), Shareholder Activism by Institutional Investors: Evidence from CalPERS, *Journal of Finance* 51 (1), 227-252.

Steiger, M. (2000), *Institutionelle Investoren im Spannungsfeld zwischen Aktienmarktliquidität und Corporate Governance*, Baden-Baden.

Steiner, M. (1998), Konstitutive Entscheidungen, in: M. Bitz, K. Dellmann, M. Domsch, and F.W. Wagner (Eds.), *Vahlens Kompendium der Betriebswirtschaftslehre*, 4th ed., München, 57-106.

Stiglitz, J. (1985), Credit Markets and the Control of Capital, *Journal of Money, Credit, and Banking* 17 (2), 133-152.

St-Pierre, J., J.M. Gagnon, and J. Saint-Pierre (1996), Concentration of Voting Rights and Board Resistance to Takeover Bids, *Journal of Corporate Finance* 3, 45-73.

Titman, S. and R. Wessels (1988), The Determinants of Capital Structure Choice, *Journal of Finance* 43 (1), 1-19.

Vella, F. (1998), Estimating Models with Sample Selection Bias: A Survey, *Journal of Human Resources* 33, 127-169.

Verbeek, M. (2000), *Modern Econometrics*, Chichester.

Verbeek, M. and T. Nijman (1992), Testing for Selectivity Bias in Panel Data Models, *International Economic Review* 33, 681-703.
Verbeek, M. and T. Nijman (1996), Incomplete Panels and Selection Bias, in: L. Mátyás and P. Sevestre (Eds.), *The Econometrics of Panel Data*, 2nd ed., Dordrecht, 449-490.
Wadhwani, S. and M. Wall (1986), The U.K. Capital Stock: New Estimates of Premature Scrapping, *Oxford Review of Economic Policy* 2, 44-55.
Wagner, J. (1999), The Life History of Cohorts of Exits from German Manufacturing, *Small Business Economics* 13, 71-79.
Warther, V.A. (1998), Board Effectiveness and Board Dissent: A Model of the Board's Relationship to Management and Shareholders, *Journal of Corporate Finance* 4, 53-70.
Wenger, E. and C. Kaserer (1998), The German System of Corporate Governance: A Model Which Should Not Be Imitated, in: S.W. Black and M. Moersch (Eds.), *Competition and Convergence in Financial Markets*, Amsterdam, 41-78.
Yermack, D. (1996), Higher Market Valuation of a Company With a Small Board of Directors, *Journal of Financial Economics* 40, 185-211.
Zingales, L. (1998), Survival of the Fittest or the Fattest? Exit and Financing in the Trucking Industry, *Journal of Finance* 53 (3), 905-938.
Zwiebel, J. (1996), Dynamic Capital Structure Under Managerial Entrenchment, *American Economic Review* 86 (5), 1197-1215.

List of Data Sources

Bayerische Hypotheken- und Wechselbank, Guide Through German Corporations (*Wegweiser durch deutsche Unternehmen*), München, yearly editions 1986–1994.

Centre for European Economic Research, Mannheim Company Database (*Mannheimer Unternehmenspanel*), Mannheim.

Federal Statistical Office, Census of Production (*Produktionsstatistik*), Fachserie 4, Reihe 3.1, Wiesbaden.

Federal Statistical Office, Foreign Trade Statistics (*Außenhandelsstatistik*), Wiesbaden.

Federal Statistical Office, Output Price Statistics (*Preisstatistik für gewerbliche Produkte, Einzelhandel und Großhandel*), Fachserie 17, Reihe 7, Wiesbaden.

Federal Statistical Office, Real Estate Statistics (*Kaufwerte für Bauland*), Fachserie 17, Reihe 5, Wiesbaden.

Federal Statistical Office, Turnover Tax Statistics (*Umsatzsteuerstatistik*), Fachserie 14, Reihe 8, Wiesbaden.

Hoppenstedt, Balance Sheet Database (*Bilanzdatenbank*), Darmstadt.

Hoppenstedt, Group Structure Database (*Konzernstrukturdatenbank*), Darmstadt, editions 3-1994, 2-1995, 2-1996, and 1-1997.

Hoppenstedt, Hoppenstedt's Stock Guide (*Hoppenstedt's Aktienführer*), Darmstadt.

ifo Institute, Business Climate Index (*Geschäftsklimaindex*), München.

Institute for the German Economy, Statistics on the Development of the Federal Republic of Germany (*Zahlen zur wirtschaftlichen Entwicklung der Bundesrepublik Deutschland*), Köln.

Monopolkommission, Market Structure Data (*Marktstrukturdaten*), Baden-Baden, editions 1996 and 1998.

University of Karlsruhe, German Finance Database (*Deutsche Finanzdatenbank: Kursdaten*), Karlsruhe.

List of Figures

1.1 Structure of this study 6

2.1 Estimation bias due to sample selection 20
2.2 Causes for selection bias 23
2.3 Truncation of the endogenous variable 25

3.1 Structure of German Corporations Database 44

4.1 Ownership structure of Dornier Aeronautics GmbH (1992) 57
4.2 Ownership structure of Boge AG (1990–1992) 61

List of Tables

2.1 Comparison of criteria for sample selection 21
2.2 Comparison of performance measures 33

3.1 Sample selection for balance sheet data 42
3.2 Sample representativeness in 1992: listed and non-listed firms . 45
3.3 Sample representativeness in 1992: industry coverage......... 46

4.1 Characteristics of firms with different number of observations . 54
4.2 Characteristics of entering and exiting firms 55
4.3 Ownership concentration 59
4.4 Ownership of large share blocks by type of ultimate owner.... 60
4.5 Purchases and sales of large share blocks 62
4.6 Size distribution of blocks purchased by new shareholders 63
4.7 Causes of control transfers................................ 66
4.8 Industry-adjusted performance as cause of control transfers ... 67
4.9 Governance changes and corporate restructuring following control transfers.............................. 70
4.10 Industry-adjusted performance following poor performance ... 71

5.1 Number of firms by reason and year of exit 81
5.2 Number of observations by time horizon.................. 82
5.3 Survival and exit of firms by industry 84
5.4 Industry-adjusted performance as determinant of exit 85
5.5 Capital structure as determinant of exit 87
5.6 Ownership concentration as determinant of exit 88
5.7 Ownership type as determinant of exit 89
5.8 Restructuring and firm size as determinants of exit 91
5.9 MNL results: four-year time horizon, without type of owner... 96
5.10 MNL results: four-year time horizon, with type of owner 97
5.11 Robustness tests: different time horizons, without type of owner 100
5.12 Robustness tests: different time horizons, with type of owner .. 101
5.13 Robustness tests: different performance measures, without type of owner 102
5.14 Robustness tests: different performance measures, with type of owner 103

5.15 Robustness tests: different measures of capital structure, without type of owner ... 104
5.16 Robustness tests: different measures of restructuring and firm size, without type of owner ... 105

6.1 Firm- and industry-specific measures of competition ... 117
6.2 Bivariate analysis of corporate governance, market discipline, and productivity growth ... 119
6.3 Effects of corporate governance on productivity growth ... 125
6.4 Effects of corporate governance and market discipline on productivity growth ... 126
6.5 Robustness tests: different measures of ownership structure ... 129
6.6 Robustness tests: different measures of capital structure interacted with competition ... 130
6.7 Robustness tests: different measures of firm-level competition ... 131
6.8 Robustness tests: different measures of capital structure interacted with financial distress ... 132

A.1 Variables measuring performance ... 142
A.2 Variables measuring ownership structure ... 145
A.3 Shareholder categories ... 146
A.4 Variables measuring changes in ownership structure ... 147
A.5 Variables measuring capital structure ... 147
A.6 Variables measuring board structure ... 148
A.7 Variables measuring corporate restructuring ... 149
A.8 Variables measuring product market competition ... 150
A.9 Variable measuring reason for non-reporting ... 151
A.10 Variables measuring other firm-specific characteristics ... 153
A.11 Variables measuring macroeconomic conditions ... 154

GPSR Compliance

The European Union's (EU) General Product Safety Regulation (GPSR) is a set of rules that requires consumer products to be safe and our obligations to ensure this.

If you have any concerns about our products, you can contact us on ProductSafety@springernature.com

In case Publisher is established outside the EU, the EU authorized representative is:

Springer Nature Customer Service Center GmbH
Europaplatz 3
69115 Heidelberg, Germany

Batch number: 10725973

Printed by Printforce, the Netherlands